The Struggle to Organize

The Struggle to Organize

RESISTANCE IN CANADA'S FISHERY

by Wallace Clement

McClelland and Stewart

Illustrations reprinted from *Careers in Fishing and Fish Processing*, Minister
of Supply and Services Canada, 1978 (No. MP70-20/23-1977). Credit: Employment and Immigration Canada. Reproduced with permission of the Minister
of Supply and Services Canada.

Canadian Cataloguing in Publication Data
Clement, Wallace.
  The Struggle to organize: resistance in Canada's fishery
Includes bibliographical references and index.

ISBN 0-7710-2158-5 (pbk.)

1. Fisheries, Cooperative – Canada – History.
2. Trade-unions – Fishermen – Canada – History.
3. Fishermen – Canada – Political activity – History. 4. Fisheries – Canada – History. I. Title.

HD8039.F652C3 1986   331'.04392'0971   C85-090781-0

McClelland and Stewart Limited
The Canadian Publishers
481 University Avenue
Toronto, Ontario
M5G 2E9

Printed and bound in Canada by Gagné Ltée.

Contents

Preface

Struggling just to survive is the most basic activity of Canada's fishers. In an industry subject to rapid social change and ruthless restructuring, loosely guided by state policies, and beset by turbulent economic conditions, Canadian fishers have created a complex of organizations to defend themselves. These can be broadly categorized as unions, co-operatives, and associations, although such groupings do not do justice to the complexity of the actions, ideologies, and politics of these organizational forms. This book seeks to understand the conditions underlying the formation and behaviour of these organizations and the fishers they include.

Why do fishers sometimes organize into industrial unions, at other times join producer co-operatives, and at still others form associations based on gear types or areas? This was initially the phenomenon I sought to explain – under what conditions do fishers organize, and what form does such organization take? In building an explanation I examined the labour processes and property relations of fishers. After five years of study I still marvel at the tangled and continually evolving web of fishers' organizations. At first I thought simply that untangling associations from co-ops from unions would suffice, but it soon became evident that each "type" itself needed to be disentangled and located.

Fundamental to comprehending the organizational terrain of the fishing industry is an understanding of class dynamics. Having identified the class dynamics and mapped out the terrain, this book seeks to make more transparent the forces at work in Canada's class formation. Fishing is an activity germane to many Canadians on both coasts and, like so many resource-based activities, is subject to cyclical booms and busts. When I began the research for this study in the late 1970s an enormous boom was on; there was great expansion on the East Coast following the proclamation of a 200-mile limit, while on the West Coast the Japanese market for herring roe created a kind of gold-rush and the salmon market was thriving. In the past few years the industry has collapsed on both coasts and undergone a drastic restructuring. This has been an exciting time to study fishing. Turbulent conditions reveal underlying social relations. As these relations are clarified through exposure to the stresses of boom and bust, it is possible to grasp some fundamentals about class dynamics that have relevance beyond the immediate industry.

If one wishes to understand the social relations of production no place presents a more interesting challenge than Canada's fisheries. At first blush penetrating their myriad of organizations and conflicts seems almost impossible. Debate ranges from the food fisheries and traditional community rights to trendy questions of "quality circles" for plant workers. The range of questions is vast: Are fishers co-adventurers, entrepreneurs, or industrial workers? Which associations, co-operatives, or unions best represent their interests? There are, of course, additional issues that complicate the social relations of production, such as international boundary disputes with the United States, international quota allocations within the 200-mile limit, the availability of international markets, and federal versus provincial jurisdiction over fisheries management or labour legislation.

While this book's motivation began with a theoretical question and selected the fisheries as a place to reflect upon issues of property relations, in the course of conducting the research I found that these abstract relations became much more concrete as I encountered the men and women who spend their lives in the entanglement. Fishing is not a romantic or exotic job; it is demanding, often dangerous, and certainly cyclical in its demand for labour. It is, however, a job where the social relations of production are fundamental. By making more clearly understood the nature of these relations in fishing and examining how they have led to organization and social action, this book seeks to contribute to a broader understanding of class dynamics. It seeks to understand how people make their own history and to contribute to an evaluation of some forms of social relations that have been created. This I seek to do in theoretically informed terms and to contribute to an enrichment of theoretical insight but in a language and expression understandable to more people than theoreticians alone.

As part of a larger undertaking that has included *Hardrock Mining* as another case study and a current project on comparative class structure, this book has both a general and a particular purpose. It is meant to be useful to persons engaged in fishing so that they can understand their situation better and evaluate their prospects for action, but it is also meant to have a broader relevance by making generalizations on the social relations for all simple commodity producers and, indeed, all workers.

Readers will soon be aware that I have not conducted the kind of detailed community studies that are typical of the fisheries literature, although I have relied upon valuable information from numerous such studies. Rather I have sought to identify patterns and relationships drawn from observation in all the major coastal fishing areas of Canada (and informed by parallel developments in Europe and Scandinavia). Investigations of communities are valuable for understanding the social and cultural aspects of the daily lives of persons associated with the fishery. Equally valuable, however, is locating broader political and economic patterns that may explain the similarities and differences in the ways people in fishing have organized themselves. Such a perspective helps make sense of more local features, although patterns can be determined only if the details have been marshalled.

There is a healthy history of research into Canada's fisheries, originated by Harold Innis and his colleagues, such as Ruth Fulton Grant on the East Coast and W.A. Carrothers on the West. A renewed interest has developed over the past five years. The oldest tradition with a continuing presence is that at Memorial University in Newfoundland, where several contemporary investigators are working within the tradition of political economy. In British Columbia there is a "Fish and Ships" group, and in Nova Scotia other research teams are engaged in intensive studies. There has been a healthy exchange of perspectives and information among researchers in these quarters, well reflected in a recent special issue of the *Journal of Canadian Studies* devoted to Canada's fisheries. In the present work I have gained greatly from these researchers and acknowledge gratefully their contribution.

Generally, however, this book differs from the others in its "distance" from the fishery as a subject (not simply because I live in Central Canada and wrote the book while living in Sweden). In this study I am seeking to illuminate some broader processes affecting labour and its organization as exhibited in the fishery. For this purpose I have chosen to draw material from both coasts. This is a most unusual research strategy in fisheries studies, which are typically confined to one of three regions – British Columbia, the Maritime Provinces, or Newfoundland (and occasionally concentrate on an inland or Arctic fishery) – and then even more specifically to a particular sub-region or community. I have attempted to "stand back" somewhat and observe broad patterns and relationships, commenting upon local conditions only to the extent that they illustrate the political, ideological, and/or cultural life of the people studied. Similarly I have devoted only limited space to exploring the technology, fishing techniques, and markets except as they are essential background for understanding relations of production central to the labour process. As far as I have utilized "organizations" as a basis for categorizing the presentation of material, it is mainly for convenience. The important factors focus on the social relations ingrained within these organizations, whatever their formal label. Hence I have adopted a format of providing profiles of the key organizations within the chapters where they are introduced, giving a capsule comment on their structure and history and the nature of their membership.

For assistance in researching the background material for the study I thank David Langille (who helped with interviews in the Maritimes), Skip McCarthy (who helped with British Columbia interviews), and Kris Schnack (who helped with Quebec). Gillian Creese and Donnan Gwashu assisted with archival work. Helpful comments on the manuscript have come from Patricia Marchak, James Sacouman, Peter Sinclair, and T.F. Wise, none of whom is responsible for the contents. Janet Craig has been most helpful as my editor and Michael Harrison has been a valuable contact at McClelland and Stewart. Elsie Clement typed the final manuscript. The study was funded initially by the Dean of Graduate Studies and Research at Carleton University (for 1981), then by the Social Sciences and Humanities Research Council of Canada (for 1982-83). This book has been published with the help of a grant from the Social Science Federation of Canada, using funds provided by the Social Sciences and Humanities Research Council of Canada. Time for the writing was made possible by a SSHRCC leave fellowship (for 1984-85). It was done at Arbetslivscentrum in Stockholm while I was a "gästforskare," and I wish to thank the people there for a productive and stimulating environment. For the first time I do not have to ask for the indulgence of my family while writing a book. Elsie, Christopher, and Jeffrey enjoyed themselves in Stockholm as much as I did.

Wallace Clement
Stockholm, Sweden
March 1985
(Revised, Ottawa,
January 1986)

CHAPTER ONE
A Fine Kettle of Fish

When John Stevens stepped off a sailing ship to seek a livelihood catching Fraser River salmon, he little knew that he would join the first fishers' local to engage in a major labour struggle on Canada's west coast. That was in 1893 in Ladner, British Columbia. And it was, of course, impossible for him to foresee that he would have a grandson, Homer, who would one day become a dominant figure in organized labour in Canada's coastal fisheries. During the brief period between 1967 and 1971, Homer Stevens of the United Fishermen and Allied Workers' Union was at the centre of two disputes (in both of which his union apparently was the loser) that were to change the direction of fishers' organizations in Canada.

One of these was the 1967 Prince Rupert fiasco at the end of which the Prince Rupert Fishermen's Co-operative had escaped from certification by the United Fishermen and Allied Workers' Union, and Homer was jailed for a year. In the second, he was a key figure setting the stage for today's unions in the East Coast fishing industry, which include the Newfoundland Fishermen, Food and Allied Workers' Union, the Maritime Fishermen's Union, and the Canadian Brotherhood of Railway, Transport and General Workers.

Following a period of uneasy truce, the United Fishermen and Allied Workers' Union, the country's most militant union (whose very right to a legal existence was then in question), was led into mortal conflict with the most successful fishery co-op in the country, a co-op that had originated as an extension of that very union. It was a bitter confrontation wherein unions were pitted against one another and the "sympathetic" Prince Rupert Fishermen's Co-operative was a not-so-innocent bystander. Having been expelled from the old Trades and Labour Congress for "communist activities" during the Cold War and certainly a thorn in the side of all forms of capital in the West Coast fishery, the undaunted United Fishermen were in a period of expansion. This union was beginning a program to organize fishery workers on the East Coast; it was combatting anti-combines charges brought in the federal courts; it was struggling to gain official recognition as the bargaining agent for its own fishery members on the West Coast, whom by law it could not represent.

The British Columbia fishing industry itself was in turmoil (a not unusual condition). The leadership of the Pacific Trollers' Association, bitterly anti-union, was seriously considering transforming the association into a union to do an end-run around the United Fishermen during strikes. The Native Brotherhood, a frequent partner with the United Fishermen in negotiations, was contemplating the same path. At the same time the Deep Sea Fishermen's Union, long a dormant force in the industry enjoying a comfortable understanding with the United Fishermen, the Prince Rupert Vessel Owners' Association, and the Prince Rupert Fishermen's Co-operative, suddenly became a tool for breaking the United Fishermen's membership in the Prince Rupert Co-operative (aided and abetted by the Canadian Labour Congress).

Incredible as it may seem, conditions in the Eastern fisheries were even more bizarre. The United Fishermen led a bitter strike in 1970 for recognition in the Strait of Canso, Nova Scotia, yet after this union appeared to have achieved what Homer Stevens called "a toehold for the future" it was ousted by a rival union, even though the United Fishermen was supported by the Canadian Seafood Workers' Union and the official Nova Scotia labour bodies, not to mention the fish workers themselves. The Canadian Food and Allied Workers' Union (known as the Meatcutters after their Chicago parent, the Amalgamated Meat Cutters and Butcher Workmen) on the one hand and the Canadian Brotherhood of Railway, Transport and General Workers on the other through voluntary recognition by the fishery companies quietly became acceptable substitutes for the militant "reds from the West Coast" led by the fire-breathing Homer Stevens. Yet in Newfoundland, spurred on by ill winds from the West, the Newfoundland

Fishermen, Food and Allied Workers' Union was able to achieve the country's most progressive fishing labour legislation in its most backward labour setting.

In all these instances the organizations mentioned continue to be dominant forces in the fishing industry, albeit in greatly modified form. Most dramatic has been the change for the Meatcutters, who were in 1985 one of the country's most powerful movements and certainly the dominant force among Eastern unions. The crumbs not swept into the basket of the larger unions have sustained yet another militant and progressive union, the Maritime Fishermen's Union, which now represents small-scale fishery workers in New Brunswick and has a significant membership in Prince Edward Island and Nova Scotia.

Homer Stevens says of the United Fishermen, "This union shouldn't exist, but it does. It hangs together because of a hell of a lot of hard work. It makes it possible for people to fight back when the chips are down, even people who politically do not see eye-to-eye but rally together with sincere, capable leadership."[1] Jack Nichol, the current president of the United Fishermen, describes the situation well when he says, "We do not have formal bargaining rights enshrined in legislation; nevertheless the companies come to the table and bargain with us in those fisheries where we can deprive them of their production. We have established our bargaining rights simply by strength, but we can run afoul of the common law. For example, in 1967 during a strike of trawlers, the courts ruled fishermen are not labour, were not on strike. They were not picketing but 'watching and besetting.' Calling someone a scab was 'harassment and intimidation.' Fishermen were in breach of contract and charged with unlawful conspiracy."

This brief sketch should indicate that the fishery is a complex industry where formal laws and appearances often are only the palest reflection of reality.

The 1980s have been particularly notable for the capital restructuring of the fishing industry; for fishery workers the years around 1970 were the most important formative period. It was during this stormy era that the contemporary organizational structure was established and all the most important current organizations took shape. The United Fishermen and Allied Workers' Union is outstanding as the key organization in Canada's fisheries because it has significantly affected the actions of all other organizations, often by defining the "space" within which they developed. It is the purpose of this study to make sense of the material basis of the various organizations within the fishery and to assess their political and ideological struggles. Broadly, it is the study of the making of a labour force and the response by that labour force to its own making.

By reviewing the mechanical and social development of the fishery and developing some social categories for its understanding, I hope to explain the occupation of "fisherman," a word used generally to designate the occupation of those who fish (we will use the gender-neutral term fisher[s]). The designation "fisherman" is an omnibus term covering many class relations ranging from the captain of a giant trawler, who is part of a fish processor's management structure, to the crew of sixteen working under his command, to the "independent" boat owner-operator who works alone. As an activity, fishing is heterogeneous, and because of the variety of class relations and types of fishing, fishers have created many organizations to represent themselves. While on the whole these fall into three main types – unions, co-operatives, and associations – they are not homogeneous within these types.

To explain the emergence of these organizations it is necessary to understand both the fundamental labour processes of the workers and the political economy of the industry. Fishing has been subject to a process of industrialization that has seen dramatic changes in the relations of production. The merchant capitalists of the salt fish trade gave way to the industrial capitalists of fresh/frozen/canning fish processing. Simple commodity producers tended to become industrial workers. Yet vestiges of the earlier relations of production remain and prove difficult to shed as industrial capitalism dominates and transforms its predecessors. These relics include not only the ideologies of those engaged in fishing but also some archaic labour laws governing the fisheries.

This is a study of class formation, that is, the way collectivities of fishers become organized and act as a class. To be sure, there are important fractions of classes that have an impact on the struggles, and these require explanation and understanding. The simple identification of these fractions and the determination of which divisions are fundamental (rather than mere rivalries) are important undertakings. But to gain an appreciation of class formation it is necessary to examine the political and cultural/

ideological struggles that are the dynamic social relations of the fisheries.

Studying the fishery is like watching a pot of boiling water – it's always in flux, it produces a lot of steam, and there is the ever-present danger that the pot will go dry. Moreover, each organization in the fishery seems to be unique. One has to take into account the organization's terrain – the differences in each location, including the prevailing class structure and level of struggle. Each location has a history, a social memory that limits or expands "what is possible" in the minds of the participants. This study is an attempt to share and transmit some of these experiences and, it is hoped, to expand for some readers on what is possible (if not on what is desirable).

The organizations studied here are the outcomes of economic, ideological, and political struggles and are undergoing constant reorganization. They are "organized resistance." Resistance is not confined to fighting the companies but includes struggling with the co-operatives, the state, and other fishing organizations. Resistance is the struggle to fight back and attempt to shape the lives of those who directly produce fish for sale.

Organizations are formed in the context of relationships with certain subjects and objects. Associations, unions, and co-operatives are not mutually exclusive forms, nor do they always have mutually exclusive objectives. Associations and unions are both found engaged in "over-the-side" sales of fish, an activity normally associated with co-operatives seeking markets. Unions and co-operatives are often formed in the context of government demands, sometimes in order to substitute a more conservative union for one that is more militant, sometimes because a co-operative is deemed the only means for sustaining a fishing community when private capital fails. Hence it is not only the catalogue of organizations that is important but also the relationships as expressed in and through organizations. Each of these organizations has its own important class content, character, and qualities demanding exploration.

But what about those who remain unorganized? To some extent they are the "silent" participants in the fishery, especially among shore workers in the Maritime Provinces outside Newfoundland. On the West Coast there are few fishers (or shore workers) not covered by one or more of the organizations examined here. The major areas where gaps appear are in the Maritimes, but even there the political and ideological "field" is defined by the organizations that are currently seeking out and incorporating virtually all fishers.

Fisheries make an interesting case to study because even the most basic, fundamental capital/labour relations are often in dispute. Fishing has recently been involved in the ongoing struggle to define the rights of capital and the obligations of labour in both legal and practical terms, thus exposing assumptions simply taken for granted in other labour processes. These relations of production have undergone rapid transformation since the Second World War, and the core of this study is the narrative of their unfolding.

In summary, this book's main argument is that the abundance of organizations and spectrum of behaviours within the fishing industry of Canada can best be understood through a theory of property relations that explains the nature of organizations and the actions of their members in terms of the social relations of production following from the rights of property and the obligations of labour. Only by understanding the property relations of those within this wide range of organizations can one make sense of both the organization's existence and its behaviour, hence the nature of conflict and struggle itself.

The theory seeks to categorize the relationships characteristic of the major fisheries organizations, examine their content, and explain their actions. In so doing, it is argued that the theory of property relations utilized here has broader applicability for understanding all class structure and action. The exercise is one seeking to demonstrate the utility of class theory for understanding very complex social phenomena. In the process, the contemporary nature of Canada's fishery will be illuminated. Some will not like what is revealed. It is hoped, nevertheless, that the understanding offered will help guide people's actions to promote progressive changes.

CHAPTER TWO
East Coast Production Patterns

Commercial fishing was the *raison d'être* for early European forays into what became Canadian waters – Norse, Portuguese, Spanish, French, and English sailors took their turns on the wide continental shelf. By the seventeenth century the combatants for possession had been reduced to the French and the British, who struggled over the spoils of the sea for two centuries. The quarry was cod – synonymous with "fish" on the East Coast.

Although the British theoretically had sovereignty over the island of Newfoundland in 1635, the French continued to use a base at Plaisance to attack the British in St. John's. "The Treaty of Utrecht in 1713 finally gave Plaisance to the British, who forthwith named it Placentia; the French lost everything but four islands: St. Pierre, Miquelon, Cap Breton, and St. Jean (now Prince Edward Island)."[1] Most of the French in Newfoundland migrated to Cape Breton Island (protected by the fort at Louisbourg) while they retained fishing and drying rights on Newfoundland's northern coast from Cape Bonavista to Point Riche, an area that came to be known as the French shore. Following further French-English warfare, the Treaty of Paris in 1763 limited French holdings to the islands of St. Pierre and Miquelon, although reduced claims to a "French shore" (running from Cape St. John to Cape Rae) remained. (The islands, captured by the British in 1793, restored to France in 1802, and recaptured in 1803, were finally returned to France in 1814; the population migrated back and forth to the Magdalen Islands.)

Regulation of the East Coast fishery appears to have begun

in the early 1850s (war having been the previous instrument of control and the means for establishing rights) in the person of Pierre Fortin, who for sixteen years patrolled the Gulf of St. Lawrence representing the colonial government and enforced (after having helped create) the new Fisheries Act. He monitored the fishing of American schooners, noted illegal practices, and recommended species quotas and conservation measures such as mesh sizes.[2]

Newfoundland, which gained responsible government in 1854, continued the traditional inshore fishery in outports dotting the island's coastline. In addition the island had two large continental shelf fisheries, the Labrador "floater" cod fishery on the northeast coast and the Grand Bank dory fishery on the south coast. The Labrador fishery is described thus by W.A. Black:

> From the beginning of the fishery to the middle of the nineteenth century, the floater fishery was organized on a feudal basis that was generally known as the "truck" system. The fish merchants owned the means of production and employed fishermen to catch the fish. In return for their labor, as money was not exchanged, the fisherman received sufficient goods to maintain himself and his family to the next season. . . .
>
> By mid-century these practices were gradually modified and the credit system emerged. As the population had steadily increased, the ability of the fish merchants to support the increasing population declined. . . . The practice developed for the fisherman in the spring to secure from one of the large outfitting merchants or one of the large mercantile concerns of St. John's supplies of salt, gear, and provisions, on credit. . . . Fish were turned over to the merchant as a "set off" against his account.[3]

There were variations on the specific organization of production, but typically in a merchant-owned vessel, which carried several trap boats and twelve men, there were twenty-five half-shares. The ship was credited with eleven half-shares, the floater skipper with a full share, and the sharesmen on the trap boats with a half-share each.[4] The fishery was carried out by crews that travelled from the northeast coast in the spring to make camp on Labrador, where cod traps and drying stages were established, the entire labour force returning in the fall to the island, where additional curing of the fish was carried out.

The most famous early social movement in Newfoundland arose from this fishery. The Fishermen's Protective Union, led by William F. Coaker, was organized at Herring Neck in 1908 in protest against the credit system and the St. John's "fishocracy." It was a populist movement, later becoming a political party that had its heyday in the second and third decades of the century as the opposition party in 1913 and a junior partner in a coalition government in 1919. The floater fishers and the sealers formed its base, but also members were loggers, farmers, and generally all the "toiling masses" within the region. The local economy was tied to overseas markets, which collapsed in the severe depression of 1908. Coaker sought to reform the export process by establishing marketing boards and to create supply co-operatives to import provisions wholesale and thus free "the people" from the grip of the merchants. By 1911 the Fishermen's Protective Union had 12,500 supporters, and by 1914 it had 20,000. The movement's reform platform included social measures such as compulsory education in outport schools, development of local hospitals, and even a system of universal pensions, in addition to elected representation on road and school boards. The movement was bound to be opposed by the St. John's merchants, but it was also attacked by the Catholic Church, which accused it of "protestantism." Wartime conditions undermined the movement, and after 1921 the party lost its political force. It represented, however, the only major social movement among rural Newfoundlanders during the next half century when the same region was to produce the Northern Fishermen's Union, which laid the foundations for the Newfoundland Fishermen, Food and Allied Workers' Union (see page 111).[5]

The Newfoundland dory fishery on the Grand Bank operated from the south coast of the Burin Peninsula. Banking schooners carrying dories began to arrive early in the eighteenth century but reached their golden age in the mid-nineteenth century. At the peak of this fishery in the 1880s there were 330 vessels from Newfoundland on the Banks; it started its decline a decade later, finally disappearing by the 1950s. This was also a cod fishery in which heavy salt was used on board ship and drying flakes on shore. The schooners were usually merchant owned, and skippers were sometimes part-owners.

The schooners had aboard crews to handle six to twelve two-man dories plus a skipper, the cook, and a deckhand (or "kedgie") for a total of from fifteen to twenty-seven men. Skippers appear to have had a high degree of discretion regarding the use of either the count or the share "lay" systems, which were competing or co-operating methods of payment, depending upon the strategy of the skipper and the experience of the crew. Each dory had trawl lines, coiled in tubs, to be baited and set. When the trawl was in place the crew would haul it over the dory, bait the hooks, remove the fish, and return the line to the water (a system known as "under-running"). Initially the schooner would sail out to the fishing banks and anchor while the dory men fished and returned with their catch to be salted in the hold. Later systems were developed whereby the dories were set out while the schooner was under sail, dropping the dories in particular patterns. When the catch had been returned to the schooner to be "green salted," everyone helped split the fish and store it away. When "on the count" (also known as a tally), each dory crew was paid according to its actual catch; when "on share" each crew had an equal proportion of the total catch.

When the fishery shifted from sail to power, the skipper typically received 5 per cent of the gross landed value of the catch plus one crew share. The ship owner took half the balance after the cost of bait and ice were deducted from the "market value" of the catch. From the remaining half were deducted the vessel costs, provisions, insurance, the skipper's commission, and premiums for the mate, engineer, and cook. The remainder of the half-balance was then divided by the number of the crew (which included the skipper, mate, engineer, and cook). Basically the payment method was a co-adventurer system whereby crews were totally dependent upon the value of the catch for their income.[6] This system is still an important point in the debates that continue to rage about how fishers should be paid, even though that specific type of fishery no longer exists.

Processing techniques also changed. The *Canadian Fisherman* reported in April 1945 that

the big port of Grand Bank which once sent twenty-two vessels to the Banks, this year is sending only five.

Perhaps the most significant thing that we notice in the sailing of the Bank fleet this year is that some will go "fresh-fishing".

Fresh fishing trips occupy about four or five days. With ten dories working, the vessels average one hundred and fifty thousand pounds of fresh cod per trip, which is iced down as soon as caught and delivered to the filleting plants at the end of the trip.[7]

Four years later, when Newfoundland was entering confederation with Canada, the fishing industry was undergoing revolutionary changes from the salt trade to frozen fish; the result was that the entire society was being restructured. The provincial government sponsored massive relocations of people from settlements that had depended upon domestic production of salt fish to centres intended to be based upon industrial processing. Commercial fish production shifted to the wet-fish trawler for its main source of year-round supply. The producers changed from being locally controlled merchants to externally dominated industrial firms. It was now evident to the fishers and fish plant workers that old paternalistic structures no longer worked. Their own material conditions had dramatically altered, as had their ideas. The government sought new ways to protect local interests and, ironically, the union would emerge as one such means, as we shall see.

Lunenburg, Nova Scotia, was another centre for offshore dory fishers working from schooners. In the late 1880s "each vessel carried from fourteen to sixteen men, depending on the vessel size. This number increased to a fairly uniform twenty-one men per vessel by the end of the century. A typical crew would consist of the skipper, cook, salter, header, throater, flunkey, and fourteen fishermen divided into seven double dory crews."[8] During the period from 1896 to 1930, the famous "Lunenburg-64" system was developed, as distinct from Newfoundland practice. Ruth Fulton Grant described it thus in 1934:

A type of co-operative enterprise has emerged in the Lunenburg vessel fishery. Each schooner is ordinarily divided into 64 shares (aliquot parts), which may be owned by the builders, the chandlers, the fishermen, or the townspeople who may wish to invest – there are possibly forty or fifty people share owners in one vessel. Credit is obtained from outfitting companies, which, in turn are financed by local banks.[9]

From the trip's gross receipts were deducted the wages of the header and throater, the captain's commission, bait, ice, and delivery costs. Half the remaining amount went to the crew after deduction of the cook's wage and the costs of insurance and fuel. The other half was claimed by the vessel owners who paid for gear, salt, and provisions.

A different perspective on the Lunenburg-64 system of shares is provided by Gene Barrett, who claims that it was primarily a device for financing a trawler voyage. Income was derived from both a "lay" for labouring on the voyage and a dividend income from shares. The share system permitted merchant capital to participate in voyages and gave merchants leverage over supplies and fish sales. After reviewing company books, which show that capitalists, not those directly engaged in the fishery, were the main shareholders, he concludes: "The Lunenburg 64 concept of profit-sharing can therefore be considered to have been dead, in its original form and intent, by the post-war (1920s) ... however, its flowering as a social philosophy divorced from all reality in either the inshore or offshore fishery reveals its function as an ideology."[10]

Barrett has identified four "basic types of labour" participating in the Nova Scotian fishery from 1900 to 1930. These were a "small but growing number of wage-earning fish plant workers," who worked seasonally in small (less than ten employees) firms in their own communities; the inshore fishers; the schooner (dory) fishers mentioned above; and the trawler crews. He reports that in 1906 about two hundred fish handlers in five Halifax plants walked out over wage demands, but plant workers were not represented by a union until the 1930s and 40s when "fish plant workers would lead the entire trade union movement in Nova Scotia."[11] Inshore fishers were heard from in the form of the Fishermen's Union of Nova Scotia, formed in 1905, but it rejected other unions and "isolated itself from the growing labour movement in Nova Scotia in general" and met its demise in the late 1920s. Although called a union, it was more like the associations, being characterized as a "self-helping order" and "lobby association."[12]

Trawler crews were the rising force in the industry and the leading edge of the shift from salted to fresh/frozen fish processing. Trawler crews worked the large "dragger" ships that catch fish by pulling huge nets behind them rather than by lines worked from individual dories as on the schooners where the fish was salted. In 1920, 80 per cent of Atlantic groundfish (particularly cod) was salted; by 1939, salt fish production had fallen to 54 per cent and fresh/frozen had risen to 34 per cent.[13] Barrett has traced the history of fishers' organizations during this period. The Canadian Fishermen's Union had eight locals in Nova Scotia in 1940, but it had been unable to renew its contracts. Barrett reports that

> in September 1943 a convention of the Canadian Fishermen's Union was held in Lunenburg, and, at the behest of the trawlermen of Lockeport, the union split into two – the Canadian Fishermen's Union and the Canadian Fish Handlers' Union. By 1944 the two unions claimed a combined total of ten locals – six among the fishermen, and four among the fish handlers – representing over 1,000 men.[14]

The National War Labour Relations Board, however, overruled a decision by the Nova Scotia board to certify the Canadian Fishermen's Union in 1946. When the two unions were reunited to form the Canadian Fishermen's and Fish Handlers' Union they divided into three divisions: inshore, deep sea, and fish handlers. Later, in the famous Zwicker decision (to be discussed in Chapter Five), the trawler crews were decertified on the grounds that they were co-adventurers and hence ineligible to be union members.

Out of this fiasco came the Nova Scotia Fishermen's Federation Act of 1947 which, Barrett reports,

> saddled fishermen with a restrictive, ineffectual, and frustrating piece of legislation for some time to come.
>
> The revised Act restricted collective organization among fishermen to one organization, the Fishermen's Federation of Nova Scotia, and excluded all groups in the industry, except the offshore fishermen, from membership. The Act further limited organization to each county, frustrating either industry-wide, or even company-wide, bargaining. . .the Act restricted bargaining to only two items: the terms or conditions of sharing, and work conditions. It still treated fishermen as co-adventurers without recourse to collective bargaining over wages or supplementary benefits, hours of work, job classification or security, or grievance procedures.[15]

Needless to say, the legislation demolished the Canadian Fishermen's Union. What remained was the shore workers' union, known as the Canadian Fish Handlers' Union, which was to become the Canadian Seafood Workers' Union (see page 106). The legislation also foreshadowed similar repressive and deceptive labour laws passed in Nova Scotia right through the 1980s. Meanwhile, conditions changed so that trawler crews became partially unionized but only after a tremendous struggle to drag the processors and provincial government out of the dark ages. Even now in Nova Scotia the struggle continues for the right to unionize small- and intermediate-scale fishers.

The primary impetus to the industrialization of the Atlantic fishery has come from the processors, who wish to regularize, rationalize, and maximize their processing capacity. "Inshore" fisheries can operate for only a few months of the year (more of them in southwestern Nova Scotia and fewer in northern Newfoundland), while "offshore" fisheries can operate virtually year-round, thus forming a continuous source of product. As the large processors concentrated on the fresh/frozen fish market and undertook to produce a continuous supply, they were required to enlarge their offshore source. Initially this supply was met by wooden side trawlers (which dragged the nets over the side), some of them company owned, others partially company financed and owned by captain, crew, and shareholders. The cost of such ships, including their expensive maintenance and financing, soon drew more and more of them into company ownership. Company ownership became the dominant form after steel stern trawlers were introduced to replace the smaller and less stable wooden side trawlers. These ships are worked by trawler crews.

When the fishery changed from salt to fresh fish, payments to crews were made before the next voyage began instead of after the fish was eventually sold. Thus an element of the "co-adventurer" illusion was eliminated. Another that persisted, however, was the idea that the trawler crews "sold" the fish caught to the processing company at a "market" price. Actually, side trawlers' lays in 1945 provided a 37-per-cent share of the gross stock for the crew, everyone receiving one share. The captain and the mate received in addition a commission; the cook and engineer had per diem wages, but the rest of the crew were paid only the percentage mentioned above with no guarantees.

Illustration 1

OTTER TRAWLING

Otter trawls are used to catch groundfish such as cod and haddock. The bag-shaped net is dragged along the ocean floor by a trawler. Fish are trapped in the closed end. Cone-shaped, the net is kept open at its mouth by iron-shod wooden doors.

Over the years some changes were made in trawler construction. Wooden side trawlers gave way first to steel vessels and then, in 1965, the method changed to fishing from the stern. The fishing gear itself – a net with trawl doors (see Illustration 1) – has changed little except that the nets and doors are more efficient. The principle remains the same: the net, known as the trawl, is towed by the trawler and spread by "doors" that plane in the water. The net, with the catch in the "cod end," is then dragged on board and opened so that the fish spill onto the deck in preparation for storage. There are some differences in the labour process between side and stern trawlers, particularly concerning the time needed to perform certain tasks such as "shooting" and retrieving the trawl and time for unloading; the larger stern trawlers are also faster and have a greater carrying capacity. Side trawlers cannot operate in heavy weather conditions as stern trawlers can and are not attractive to crews for productivity and safety reasons. Moreover, they have less comfortable quarters and make less money.

Aboard a trawler the captain is the company's representative.

Each captain has a great deal of autonomy in catching the fish and running "his" boat, although there are some directives from the processor concerning desirable species and landing times. Companies obviously keep close watch on the captain regarding productivity, and for a crew member there can be a considerable variation in income (in the range of $10,000 a year), depending upon the captain. As the director of a major trawler fleet said, "Somebody will be highliner and somebody has to be on the bottom, but it need not be the same guy every time." Captains lead a very competitive life; either they perform or they are "retired." Nevertheless, they do control recruitment of their crews and are pretty much on their own once they leave port. Captains are supposed to be "at the source of up-to-date information" and knowledgeable about where the fish are, but they are increasingly directed to particular grounds and species by the companies as state-set quotas rather than competition govern the catch.

Trawlers usually fish for eight to fourteen days with a sixteen-member crew aboard (most have eighteen or nineteen men in their rotation system, allowing some to remain ashore). Each has a mate who supervises the crew and net operations, a boatswain in charge of the deck work and one watch, two engineers, a cook, and ten deck hands. In a typical trip sequence after a minimum of forty-eight hours in port, the trawler leaves port at 9 A.M. for the place where the captain has decided he is going to fish (the shore staff having indicated the species they want). The mate looks after the fishing gear and preparations while the ship is steaming to the fishing grounds. Once on the grounds, the crew fishes in a continuous twenty-four-hour operation of set-haul-set for seven or eight days with irregular eating and sleeping breaks. The length of the trip is determined by the first catch of fish, as they try to return to port before the first fish caught is ten days old. The fish are washed, gutted, stowed, and iced by the crew. Although icing tends to be a specialized task, the whole crew is expected to fulfil a range of tasks from dressing fish to hauling nets and repairing gear.

Canadian stern trawlers are generally 150 feet (46 metres) long and weigh about 750 gross tonnes. They should not be confused with the factory trawlers, which operate on the same catching principle but process the catch into frozen fillets. Canadian trawlers are, at maximum, whole-fish freezer trawlers that only gut the fish before freezing it. (Late in 1985 two factory freezer trawlers were licensed by the federal government for use by Canadian companies.) The factory freezer trawlers make up the foreign fleet that operates off the coast and first appeared in the early 1950s. Their standard equipment is the stern ramp, the multi-plate freezer, and the Baader filleting machine.[16] At over 2,600 gross tonnes in size and with crews of one hundred persons, these boats dwarf the Canadian trawlers. The catch is processed on board into oil, meal, and fillets. The stern ramp system was adopted from that used by whaling ships in size and design; the nets are recovered from behind, which allows the ships to move rapidly in the water and pull the net and fish even in rough weather. The range of these trawlers has been greatly extended by their freezer capacity utilizing the multi-plate freezing technique invented by Clarence Birdseye. The automated filleting machines they use were developed by the Nordischer Maschinenbau Baader company of West Germany. These developments opened the Grand Banks to the European "fresh fish" trade. The British began in 1953 with the trawler *Fairty*, the Soviets followed in 1956 with the *Pushkin*, and by 1959, 35 Soviet factory ships were working the Banks. By 1965 there were 106 foreign factory trawlers and 30 mother ships. The size of the fleet has subsequently declined markedly. According to William Warner, "from a peak of slightly over one hundred ships, the West German distant water fleet now counts only twenty-eight."[17]

Since 1977 and the declaration of a 200-mile coastal management zone (see Chapter 5), the foreign fleets have all but disappeared with the exception of those fishing for specified quotas of underutilized species or having historic claims (for example, those of the French based on possession of the islands of St. Pierre and Miquelon). Initially it appeared that the declaration would be a bonanza for Canada's trawlers and near-shore fleet. Indeed, a boat-building boom was the response to the prospect. But high interest rates and the cost of fuel formed a new "tax" that these boats could not meet, especially when it was combined with weak markets.

East Coast fishing is by no means entirely on such a grand scale. Most fishers still work on much smaller boats and much closer to shore. Very close to shore are the cod traps (see Illustration 2), which are still the mainstay of Newfoundland fishers. Cod traps tend to be worked as family operations, with several traps to a family. There is an investment of about $10,000 per trap

Illustration 2

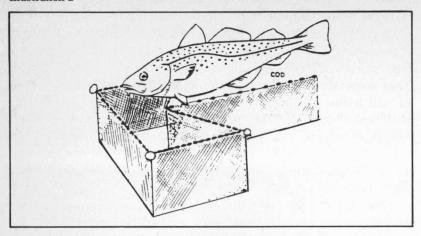

COD TRAPPING

The cod trap, the mainstay of thousands of Newfoundland inshore fishermen, is set in varying depths of water. It resembles a huge room of net without a roof extending from the surface to the ocean bottom. Cod swim into it and are trapped. Fishermen haul the trap to take their catch.

for materials and a minimum of $30,000 for a boat to work the traps. Berths, as trap locations are called, are sites either held traditionally for generations or assigned by an annual lottery. Such tenure practices, which may vary throughout the province, have a lengthy tradition and even legitimation by government regulation.[18]

Besides traps, the other main types of fishing gear are baited hooks, hand-held jiggers, and gillnets. Until the 1960s there was little change in the techniques, although the addition of depth sounders and radar was most important for finding the fishing banks. This had been done earlier by calculations based on time, direction, and the speed of the boat, but variables such as wind or tides could make this method unreliable (especially since fish and fog are said to go together). Now it is much easier to find both the fishing places and home port. A major change was the introduction of gillnets, particularly as the market for species other than cod developed with the frozen fish trade. Gillnetting included the introduction of power gurdies for hauling nets and new types of netting. Before 1950 only baited lines and traps were used in Newfoundland. Power gurdies have also made it possible for crews of about three to work four or five traps; earlier, up to six were needed for one trap.

In considering the background of the Newfoundland fishery it is important to recall that the close family life in the outports was based on the preparation of lightly salted, sun-dried cod. That domestic form of production depended upon family labour in which the men caught and the women (often aided by the children) cleaned and "made" the fish. When the market for salt fish declined and there was an industrialization of production, the Newfoundland government responded with its famous resettlement programs from 1957 through 1965 to move people from their villages to what were optimistically called employment centres. Domestic fishery labour was no longer required, but the new processing plants certainly needed a supply of available wage labour.[19] An excellent illustration is Arnold's Cove, which grew as a result of the resettlement program. In 1966 there were only fifteen families in Arnold's Cove; now there are 1,500 people (many still living in trailers), brought from the islands of Placentia Bay initially to work for the now bankrupt oil refinery at Come-by-Chance. National Sea Products Limited subsequently opened a modern processing plant there in the fall of 1979 at a cost of $6.5 million that employs most of the community's women and buys from 750 inshore fishers. The men go back to their old berths for five days a week to fish. Since 1972 collector boats have been making daily rounds to the fish camps between April and October. People can be relocated, but not fish, and even fish are more reliable than the Come-by-Chances of our era.

Beginning in the early 1960s fishers were encouraged to break away from their old patterns of cod traps and move into longliners, which were supposed to turn them into a mobile fleet. "Longliner" is a general boat term in Newfoundland and is not restricted to the baited-hook fishery with the same name.[20] The main advantage of these vessels was to be their expanded range of operation. Most used gillnets, some otter trawls or Danish seines, longlines (hooks), or crab traps. Since their introduction, longliners have been nothing but trouble for the fishers, drastically increasing their production costs with interest payments and fuel bills yet not making significant new products available except for holders of special licences, such as those for crab, which have been lucrative. A multitude of gear arrangements are possible with a longliner and as many different systems of payment.

The longliners were intended to assist the rationalization of processing plants by supplying fewer plants from greater distances. They also make a wider area available to inshore fishers, hence making both fishing and processing less seasonal.

Processors are, moreover, demanding species beyond the capacity of the inshore cod traps and catchable only by the gillnets carried on the longliners, which can, in turn, deliver to the more centralized collection points. On the other hand, the boats cost more, in both investment and operating costs, thus requiring a larger catch and longer seasons to meet expenses. The result is that the longliners run into competition with the trawler fleet for access to the resource.

The longliner and the cod trap are based upon the same fundamental social structure. Both are intermediate-scale in their labour requirements (about four or five crew) and based, in Newfoundland, upon a patriarchal structure of kinship (father-sons/brothers). Family ties often condition the class relations between skipper and crew and may be determinant in the first instance. Similar patterns prevail among the herring seiners in southwestern Nova Scotia and the salmon seiners of the Native Brotherhood of British Columbia. In all three instances "family" is further affected by region and/or ethnicity, additional factors that mediate broader class forces; that is, the relationship between the owner/skipper and the labourers/crew in intermediate-scale situations (longliners, cod traps, and seiners) with strong family ties and strong regional or ethnic cultures can weaken the tensions between capital and labour within the immediate process. Such patterns influence membership in organizations and the nature of those organizations. It will be noted, for example, that in both the Newfoundland Fishermen, Food and Allied Workers' Union (see page 111) and the Native Brotherhood (see page 93) the skippers of intermediate-scale vessels are members of the union along with the crews of these vessels, even though formally the skippers employ the crew members. This practice has significant class consequences to be explored later.

The closest parallel in the Maritime Provinces to the Newfoundland cod traps is the herring weir fishery of the Bay of Fundy (see Illustration 3). As John Kearney says, "for the first 60 years of the twentieth century, the weir ruled supreme in the Bay of

Illustration 3

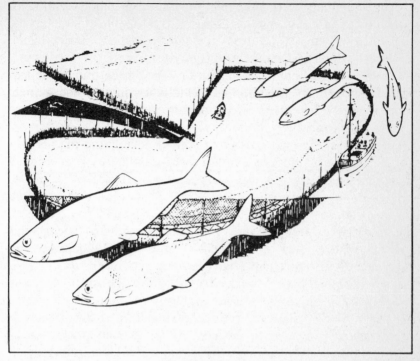

WEIR FISHING

Weirs – large corral-like structures – are used near shore to catch immature herring commonly known as sardines. Fish are diverted into the weirs by fences stretching into shore; fishermen run a seine net around the inside of the weir gathering the catch within.

Fundy. The expansion of the weir fishery was caused by the invention of a technique for canning fish."[21] That canned fish is widely known as the sardine, and the weirs average 25,000 metric tonnes of the herring used to can sardines each year. Kearney reports that a Weir Fishermen's Union was formed in 1906:

> In the Union, all the fishermen agreed to sell their fish to the canners for not less than a certain minimum price. In the years when all the weir fishermen stuck together in the Union, herring prices stayed high. But more often, some weir fishermen would make special deals with the processors and as a result, the price would begin to drop as more and more fishermen began to break ranks with the Union.

In 1925, the Union died for good, and thereafter, weir herring prices remained very low.[22]

As will be evident in Chapter Eight, weir fishers have again joined in an important association (and are acting more like a real union than the original one appears to have done). In the 1930s the weir fishers' source of supply was threatened by the first seiners. Seiners are highly mobile intermediate-scale boats with crews of five to seven that capture fish by encircling the schools with large nets that are then "pursed" or drawn together at the bottom and hauled back on board. These very efficient boats were banned in the Bay of Fundy during the weir season and restricted to winter fishing. The seiners then began in the mid-1950s to fish for adult herring during the summers and moved away from the Passamaquoddy area in search of herring to make meal and pearl essence. A food herring fishery developed after 1976, sustained by over-the-side sales. This will be an important topic later.

Most characteristic of the small-scale producers in the Atlantic region are lobster fishers (see Illustration 4) who tend their traps on their own or with a partner/helper close to shore. They are under strict government controls regarding open seasons and number of traps allowed. Few of them fish simply for lobster but combine it with gillnetting for herring, small-scale scallop dragging, gillnetting for groundfish, or even jigging for cod or squid. Basically, however, the organization of production for lobster is characteristic for all so-called inshore fishers. There are a few offshore lobster fishers sailing out of southwestern Nova Scotia (involving fifty-six full-time fishers with an average of seven crew per vessel, making four-day trips and limited to 1,000 traps per vessel), but they are highly specialized boats. This fishery was initially limited to six former sword-fish boats after unsafe mercury levels called a halt to that fishery. Two more licences were added later.[23] Most lobster fishers, however, return home daily and fish about three hundred traps (the number varying by region), which are set out and anchored to buoys. Besides the daily checking of traps, gathering the catch, and re-baiting, lobster fishers must also make and maintain their traps in the off-season. Like most small-scale fishers, they also spend a good deal of time maintaining their boats.

Taking a somewhat wider view of the Atlantic fishery, we should

Illustration 4

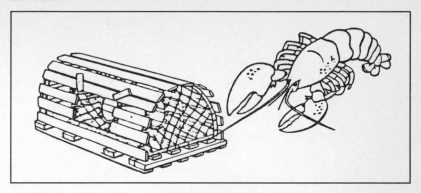

LOBSTER FISHING

The lobster trap constructed of wood laths and twine is baited and weighted with stones to keep it on the ocean floor. Some fishermen tie a number of traps to a line; others fish one trap from each line. Metal traps are also coming into use in this inshore fishery.

note that the bulk of production is located in Newfoundland (42 per cent), although Nova Scotia has the largest share of value (47 per cent) while New Brunswick has about 10 per cent of each category and Quebec about 8 per cent. Prince Edward Island has only 3 per cent of volume but 6 per cent of value.[24] Nova Scotia has a high share of the value because of the scallop fishery, which constitutes only one sixth of its volume but one third of its value. Since 1942, Quebec's fish catch has had a value about equal to that of Prince Edward Island's and about half the value of New Brunswick's landings. Nova Scotia's catch is worth about twice that of Newfoundland (roughly equal to the British Columbia catch).

If we ignore the *relative* importance of fishing to each province, British Columbia and Nova Scotia have been the major Canadian producers since the Second World War, followed by Newfoundland, New Brunswick, Quebec, and Prince Edward Island.[25] Of the twenty trawler ports on the East Coast, Quebec and Prince Edward Island have one each, New Brunswick has none, Nova Scotia has six and Newfoundland twelve.

Since 1946, lobster has surpassed cod (and all other species) in value. Especially since 1956 scallops have been increasingly profitable, joining these two species, which are followed, at about half the respective value, by herring, redfish, and haddock. (On the West Coast, salmon is the most valuable species by far; only herring and halibut have value about equal to that of the other major species.) In Newfoundland cod reigns, but in the Maritime Provinces the species are heterogeneous. There lobster, scallops, and herring are just as important as groundfish, yet sub-regions often depend upon a single species.

A sense of fishing's importance is indicated in the recent statement of the Economic Council of Canada that "during the 1980s, 75 per cent of all the communities in the Atlantic provinces had some connection with the fishery, and 20 per cent of them had no other local industry."[26] The Kirby Commission inquiry into the Atlantic fishery recently found that "about 700 processing facilities are located in 440 fishing communities throughout the region. The jobs provided by these plants employ about 21 per cent of the labour force in those communities."[27] Licensed fishers in Atlantic Canada increased from 36,500 in 1974 to 53,500 in 1981 (there had been 49,000 in 1965). The number of fishers who actually used their licences in 1981, however, numbered only 23,400 full time and 17,455 part time.[28] It is estimated that the part-timers are actually equivalent to about 4,360 full-timers; therefore "a total of 27,794 active fishermen whose primary source of earning is fishing activity" work in Atlantic Canada.[29]

How does the future look for these people? Since the 200-mile limit was set, both the volume and the value of the catch have risen, along with the number of fishers, yet the industry is in crisis and currently undergoing a dramatic restructuring. This is particularly alarming when "one-quarter of the population of the four Atlantic provinces live in small fishing communities, more than half of which have single-sector economies that are dependent almost entirely on fishing and fish processing."[30] The economic problems of these people have a political basis as much as anything else and can no longer be blamed on the foreign fleets, biology, or even the weather. The answers will have to come from much closer to home and be addressed in much more human terms.

CHAPTER THREE
West Coast Production Patterns

Unlike the Atlantic, the Pacific Ocean has a narrow continental shelf. For that reason most fishing is done on a relatively narrow coastal band instead of over widely distributed banks. Moreover, salmon is the dominant species in the West Coast fishery, and the fish are captured on their spawning runs to the rivers. The frequent and open class conflicts over its capture and value are strongly coloured by ethnic and racial tensions, more evident here than elsewhere in Canada. Salmon has been at the heart of the Native people's domestic economies for all of recorded time on the West Coast. It became valuable as a commodity, however, only when it could be canned (and later frozen) for transport to the world's markets. The fishery did not become commercial until canning techniques were developed, but when they were the canneries blossomed, especially along the Fraser River but spreading north to virtually all coastal communities as far as Alaska.

Ten canneries opened in British Columbia in 1878 and by 1895 there were at least forty-eight, thirty-one of them on the Fraser River. Cannery work was labour intensive and performed mainly by males, with 2,500 men working in the fishery for the Fraser River canneries in 1879, many of them Chinese and native Indians. The Chinese were concentrated in can-making and fish-cleaning and organized through a labour contract.[1] Many of the Chinese had been attracted to North America during the gold rushes of earlier years, but later arrivals were recruited directly as cannery labour, each operation having a so-called China House for the accommodation of usually two hundred workers.

At the turn of the century three-quarters of cannery labour was being performed by Chinese workers. Duncan Stacey has described the contract system that prevailed until the 1940s:

A Chinese crew worked for a Chinese contractor who had an agreement with a canning company to put up a pack for a certain amount of money per case. The contractor then sub-contracted the work to his crew, which was paid various rates for specific jobs such as butchering, filling, soldering, and so on. The contractor also provided his crew with room and board during the season in the cannery's China house. These Chinese contractors usually were backed up by a firm of Chinese merchants who provided working capital.

Under this system the contractor gave advances of $30 to $40 to each China crew member at the opening of the season to induce him to come to the cannery.... This system had many advantages for the canners. The contractor took respon-sibility for employing sufficient hands, especially for expert cannery labour needed for the manual canning systems, and cannery owners believed that the China boss could get more work out of his Chinese crew. Contrary to the popular view that Chinese labour was a docile workforce, the historic record is one of often violent strife.[2]

Sweeping changes were already taking place in cannery tech-nology with the introduction of machinery, a subject Stacey has studied in detail. Using evidence from the Royal Commission on Chinese and Japanese Immigration in 1902, he says

one washing- or wiping-machine with, at most, three people could process up to 2,000 cases every day whereas the old manual system demanded 20 to 30 hand washers. Two men with a capping machine put up 1,500 to 2,000 cases per day; under the old system this process involved 20 labourers. The fish-cutting machine saved the labour of five men on 1,500 cases per day. The labour of 15 or 20 more was saved by the application of an automatic cooking process, a tester, and an automatic washer. Two men did as much work with a soldering machine as 75 men working by hand would have done.[3]

Cannery owners took advantage of the newly developed technology to centralize control and rationalize production (that is, make it more profitable). The benefits of the new capital-intensive system accrued to large-scale capital. The British Columbia Packers Association was formed as a consortium in 1902 to buy forty-two coastal fish plants, accounting for 55 per cent of production.

As cannery production spread northward along the coast, typically locating at inlets and estuaries where the major salmon runs were concentrated, more Native people were utilized as labour. The men generally fished for the companies while the women (and children) worked the canneries. "By 1919 there were 97 canneries on the coast from the Fraser River to the Nass River, on Vancouver Island and on the Queen Charlottes, employing more than 9,000 people, the majority of whom were Indians. And more than one-third of all salmon fishermen were Indians."[4]

Although there had been sporadic work stoppages and attempts at organization earlier, the first notable fishers' organization was the Fraser River Fishermen's Protective Union of 1893 (which refused admittance to Japanese fishermen) with about 1,600 members. This organization attempted unsuccessfully to negotiate with Fraser River cannery-owners who joined forces during a strike in 1893.[5] Fishers had been paid a daily wage, but after the strike the canneries shifted to a piece-rate system, paying them by the piece or the pound and deducting rental payments for the gear and boat from their pay.[6] The number of licences was also dramatically increased from the previous limit of 500 (350 held by the canneries and 150 by "outside" contracts), thus making it more profitable for the canneries to buy fish than to pay daily rates.[7] More rather disorganized strike activity occurred in 1899 at Rivers Inlet and was broken by scab labour, but the benchmark strike took place in 1900.

The 1900 strike focused on the fishers' demands for twenty-five cents a sockeye against a company offer of twenty cents. The companies formed a consortium through the Fraser River Canners' Association "with power to set maximum fish prices and production quotas for each cannery, and to levy fines on violators of its decisions."[8] The Association refused to negotiate with the Union but made an agreement with Japanese fishers that eventually broke the strike. The force the canners and the state were willing to use, including the warship *Quadra* and troops labelled the Sockeye Fusiliers, convinced the fishers of the need for unity, and in 1901 the Grand Lodge of British Columbia Fishermen's Unions was formed as the earliest coast-wide forerunner to the United Fishermen and Allied Workers' Union.

Another noteworthy strike occurred in 1913 when 5,000 gill-netters united across racial lines, including an alliance of white and Native fishers with a Japanese fishers' union.[9] But no lasting labour organizations were set up until the 1930s. In 1931 the Fishermen's Industrial Union was formed for shore workers (changing its name to the Fishermen and Cannery Workers' Industrial Union in 1933), and for fishers the B.C. Seiners' Association, which quickly changed its name to the United Fishermen of British Columbia (and later to the United Fishermen's Federal Union), made its appearance. These new unions included, for the first time, a mixture of races – Japanese, Chinese, Natives, and whites – thus marking an important break with the practice of racial segregation. In 1935 the United Fishermen's Federal Union expelled owners of "large boats" (at that time vessels over 10.5 metres long), establishing a significant ideological position that would characterize this union and its successors.

In 1936, however, Alert Bay Native fishers formed the Pacific Coast Native Fishermen's Association as a result of their treatment during a strike.[10] By 1942 this association had joined with the Native Brotherhood of British Columbia, which was recognized in 1945 as the bargaining agent for its members (see page 93). During the Second World War the position of Native people in the fishery improved because of a strong demand for fish and the Japanese expulsions, which made boats available at low cost. In Percy Gladstone's estimation, the Native organization sponsored a form of "conservative unionism" in contrast to the "militant" practices of the other fishing union.[11]

With the notable exception of the Native Brotherhood, virtually all British Columbia fisheries-related unions joined together in 1945 to form the United Fishermen and Allied Workers' Union (see page 91). The new union had a membership of 3,000 fishers and 2,000 cannery workers. For the first time contracts were negotiated that included women and Chinese workers.[12] The new industrial union also sought to redress injustices suffered by Japanese fishers who were expelled from the coast in 1941 by the federal government. This was not an easy task as the following account from *Canadian Fisherman* of April 1945, reporting on the Union's founding convention, indicates. Addressing the two hundred delegates, Vancouver mayor J.W. Cornett "expressed his belief that it was better for the community generally that the Japanese had ceased to be a factor in this industry. He said B.C. had been faced with the Japanese problem for the past 40 years, and it did not want a return of these people after the war." The mayor was reprimanded for his racism, and Alex Gordon reported, on behalf of the cannery workers, that "half of the Chinese in the industry had already joined up, and that there were hundreds of women members of the organization."[13]

A parallel development of importance during the thirties was the formation in 1931 of the Prince Rupert Fishermen's Co-operative (see page 98), although the modern organization of the same name was not formed until 1939 as a result of the merger of its namesake and the North Island Trollers' Association. Guiding the co-op's birth was Norman McKenzie, lent by the Extension Department of St. Francis Xavier University (Antigonish, Nova Scotia) on a grant from the Dominion Department of Fisheries.[14] During this period its relations with the Pacific Coast Fishermen's Union, forerunner of the United Fishermen, were close, but signs of tension surfaced by 1944 when the Fishermen's Co-operative Federation (predecessor of the Prince Rupert Fishermen's Co-op) was formed to market fish coast-wide. A.V. Hill, a leading co-op supporter, commented:

> ... with the FCF sales agency, fish caught by Kyuquot Trollers would no longer be sold in the markets which affected the coastal unions, so that the necessity for sympathy strikes was finally eliminated. Indeed, many trollers, with the tradition of independence, apparently wondered why they should need a union, now that they no longer had business dealings with private enterprise companies. Some trollers had already dropped their Union membership after the Co-op was formed (West Coast Trollers' Association, in 1939, had merged into the Pacific Coast Fishermen's Union), but some Co-op members with strong Union loyalty still agitated for dual membership in Co-op and Union.[15]

Readers who detect a note of cynicism here are correct, but an explanation will have to wait until Chapter Six. One of the significant actors in that account will be the Deep Sea Fishermen's Union, which was originally the Pacific Halibut Fishermen's Union, organized in 1909 as an affiliate of the International Seamen's

Union. It was a type of craft union with only seventy-five to ninety-five members fishing for halibut. This union negotiated a master agreement with the Prince Rupert Vessel Owners' Association but left all other fishers to the jurisdiction of the United Fishermen.

The Prince Rupert Vessel Owners' Association, formed in 1941 as the Canadian Halibut Fishing Vessel Owners' Association and renamed in 1950, had originally twenty owner-members concentrated in northern British Columbia. They negotiated a master agreement with the Deep Sea Fishermen's Union, which had broken away in 1932 from its Seattle headquarters and chartered as Local 80 with the Canadian Trades and Labour Congress. Another important organization has been the Fishing Vessel Owners' Association of British Columbia, established in 1935 (incorporated in 1938), whose membership, according to its constitution, included "owners and part-owners owning one-third or more of such fishing vessels and fish carriers . . . [with] a registered tonnage of nine tons or more . . . requiring a crew of three or more in addition to the skipper." Explicitly excluded are processing-plant owners. Its membership of about 165 continues to have a master agreement with the United Fishermen concerning lay arrangements and working conditions aboard boats.

To understand the basic production patterns in the West Coast fishery it is necessary to identify the primary gear types. The basic structure of fishing is more homogeneous on the West Coast than on the East Coast. There are a few trawlers like those of the East Coast, although the boats are considerably smaller in most cases, and a few remaining halibut fishers who use a longline technique. The most common methods of fishing, however, are trolling, gillnetting, and seining. All three techniques are used for salmon; boats using gillnets and seines often catch herring as well during a very short fall opening.

Trolling is the technique of the most independent fishers (see Illustration 5). Their "opening" (the season when fishing is permitted) is the longest of any allotted to salmon fishers; they range the entire coastline following the salmon. Their catch – mainly coho and chinook (or spring) salmon – is prized for the fresh fish market because it is not damaged by nets and is immediately gutted and iced when caught. Trollers usually fish alone, operating six lines at a time strung on a complex system of tall poles and gurdies with bells that ring when a fish strikes. When fishing

Illustration 5

TROLLING

The salmon-catching troller, which varies in length from 30 to 48 feet, is marked by long poles which extend over the sides of the vessel while fishing. To these poles are attached weighted lines bearing lures which are dragged through the water at a slow speed. The salmon are caught on the lures.

they operate the boat from the "pit" in the stern, where all the controls required to steer the boat and the equipment needed to fish and clean are readily at hand. They go out for long periods of time, searching for exactly the right conditions, sleeping on their boats in the innumerable coves along the coast. Their trips have been extended by the shift into freezer trawlers, which can keep the catch "fresh" longer than conventional ice-boats. They carry a store of different bait and lures that are frequently changed according to conditions – tides, winds, time of day, depth of water, location, season, type of salmon, and so on – all of which enter into the mystique of trolling. Recently trollers have developed techniques for catching pink and sockeye salmon as well as their traditional chinook and coho, thus allowing them to participate in a somewhat different market situation than earlier.

Recently many gillnetters (see Illustration 6) have added trolling

Illustration 6

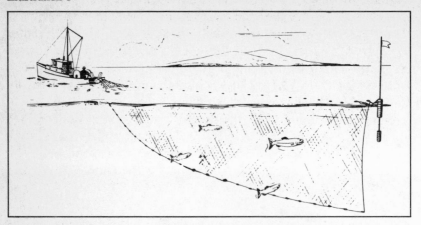

GILL NETTING

The gill netters, usually operated by one man, range upward from 28 feet in length, with large multi-purpose gill netters reaching 38 feet. These are the most popular craft for salmon fishing. From a drum at the stern the net is set out and hangs like a curtain in the water. The fish are caught by becoming entangled when they swim into the net.

equipment to their boats to extend their season. These combination boats, as they are called, account for about 10 per cent of all troll-caught fish (2.5 per cent of all salmon). Gillnetters have very limited seasons governed by the "open days" declared by the federal Department of Fisheries and Oceans that usually allow only one or two days of fishing a week during the salmon runs, so combination fishers switch to trolling as a supplementary activity.

The gillnet used on the West Coast is attached to a boat, not set separately and checked periodically as it is on the East Coast. It is a mesh suspended in the water, connected to a buoy, with a float-line on the top and lead-line on the bottom. Fish are captured in the curtain when their heads jam through the mesh and they are unable to pull back because of their gills. Operators of gillnets often work alone, although they may have a helper. Generally their boats are the same size as trollers' (30 to 50 feet, or about 9 to 15 metres). Since the installation of hydraulic drums to help haul the nets, gillnetters have been able to increase their number of sets per hour and decrease the need for additional help. Depending upon conditions, gillnetters leave their nets in the water anywhere from a few minutes to several hours before hauling them in. They, like the trollers, must be able to "read" the conditions and find the appropriate places to set their nets. They are, however, under much more intense time pressures because of the shortness of the openings. As will be discussed, they also have a much more limited market for their catch, which is made up mainly of sockeye, chums, and some pinks used for canning as well as incidental catches of coho and chinook.

Similar to gillnetters in the species they catch are seiners (see Illustration 7), although they have a greater share of the pink salmon, about the same amount of chum, and somewhat less sockeye. All net-caught fish tend to go to the canneries. Seiners have the same limited openings as gillnetters. Their boats tend to be larger (15 to 24 metres) and have a crew of five to seven. Traditionally the seine was set from a table (as shown on the back of a five-dollar bill), but since the 1950s it has been commoner to use a drum like that of the gillnetter but larger. Other changes have included hydraulic power blocks and synthetic nets. Seining is a more active method of fishing than gillnetting; the seiners encircle schools of fish by sending out a small skiff from the main boat to let out the net. Once the top is together, the bottom is "pursed" or drawn together, preventing the fish from escaping. The net is then hauled in and the fish are taken aboard with a "brailer" or dip net attached to a winch and a long pole.

Division of labour aboard the seiner tends to be low; the captain also works on deck and crew members serve as engineer, cook,

Illustration 7

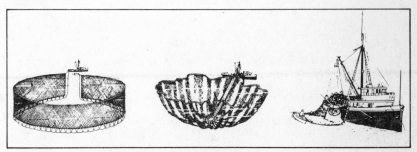

PURSE SEINING

Purse seiners ranging in length from 50 to 80 feet catch salmon and herring. The huge net, or purse seine, is set out from a platform or table at the stern and is manoeuvred to encircle a school of fish. The seine is then drawn together and the fish are dropped into the boat with a brailer, a large dip net on a long pole.

and skiff operator. Captain and crew share information about fishing, and the crew have a good deal of autonomy in handling nets and lines. A share agreement system was originally established during the era of table seines, when there were seven crew members rather than the five common now. The cost of fuel and oil are deducted from the gross value of the catch, leaving a balance that is divided into eleven shares. The "boat and net" get four shares. The cost of provisions is deducted from the remaining seven and the balance is divided evenly by the number of crew (including the captain). The price for salmon is negotiated between the United Fishermen and the processors and is the basis for determining the value of the catch. For herring roe, however, there is no lay arrangement. Instead, a labour rate is paid by the processors to the crew for each ton of herring landed. Seiner captains may hire their own crew as long as they are union members; if none are available, new hires are taken on as new union members.

The following table illustrates at a glance the distribution of salmon catch by sector:

Salmon Catch by Sector (1971-80 average per cent)[16]

	Seine	Gillnet	Troll	Sport*	Indian*	Total
Sockeye	35	53	6	0	6	100
Chum	48	49	1	0	2	100
Pink	69	15	15	0.5	0.5	100
Coho	12	11	61	15	1	100
Chinook	4	8	66	21	2	100
All	43	27	23	4	2	100

*"Sport" refers to non-commercially caught fish and "Indian" to the traditional food fishery of Native peoples.

It is clear that sockeye, chum, and pink salmon tend to be net caught while coho and chinook are usually line caught (by troll and sport fishers). The product of the salmon troller's labour is a finished product (dressed coho and chinook), not the raw material of the net fishers, whose catch is destined mainly for canning. The troller's catch commands a premium price and can be sold on a more competitive market (there are as many as a hundred cash buyers on the fishing grounds at times). The troller has, therefore, been less affected by the union-negotiated minimum prices for fish sold to the processors. Moreover, the troller has a much longer season opening (from spring to fall) than the day-a-week available to net fishers. The East Coast lobster fishers most closely resemble the troll salmon fishers, but they are restricted to a shorter season and actually have two products, smaller canning lobsters and live lobster. While they may be able to sell the live lobster to cash buyers, the only regular market for the canners is the processor.

The above account shows why the salmon trollers are the most independent commercial fishers. They typically fish alone, own their own boats, and sell a finished product on a competitive market. Not being directly affected by minimum price agreements with processors, they have less interest in unions than other fishers. Their own concerns are usually expressed through area-specific gear associations – the Pacific Trollers' Association, the Northern Trollers' Association, or the Gulf Trollers' Association – which lobby governments regarding enhancement, openings, licensing, environment, and restrictions on gear (such as the number of lines they may use). Trollers have also traditionally been co-op supporters, attempting to gain further independence through marketing arrangements for fresh and/or packaged fish that requires virtually no processing.

Combination fishers using both troll and gillnet are usually gillnetters who supplement their catch by trolling. Because their principal activity is gillnetting, they tend to be union supporters, as are virtually all seine boat crews, with the exception of those aligned with co-ops or the Native Brotherhood.

What is the fundamental difference between the operators of trollers, gillnetters, and seine boats? They may own their own boats and command their own labour in the sense that the boats are their means of realizing their labour. The fundamental difference, however, is that the seine boat skipper must also command the labour power of others. While gillnetters and trollers work alone, or at most with a helper, seiners require five to seven crew to fish (the number depending upon whether the catch is salmon or herring). In order to realize his own labour power, the seine boat skipper relies upon the labour of his crew. They are under his command; he organizes, directs and supervises their labour. Yet the crew, unlike workers in most labouring situations, share in the proceeds of their labour through a lay arrangement. A portion of the catch is allocated to the boat, which means capital, and the owner of that capital; the rest is allocated to labour, which includes the skipper. Skippers who are boat owners receive both a capital and a labour share. In addition, the skipper often receives a year-end bonus for delivering "his" catch to a particular processor.

After reviewing the general situation with respect to corporate control of processing, markets, and state policies in the next chapter, Chapter Five will be devoted to developing some theories of property relations which take into account the labour processes introduced here as a way of explaining the post-war history of the fishing industry. That history, to the present, will constitute the heart of this study.

CHAPTER FOUR

Unusual Markets and Stranger State Policies

"From the gnashing of teeth to the licking of lips" was federal Fisheries Minister Roméo LeBlanc's picturesque comparison of the bust that started the 1970s to the boom that ended the decade.[1] As is typical of resource-based, boom-bust economies, the fisheries wound down in the 1980s. Throughout these cycles the fishery remains an essential part of the livelihood of coastal Canada, especially in Atlantic Canada where it is the largest employer (aside from the state), accounting for 30 per cent of all jobs. To quote a more recent Fisheries minister, Pierre DeBane, the fishery "employs more people in absolute figures than the automobile industry of Ontario ... 92,000 versus 72,000.... It is the third largest foreign exchange earner after grain and lumber."[2] Canada is the world's number one exporter of seafood (and an abysmal twenty-fifth on the list of seafood eaters).

Product Markets

The shift from salt to frozen fish had its great boost when the "great fish-stick boom" began in 1952 in the United States.[3] As recently as 1984 the *Globe and Mail*'s "Report on Business" could still report about Newfoundland that "about half of what is handled each year is sold on the U.S. wholesale market in large frozen blocks, which are processed into products such as fish sticks and fish cakes. The rest are sold on the retail market in frozen fillet packs."[4]

Pierre DeBane, trying to comfort fishers about the recession

47

of the eighties, told them through the *Financial Post* that "the problem isn't a shortage of fish being harvested – the volume landed has more than doubled since 1974 and will grow substantially in the next five years – rather the problem is a lack of market opportunity."[5] Finally, in the summer of 1984, the federal government promised as much as $14.5 million for price stabilization "designed to reduce an inventory of about 30 million pounds of frozen cod destined for the U.S. market" by means of a Fisheries Prices Board.[6] Besides groundfish, which are the staple of the Atlantic fishery, other key fish species are oriented to the U.S. market. Over three quarters of Canada's scallop catch, for example, is sold to the United States. Atlantic herring, on the other hand, are more diverse in both their sources and their markets. Half are caught in New Brunswick, 30 per cent in Nova Scotia, and 20 per cent in Newfoundland. The United States takes 26 per cent of the catch, but West Germany (20 per cent), the Caribbean (16 per cent), and Japan (15 per cent) are also significant markets.[7]

On the West Coast the fishery is similarly export-directed and has been so for a long time. H.R. MacMillan, then president of British Columbia Packers, reported in 1934 that "the British Columbia salmon industry, which sells over 98% of its product outside British Columbia and over 50% outside Canada, is peculiarly exposed to any form of provincialism or nationalism that tends to restrict markets."[8] Even so, within the world market British Columbia producers are dwarfed by the Alaska salmon pack. In 1933 British Columbia was contributing only 8 per cent (compared to 70 per cent from Alaska), and fifty years later there was little change, with British Columbia holding 13 per cent of the market and Alaska 50 per cent.[9] Generally, British Columbia producers sell farther afield than in the U.S. market that predominates for East Coast companies; the British market is particularly significant for salmon, and the Japanese market, although fickle, is important for herring roe and salmon.[10]

Viewing the entire Canadian situation in the post-war era, it can be said that the main change has been the increase in demand for frozen filleted products accompanied by a decline of the market for whole fish and canned products. Whereas in 1945 (the first year when statistics for fresh and frozen fish were stated separately) fresh fish accounted for 38 per cent of value, thirty years later this product had declined to 21 per cent; the proportion of the market held by frozen fish increased over the span from 12 per cent to 53 per cent; canned fish, meanwhile, fell from 30 per cent to 14 per cent of the market.[11]

Port Markets

"Port market" is the latest catch-phrase for the point at which fishers sell their fish to buyers. Receiving the most notice recently on the East Coast have been over-the-side sales (about which more will be said later because of their political importance), but they account, surprisingly, for "only about 2 per cent of the catch."[12] There is, however, a considerable variety in port market situations, the most innovative of which occurs in the most marginal fisheries. For instance, virtually all inland/fresh-water fish are sold through a single buying organization, the Freshwater Fish Marketing Corporation, reaching northern Ontario, Manitoba, Saskatchewan, Alberta, and the Northwest Territories. It is a federally operated Crown corporation. Similarly, following recommendations of commissions in 1953 and 1963, the federal government created the Canadian Saltfish Corporation in 1970 (albeit minus the "development" role the commissions had suggested).[13] Although this was long after salt fish had had a major place in the Newfoundland fishery, the exceptional success of the Crown corporation has dramatically strengthened the salt fishery. The Canadian Saltfish Corporation had been a last-ditch effort on the part of the government after the collapse of private markets and major subsidies in 1967. Both these Crown corporations operate like co-ops, paying the fishers the estimated price at the start of the season and adding final payments after the returns are totalled. Their success has often caused questions about how the major private buyers have functioned and serves as a basis for suggestions about marketing boards.

When discussing marketing boards, however, one should keep in mind that they deal only with prices paid for fish (as do fish auctions, such as those for halibut in Prince Rupert) and do not address working conditions, benefits, or the organization of workers for a united voice. Such boards help to set prices; they do not negotiate prices as a proxy for wages. Most fishers face a port market that is a large processing company with intricate controls over the conditions of sale. The most obvious example is the crews of trawlers directly owned by the processors and whose "prices" have no market other than labour market rate negotiations carried out with unions. Often when fishers are the nominal owners of their own boats, they are tied to particular processors through a variety of bonds such as loans and advances, servicing arrangements, or, quite simply, a buyer's monopoly. In most cases the only effective resistance to the total domination of port markets by processors comes from unions that negotiate minimum price agreements, thus again altering the so-called markets from the market for fish to the market for the labour that catches the fish. There are, to be sure, some competitive port markets where prices are set in the interface between many producers and many buyers, such as in the sale of some troll-caught salmon on the West Coast and some lobster on the East Coast. Overall, however, these are fairly minor markets and could not sustain the total actual volume of production in either situation.

Prices are often not what they appear. Imagine a situation in which a lobster fisher is faced with selling either to the company/ co-op or to a "pick-up" buyer who is paying twenty-five or fifty cents more a pound. As tempting as the higher price may be, the lobster fisher usually sells to the company/co-op because the pick-up buyer cannot provide services such as ice, wharfage, bait, or boat repairs, nor does this fly-by-night buyer offer a reliable, steady market during the full season and possibly for other fish during other seasons. As an example of a different type of market, salmon in British Columbia has three prices. The first is the "minimum price" negotiated by the United Fishermen and Allied Workers' Union with the Fisheries Association of British Columbia, which acts on behalf of processors. The second is the "posted price," which may be above the minimum for net-caught fish (troll-caught fish are nearly always above the minimum); and the last is the "final price," which is the posted price plus the year-end bonus (or final payment). Crew shares are based on the posted price. According to the Fisheries Association, the bonus came about because the union refused to renegotiate the seiners' seven-elevenths share agreement, and the additional payment compensates boat owners for boat costs. It is "partially an incentive and partially equalization." Such bonus payments work in tandem with another practice reported by the Pearse Commission in its inquiry into the West Coast fishery whereby "some processors provide fishermen with services at less than cost. These include packing and collecting services, boat and gear storage, repair facilities, credit and capital financing, and commitments to purchase all fish delivered."[14] So-called boat charters were reported to be "as high as 17 per cent for sockeye, 15 per cent for springs and coho and 10 per cent for pinks" according to United Fishermen's business agent Bill Procopation.[15] A third illustration can be found in the Kirby Commission report, which says that on the East Coast "offshore 'prices' are not really prices at all and bear almost no relation to the prices paid to independent fishermen . . . the 'prices' are negotiated with the trawler unions with an implicit target annual income in mind."[16] Nothing is as it appears in the fishing industry!

Readers should similarly not be confused by the fact that the proportion of the catch coming from company-owned fleets is declining on both coasts. This does not mean that the port markets are more competitive or that fishers have more "autonomy"; other means have been substituted for direct ownership to ensure secure sources of supply. Major port markets are synonymous with the big processors: British Columbia Packers, National Sea Products, and Fisheries Products International.

Corporate Markets

Sales for the big three processors in 1981 were for British Columbia Packers, $301 million, National Sea Products, $314 million, and Fishery Products, $175 million.[17] Reporting on the West Coast, the Pearse Commission concluded that

> most fish are purchased by long-established processing companies or their agents. Between 1973 and 1977 these processors, who are involved in canning as well as fresh and frozen sales, accounted for 95 per cent of the purchases of raw salmon. . . . In 1980 the largest processor, British Columbia Packers Limited, increased its share of salmon processing capacity from about 33 per cent to about 42 per cent through acquiring assets from the Canadian Fishing Company.[18]

On the East Coast National Sea Products is the giant, having emerged from a complex restructuring involving its takeover of H.B. Nickerson & Sons (a privately owned processor), which once controlled National Sea. In 1980 National Sea Products had a fleet of fifty trawlers that supplied over half its raw material and twenty-two plants, twenty in Atlantic Canada and two in the United

States, of which twelve operated year round. Fisheries Products International (the federally restructured outcome of its predecessor, Fishery Products Limited) has sixty-one trawlers and thirty processing plants in Newfoundland plus twelve scallop vessels in Nova Scotia and two secondary processing plants in the United States. It employs over 17,000 plant workers and fishers. Cod blocks, which are commercial-size pieces of frozen fish, constitute two-thirds of Fisheries Products International's output.[19]

Fish buyers and marketers are well organized under the umbrellas of various trade associations, including the Fisheries Council of Canada with its nation-wide membership. Provincial associations are more or less significant factors depending upon the strength of the provincial fishers' organizations since these associations provide both marketing assistance for the companies and industry-wide bargaining when the fishers are organized into unions. The Fisheries Association of British Columbia is an excellent example, serving as a type of "management's union" (its director's description) representing about 85 per cent of all salmon production in the province and an equivalent proportion of herring production. The Association signs labour contracts with shore workers and minimum price agreements with fishers belonging to the United Fishermen and Allied Workers' Union. The Association, which has operated under various names since 1892, adopted its present name in 1951 and has been led by such prominent figures as James Sinclair (former Minister of Fisheries) and Kenneth Campbell (long-time head of the Fisheries Council of Canada).

By contrast, the New Brunswick Fish Packers' Association, which represents about fifty-five companies with about 85 per cent of the provincial production, does not negotiate prices or labour agreements. (Until recently there were no price negotiations for fish in New Brunswick.) This association dates back to 1918 as part of the Canadian Manufacturers' Association and was called the Maritime Canned Fish Section until 1946, when the New Brunswick and Nova Scotia sections separated. The Seafood Producers' Association of Nova Scotia represents twenty-two companies and again about 85 per cent of the production in the province. It does not have a part in "industrial relations," although it does become involved in setting herring prices in southwest Nova Scotia. The Fisheries Association of Newfoundland and Labrador, like its counterpart in British Columbia, negotiates with a union, this time the Newfoundland Fishermen, Food and Allied Workers' Union, for labour rates in processing, prices for inshore fish, and a combination of per diem and fish prices for trawler crew.

No matter how powerful processors are *vis-à-vis* fishers, they are themselves in a chain of dependence. British Columbia Packers is a subsidiary of George Weston Limited, the giant food conglomerate (as is Connors Brothers Limited on the East Coast, Donald A. McLean currently serving as president of both fishing subsidiaries). Virtually all other processors on both coasts have become wards of the banks, governments (through loan guarantees), and/or highly concentrated export markets (which account for about three quarters of their production). Just as small processors depend upon larger ones to market their fish, so the larger processors are tied into financial and marketing arrangements with larger capital.

Viewed from the perspective of the workers, most large processing plants are industrial factories. There are still many small, seasonal plants (especially in Atlantic Canada) employing only a few workers who are often unorganized. In general, however, the industry has been subject to centralization, which has meant the closing of smaller plants and shifting of processing to larger, more populous locales. Recall the earlier discussion of Arnold's Cove where women and children were resettled while men returned to their original fishing grounds. On the West Coast the consolidation of canneries had a particularly strong effect on Native women because the small canneries formerly scattered along the coastline were their main source of work. From 1968 to 1971, for example, there were nine closures of these canneries, in seven of which Natives were in the majority, so that over a thousand women were out of work in villages where the fishery had been the main employer.[20]

As will be clear in later chapters, process workers are germane to an understanding of the fishing industry. The Kirby Commission reports that "in the Atlantic region as a whole, processing plants create as many jobs (and almost as much income) as fishing itself."[21] Moreover, there is at least one fish plant worker to about one of every five fisher households, especially in New Brunswick and Newfoundland. Frightening for shore workers has been the erosion of their jobs because, as Kirby reports, "the degree of upgrading of Atlantic coast fish products has been declining since 1976."[22]

In other words, the secondary processing of fish is being done elsewhere. Eighty per cent of Canadian fish products are exported, and the upgrading of the frozen blocks and fillets takes place outside Canada to avoid tariff barriers. To use an even more specific example, Liberal fisheries critic Azor LeBlanc (himself a thirty-six-year employee of National Sea), has said: "If you section 100,000 lbs. of crab, you only need hire 20 people for an eight hour day. To process that same amount, a fish processor needs 175 workers for an eight hour day." The result of shifting to sectioning meant 3,000 fewer jobs in 1982.[23]

Processors, however, are squeezed by the so-called market on the one hand and the costs of production on the other. According to Gus Etchegary, head of Fisheries Products International, "In the last three years, doing the same volume of fish, our energy costs went from $3.5 million to $11 million. The cost of interest jumped from $7 million to $18 million."[24] The trawler fleet has been particularly burdened by high interest rates because it is so capital intensive. Among these ships, according to recent figures, "$1.7 of capital is required to produce $1 in output in comparison with $0.7 in the inshore fleet."[25] After the 200-mile limit was announced in 1977, the banks "opened their vaults" to the fisheries, thus intensifying the boom period and making inevitable the subsequent bust. The result was that by 1983 Fishery Products, the Lake Group, and John Penney and Sons together owed $85 million more than they were worth. An unavoidable restructuring followed.

Strange State Policies

The past hundred years have witnessed over a hundred official commissions set up to investigate Canada's fisheries. The Canadian state cannot make up its collective mind about what to do with the fisheries. For nearly a decade Roméo LeBlanc was touted as the fishers' friend while he was actually overseeing their demise; following his departure there has been a rapid succession of Fisheries ministers in two years. Adding to the confusion is the question of jurisdiction, encapsulated in the expression "Live fish are federal, dead ones provincial." For the most part, the federal government controls the harvesting of fish while the provincial governments license processing, but (and there are always buts in fisheries policies) until recently, Quebec had its own jurisdiction over harvesting and, of course, the federal government owns Fisheries Products International and the Canadian Saltfish Corporation, which encompasses virtually all Newfoundland's processing and marketing capacity. That should really not be surprising; the provinces only *appear* to control processing through their licensing capacity; in fact, the federal level has control through trade export and standards. And this is all very simple compared to the question of jurisdiction over labour legislation in the fisheries (where for the past twenty years the courts have tossed the question back and forth between them, leaving the matter in juridical limbo). Of related interest are the Anti-Combines and Restraint of Trade actions the federal government has pursued in this highly concentrated industry not, as might be thought, against the fish companies but against the unions. Unravelling these rather strange facts will have to await some theoretical insights from Chapter Five.

Since 1977 Canada has had a 200-mile management zone and has dramatically increased its catch, which rose from 895,000 metric tonnes in 1976 to 1.1 million in 1980. This represents an increase in Canada's share of fish taken within the area from 42 per cent to 75 per cent over the period. Outside this zone, Canada participates in the Northwest Atlantic Fisheries Organization, formed in 1977, which arbitrates disputes concerning additional access to fishing grounds. Canada's quota of cod on the Grand Bank increased from 11,650 to 15,955 tonnes for 1985 (almost half the total allowable catch). The Grand Bank, an ideal fishing ground with little ice and warm currents, is close to port for the hundred or so Canadian offshore vessels that fish there.[26] It gives an appearance of bounty and potential wealth. Biologically, the fish stocks are generally healthy and recovering from the decimation they suffered from the factory freezer trawlers. In any case, biology cannot be offered as the sole reason for either state regulation or the industry's collapse in the 1980s. The fisheries are inherently political, and the only way to understand them is to understand power relations. Power relations themselves are based on class relations, and class relations underlie the organizational formation of the fishery, which will be explored in the core of this book.

State Practices

An encyclopaedia would be required to document the full range of the state's practices in the fisheries of Canada. Yet because these practices and regulations are so central to understanding the development of all activities related to the fisheries, at least some of their aspects must be noted before we proceed with a more chronological account. The range extends from the certification and training of skippers in navigation and safety under Transport Canada to programs for engineers and deckhands under Canada Manpower at the Fisheries School in Pictou, Nova Scotia. More controversial, and clearly related to class struggles within the fisheries, have been the Unemployment Insurance and Workers' Compensation programs that help delineate class cleavages.

Cynics may say government practice has been to adopt the "Parcival Copes approach" to unemployment and the fisheries – in other words, to get rid of the fishers and there will be no fisheries unemployment (because the fishery is more of a liability than an asset). Actually the federal government has chosen to use unemployment insurance as a way to cushion the seasonal cycles in the demand for labour and maintain an available labour supply. The original Unemployment Insurance Act of 1940 excluded fishers (along with lumber workers, water transport workers, and stevedores). Each group was eventually covered, fisheries workers in 1957, under a seasonal benefits program (wherein 90 per cent of payments are made by the federal government compared to the ordinary 22-per-cent federal share). Various changes in the regulations have occurred; for example, since 1980 "an estimated 10,000 women who work with their self-employed fishermen husbands" are eligible for unemployment insurance benefits, reversing a 1957 ruling.[27] The coverage requires the women to work directly at capturing fish (thus excluding baiting of hooks at home and handling of fish on shore).

Some say that it is unemployment insurance that makes the fishery run on the East Coast. Certainly many practices have been adapted to the regulations. Its impact, however, is uneven and often exaggerated. According to a detailed investigation carried out for the Kirby Commission, "On average, full-time fishermen received $2466 in UI benefits in 1981, while part-time fishermen received an average of $1483." Although unemployment insurance payments constituted 32 per cent of the average fisher's income in northeastern Newfoundland, in western Nova Scotia they made up only 6 per cent.[28] Plant managers complain, however, that fishers concentrate their catch and delivery in short periods in order to maximize the payments they receive, thus at times causing gluts and at others gaps when fishers could be catching fish, albeit with marginal returns. Processors want the catch to be spread over as long a season as possible. Changes in the insurance regulations following the Kirby Report have addressed this problem by calculating benefits on the basis of the best ten weeks rather than the last fifteen weeks, although the recommendation to dismantle the program and replace it with an income stabilization plan was not accepted. Unemployment benefits are still an important means of supplementing the incomes of these workers and, in so doing, ensuring the reproduction of fishers even with depressed prices. The costs are high; "benefits totalling $135-million were paid to workers in the east coast fishery in 1980 – $72-million under the 25-year-old fishermen's unemployment insurance program, and $63 million in regular unemployment benefits to fishplant workers."[29]

If unemployment insurance benefits have been the subject of controversy among the public, licensing has been the most irritating issue among those engaged in the fishery. Licensing the fishery has become an exceedingly complex subject. It is based upon the principle that a person and/or a boat must be granted special permission in order to fish. Access is therefore not open to everyone who wishes it. A licence does not guarantee the holder a catch, but it does confer a property right upon a privileged few while excluding others. The effect of licensing varies greatly by fishery and region. For example, in the shrimp fishery of northwestern Newfoundland, "a regional economic elite of mobile gear skippers" was formed by licensing practices.[30] Such is not universally the case.

Licensing affects the big as well as the small participants. Company licences for offshore trawlers are limited in number and type. A limit was first placed on trawler licences in 1973, when a three-month moratorium ended in a "replacement rule" whereby new boats can be introduced only when "equivalents" are retired. Companies are often heard to complain about the ban on freezer trawlers. In fact, the Ministry of Fisheries' policy (as announced on 30 November 1979) permits their use but only for "non-traditional species" such as squid, silver hake, and capelin and not for filleting traditional groundfish, which the processors say is essential for their viability. (Two factory freezer trawler licences were issued late in 1985.)

The most prominent licence limitation program was the Salmon Vessel Licence Control Program of 1968, known as the Davis Plan, which was designed to reduce salmon fishing capacity on the West Coast. As is now well known, it had quite the opposite effect despite considerable spending on "buy-backs." Initially, the plan was to designate "A" licences for vessels that caught over 10,000 pounds of salmon in 1967-68 and "B" licences for those that caught less. Only the A's were replaceable. The B's were given a ten-year maximum life; fees were increased and revenues provided to buy back A licences as they became available. In 1971 special provisions were made for Native fishers and fishers who had been in other fisheries during the qualification period. The buy-back ended in 1973, but the "unintended consequences" were monumental. The effect was to remove low-effort boats and replace them with more effective boats, particularly by a scheme of pyramiding gillnetters and trollers on a foot-for-foot basis into seiners. Equally devastating was the increase in the "value" of boats because licences themselves began to cost independent of the use-value of the boat thus escalating out of proportion the fishery's entry cost.

Licensing has changed the character of the fisheries. The Pearse Report states, "Only 14 years ago [1968] anyone could fish commercially for any fish on the Pacific coast.... Eleven forms of restrictive licenses are now in place on the Pacific coast."[31] As if it were an echo the Kirby Commission reports: "Federal licences are now required for (1) all groundfish fishing vessels 35 feet or more in length; (2) shrimp fishing; (3) scallop fishing; (4) herring fishing with mobile gear; (5) sealing from vessels 35 feet or more; and (6) fishing outside the Gulf of St. Lawrence."[32]

Another side of licensing is that neither the companies nor the unions want marginal fishers to operate. They cut into the income of bona fide fishers by creaming only the most lucrative fisheries at the best seasons. They are said to add to the cost of supporting the average fishing income. More fishers also put pressure on the government to increase the inshore quotas at the expense of the trawlers (company boats), so companies resist increased numbers. Since the part-timers fish inshore, they add to the already heavy glut problem for processors.

The tale of government subsidies and who benefits is well illustrated through evidence given by Gregory R. Thompson, a New Brunswick longliner, before the Kirby Task Force:

A few years ago, I was longlining for codfish and landed the gutted fish for 14 cents a pound. The government announced a subsidy of 2 cents per pound on gutted fish to be paid to the fishermen. The price of fish immediately dropped to 12 cents per pound. Who got the subsidy?

The government, several years ago, announced a subsidy to be paid to fishermen which was 38 per cent of the cost of new boat construction. The price of boats immediately went up 50 per cent. Who got the subsidy?

The government offered a 50 per cent subsidy to anyone who would buy a fiberglass box for carrying fish. Before and after the period of the subsidy the boxes were selling for $350 each, during the subsidy period, they sold for $650 each. Who got the subsidy?[33]

It would be difficult to find any aspect of fishing not regulated and/or subsidized, but subsidy is also often much more complex in its impact than first meets the eye. Thompson's testimony illustrates the fact that subsidies often "pass through" fishers to the suppliers. In other cases there are conditions on the subsidies that clearly target them to specific users. The 1953 regulations that provided subsidies for large trawlers, for example, were "contingent on them being affiliated with a processing company."[34] The development of the longliner fleet in Newfoundland has been subject to especially high subsidies. A breakdown of the construction costs during the mid-1970s is as follows: a federal subsidy of 50 per cent, a provincial subsidy of 12 per cent, a Fisheries' Loan Board ten-year loan for 28 per cent, and a fisher's down-payment of 10 per cent. Bonnie McCay reports that "provisions were made that part of the down payment could be met by labor in building the longliner at the shipyard, and by cutting and delivering timber."[35] To add to the strangeness, the longliners, the Newfoundland Union claims, are "totally unsuited to the purpose the boats are being used for" with fundamental problems in design such as "hard to handle, poorly designed for loading fish, and in some cases downright dangerous." The Fisheries Loan Board, however, will only subsidize longliners built to their own design and specifications, even though the fishers claim they are not good for their needs.[36]

Donald Patton's studies of manufacturing linkages from fishing document a classic case of failure to capture the benefits of backward linkages from staples production. He finds that "Canada now imports approximately 70 per cent of the fishing gear and vessel hardware used, and almost all marine electronics come from abroad."[37] Like most Canadian imports, two thirds of these come from the United States. In addition to the increasing export of raw material rather than processed products mentioned earlier, Patton finds that "almost all of the automatic fish-processing equipment used by the East Coast fishing industry is imported."[38] Each year about $80 million is spent on imported fisheries-related technology by the world's foremost fish exporter! It must also be the world's leading job exporter.

While there is much more that could be said about state policies, some of it will have to wait until later chapters. Particularly important will be the state's role in creating what are known to the unions as "splinter groups," to the government as "advisory groups," and to the associations themselves as "interest groups." These are the associations of fishers and often co-operatives, only occasionally the unions, which thrive on state sponsorship in the struggle for the fisheries' spoils. To conclude this chapter as it began by quoting from the dean of Fisheries ministers: "This sharing out of fishing privileges is one of the most difficult and contentious areas of management, and when battles arise, fishermen need their own generals."[39] The question is whether the generals should be ones of their own choosing.

CHAPTER FIVE
The Need for an Explanation

Making sense of the preceding discussion requires some systematic way to organize thinking about the fisheries. This chapter provides such a framework for an explanation, which will be needed for the subsequent analysis. It will move from a somewhat abstract level of analysis to more concrete illustrations, providing at the end a set of social categories relevant to comprehending the development of the fisheries. These social categories become the language and analytical tools used in the substantive account of the fisheries in the post-war era. This chapter begins by discussing the meaning of class and property relations and follows with an attempt to clarify some widespread confusion about the "tragedy of the commons," then some specific features of labour and capital within fisheries, concluding as noted with a set of social categories that will make sense of some organizations and actions that may otherwise appear incomprehensible.

Property is a set of enforceable claims or rights that order the relations among people and between people and things. These social, political, and economic relations are the essence of class analysis.[1] Class can be defined as relationships to property and control over labour power. Under capitalism, the core relationship is between capital (which appropriates the value of labour) and labour (which supplies labour power). The traditional "petite bourgeoisie" as a class combines capital and labour since it owns its own property and uses its own labour power. The dominant tendency of capitalism is to subsume petty bourgeois property for two reasons: to transform the individual property of the petite bourgeoisie into social property and immediate producers into wage labourers.[2] Typically, with the development of capitalism, the petite bourgeoisie experiences proletarianization so that former independent producers become wage labourers (the proletariat). The subsumption of the petite bourgeoisie, however, does not necessarily fully proletarianize these producers in the sense of transforming them into wage labourers. Subordination may occur yet leave the *appearance* of petty bourgeois relations of production.

In the fisheries, by supporting a distorted form of petty production, capital can shift considerable risk and the supervision of labour onto the producers themselves. Firms can exercise sufficient control over supplies of fish through contractual obligations and market domination while minimizing capital investment and expenditure on supervision. Since small producers do not "own" the resource (fish) there is little pressure for capital to appropriate the means of production directly, a point clarified by the discussion of common property to follow.

By understanding property as a set of rights, it is possible to specify degrees of independence for direct producers. The minimum independence may be the producers' freedom from wage labour through ownership of the means of realizing their labour. This minimum, however, is not sufficient for an understanding of the dynamics of capital's relationship with direct producers. It is necessary to specify aspects of property relations further.

The initial distinction is between legal (or juridical) and real (or active) ownership. *Legal ownership* may be basically passive in the sense of the owner's (rentier's) claim to derive revenue from dividends; it may, therefore, be only nominal or serve as a basis for *real ownership*, which includes control over the rights to direct labour and the products of labour. Within real ownership there are two levels of control that may be designated as economic ownership and possession. These can become differentiated through the division of labour as capitalism matures. *Economic ownership* is control over production in the sense of directing the use to which production is put and disposal of the products of production, including accumulation and investment. *Possession* is the capacity to put production into operation, including the direction of the labour process, and is subject to a division of labour.[3]

The capitalist class controls both forms of active ownership, while the working class has neither command of labour's products nor control over the labour process. Among direct producers, both formal ownership and possession can be distinguished from economic ownership. The *form* of the petite bourgeoisie may remain while the *content* (in the sense of economic ownership) may have been captured by capital. Although "proletarian" means to be reduced to performing wage labour (thus being separated from the means of realizing labour power), to experience proletarianization means that direct producers can retain possession of the means of realizing their labour (and formal ownership of the means of production) yet lose real economic control (over the use to which the means of production will be put and disposing of their products). Proletarianization is thus a *process* by which capital progressively appropriates the property rights of independent producers, thereby reducing them to performing the obligations of labour while maintaining the outward appearance of their earlier form. Producers who experience proletarianization may retain the direction of their own labour power (possession) while the means by which capital is accumulated, the disposal of the products of their labour, and the technical development of the labour process (economic ownership) may be dominated by capital.

Five production patterns relevant to Canada's fisheries can be designated:

1. Subsistence production

Subsistence production is for use value, not exchange value. The producers consume what they produce and do not sell the products. Native food fisheries and household production for personal consumption are examples where fish are caught to be used as personal or family food rather than for commercial sale.

2. Capitalist (or proletariat) commodity production

Capitalist (or proletariat) commodity production separates the direct producers from the means of realizing their labour and compels them into wage labour (or its equivalent, such as shares or piece-rates). Capital directly organizes production based on social labour, and the proletariat controls neither its product nor the labour process. An example is trawler crew on processing company-owned draggers where the captain (representing capital) is separate from labour. A further example are skippers who own longliners or seine boats with crews of four or more. Here crew are proletarian and skippers are small capitalists (unless the skippers are themselves in dependent contractor relationships with larger capital). On the other hand, when skippers of intermediate-scale boats rent or "charter" a boat they are best understood as supervisors in work groups with ambiguous class positions where political/ideological factors are determinant, such as with the United Fishermen and Allied Workers' Union, where the skippers are included as union members under these conditions.

3. Independent commodity production

Independent commodity production links the producers with capital through the mechanism of the open market. These persons are the traditional petite bourgeoisie. There is a unity between the direct producers and their means of realizing their labour. Production is a unity of formal ownership, economic ownership, and possession with a non-exploitive labour relationship. Examples include some salmon trollers on the West Coast and some lobster fishers on the East Coast, if they have free market availability and are free of contractual obligations to capital.

4. Dependent commodity production

Dependent commodity production exists where open market relations are bypassed and the direct producers are compelled to enter a contract or monopoly relation with capital. Since they are often compelled to specialize, dependent commodity producers tend to become detached from subsistence production. Capital directly penetrates the relations of production by dominating economic ownership while the direct producer retains formal ownership (in cases of rental fishers, not even that) and possession. This kind of production is based on individual/family labour but only in terms of labour control and surveillance; in terms of co-ordination and unity, it becomes social labour organized by capital. Most gillnetters on both coasts whose only sales outlets are non-competitive processors and any fisher bound to a buyer by contract are examples of dependent commodity producers.

5. Co-operative commodity production

Co-operative commodity production prevails when there is individual ownership internally (among members) but there are corporate relations externally; that is, producers co-operate in the distribution of their products, not their production. Co-operatives are based on principles of exclusion and inclusion. Fishers may own a share in a co-operative without having control of it – that is, their formal ownership entitles them only to dividends based on patronage and a vote in deciding the directors – while managers of co-operatives may have the real economic control of the co-operative without having any shares (formal ownership) or even being members. A board of directors exercises control in terms of economic ownership; the managers have possession in terms of operating the plant and economic ownership through access to markets; the fishers have possession and formal ownership of their boats. Theoretically, co-operation excludes exploitation, but in practice co-operatives have employees both as crew and as shore workers (who may be excluded from membership in the co-operative), have members with different class positions (if both captain and crew are included), and may exclude potential members. Practices vary from one co-operative to another concerning selection and numbers of members, capital costs for membership entry fees, and the eligibility of employees or crew. Co-operative producers may resemble either independent producers or capitalist producers in the way they organize their own production and may be capitalist in their conduct of relations with employees and the external market. Co-operative ownership is both individual and social.

Rather than seeing themselves as "workers" in confrontation with private corporations, successful co-op producers often regard themselves as outside private corporate relationships; the notion of being "on permanent strike against the big companies" suggests that they are not simply outside but actively in opposition. Their reason for forming a co-op is to free themselves from the companies. Co-op producers sometimes have an affinity for those continuing to work for companies but have chosen a separate path of resistance. When unions representing fishers are on strike against the processing companies, co-op fishers often continue to fish because they do not sell to the companies. The unions, however, seek to set a minimum price for fish, and that price will determine the going rate at which co-op fishers will be paid. There is thus considerable room for tension, and this tension has been concretely manifest in relations between the co-ops and the unions on both coasts. When co-op producers represent themselves as being outside the capital-labour relationship, union fishers see this as something of a free ride: the unions are struggling to set a minimum fish price, and it will, in turn, be adopted by the co-ops for their members.

At the market level co-ops are in competition with private processing companies. As processors both groups face similar relations of production because wage labour prevails within processing and these workers are typically represented by unions. In very few cases are shore workers members of the co-ops (the Central Native Fishermen's Co-operative was a rare example; see page 141), and even when they are the meaning of "membership" is questionable. Moreover, in some cases only owners of intermediate-scale boats are members of a co-op (the Atlantic Herring Fishermen's Marketing Co-operative and the South-West Seiners are examples; see Fundy Co-ordinator, page 134), and the crew are excluded from membership (in these cases represented by the Scotia-Fundy Seiners' Association).

Co-operatives in fishing, for the most part, exist for the co-ordination of selling or marketing efforts for fish, not for co-operation in either catching or processing of fish. The catching capacity remains individualized and privately owned. There are cases, however, where financing is co-operative, as in the Prince Rupert Fishermen's Credit Union.

In the seams between the domains of the giant processors, some fishers have managed to carve out specific niches, most often using co-operative forms of ownership. These range from the highly successful Prince Rupert Fishermen's Co-op with its thousand-plus members to the twenty-five-member co-ops of southwestern Nova Scotia, which offer membership to the skipper-owners of intermediate-scale boats, all of whom have come together to attempt some control over their markets. Co-op fishers seek to socialize distribution while maintaining individual ownership of production. They are not exempt from the contradictions between employers and employees, as discussion of the Prince Rupert Fishermen's Co-op (see page 98) will make clear, nor are co-ops exempt from struggles led by dependent commodity producers, as the relation between the United Maritime Fishermen's Co-operative (see page 84) and the Maritime Fishermen's Union (see page 126) will make clear. Co-ops are organizations designed to cope with capitalist market relations but are also frequently used to avoid powerful unions.

Social categories, of course, designate relationships into which people enter. A person may shift between relationships or experience more than one simultaneously. Property relations of economic ownership and possession are crucial for understanding commodity production, but so too are product/market relations for commodities, sources of finance, and sources of essential supplies. Commodity producers can be subordinate to capital in so far as they relate to capitalists in the capital, supply, and sales markets. Concentrated financial capital in the money markets (mortgages on boats), industrial capital in the product markets (sales of fish), or merchant capital as a supplier of instruments of production (equipment) are possible areas in which the subordination of producers to capital can give capital real economic ownership. Often all three types of capital are combined in a single processing company that can make loans to fishers, supply equipment, and provide essential services (packing fish, transporting nets, supplying bait, ice, or wharves).

To the extent that commodity producers are subordinated they are no longer "independent"; they lose some rights of property and experience proletarianization, thus becoming "dependent" commodity producers. Dependence and independence are thus directions or tendencies within a process, a process with a strong material foundation but an important cultural/ideological element. Whether fishers actually become fully proletarian depends upon whether they are stripped of all the rights of capital (including possession).

Why would capital promote dependent commodity production rather than proletarian production? The answer is that it can ensure supplies of product yet free itself from the risks of weather, natural disaster, or stock depletion, the need to invest (without guaranteed returns through interest) in the first stage of production, and, most important, the requirement of supervising labour. The final point includes the cost of direct supervision, recruitment of a labour force, development of skills training, and reliance on producers to exploit themselves and their families by working long hours and engaging in intensified labour.

While capitalism and simple commodity production are articulated, they are simultaneously contradictory. Under some conditions (such as trawler fishing) fishers become proletarian. Under other conditions, when simple commodity production has become sufficiently consolidated to accommodate available levels of technology, capital can capture these producers by proletarianizing them. A dual process operates whereby capital requires the producers to reorganize and intensify production while the producers compete among themselves by expanding their operations and reducing their overall numbers. Formal ownership continues to be individual, but real economic control is social; in other words, dependent commodity producers become extensions of capital.

Frequently, as has been seen, the state is called upon to subsidize production, thus reducing the price of fish necessary to sustain the producers. Political and cultural factors also strongly enter into the dynamic, as will be seen. The central ideological characteristic of the traditional petite bourgeoisie has been "independence," in the sense of "working for oneself" or "being your own boss." Dependent commodity producers, however, must confront capitalist assumptions of "rationality" such as the adoption of technology to increase productivity and an assessment of the value of their labour power. This suggests that there is a much greater prospect that dependent commodity producers would ally themselves with the proletariat than would the independent commodity producers.

Since property relations focus the study of class on relationships between classes and struggles between them, political and ideological confrontations are focal points of analysis. Struggles over the benefits or use of property rights constitute the political dimension; the justification of their interests by those controlling or those excluded from property rights constitutes the ideological dimension; the history of local/regional attitudes, traditions, and practices constitutes the cultural dimension. There need not be a direct mechanical correspondence between or among the economic, political, ideological, or cultural. The concrete nature of their interaction constitutes the practices explored in the next four chapters.

The Common Tragedy

For the past thirty years one concept has dominated government planning and economists' theorizing about the fishery. It was inspired by H. Scott Gordon's famous article, "The Economic Theory of a Common-Property Resource: The Fishery," in which he argued that "common-property natural resources are free goods for the individual and scarce goods for society. Under unregulated private exploitation, they can yield no rent; that can be accomplished only by methods which make them private property or public (government) property, in either case subject to a unifying directing power."[4] Note that for Gordon the problem is one of the state, acting as a kind of resource landlord, capturing rent. At an abstract level, it is questionable whether "common property" should be regarded as the absence of rights (à la Gordon) or the claims of the collectivity, that is, the positive presence of rights of access ("the right not to be excluded from the use or benefit of something"). What is more important than this abstract difference, however, is that Gordon (and, in more extreme cases, his followers) conceives of common property in the fisheries as a closed system where there are no other opportunities for labour or economic gain (hence the conclusion that fish will always be overexploited). It also fails to acknowledge the intervention of social organizations between the irrational, insatiable individual and the resource – such organizations as co-ops, unions, and even corporations with more than an immediate need to satisfy their collective short-term desires. The so-called Tragedy of the Commons has become the common tragedy of virtually all economists and official commissioners.

One extreme is the "try harder" line of thought, which contends that

no matter how militant they are, the fishermen cannot fundamentally alter their position while the resource remains common property. In this light, organization and militant activity among fishermen must be viewed as an inchoate protest against the common-property situation. . . . The need to secure decent prices presents a constant and immediate challenge to fishermen, and diverts their attention from the fundamental problem of free entry. They are so involved in their industrial relations with processors that they are unable to devote sufficient effort to fighting open access.[5]

This position is simply silly, contending as it does that fishers just need to devote more "effort" and illustrates how all-consuming the notion of common property as tragic has become. It is significant when the notion totally dominates the thinking of official inquiries.

The Pearse Commission clearly states its basic assumption that "all these effects – stock depletion, poor economic performance and instability – result from treating the resource (the fish) as common property until they are caught, and are normal wherever resources are treated this way. It is 'The Tragedy of the Commons'."[6] Michael Kirby is even more definite: "There is no longer much doubt that the most fundamental economic problems in the harvesting sector are rooted in what is called 'common property'. This has been the conclusion of the Economic Council of Canada, of Dr. Peter Pearse in his study of the Pacific fisheries, and of the Task Force."[7] The essence of their position is succinctly articulated by the Kirby Report when it says:

> The most fundamental problems of fisheries management arise from the "common property" nature of the resource. The fact that fish in the sea are not owned by individual fishermen, and that a fisherman cannot own an area of the sea as a farmer does a plot of ground, has two consequences: (1) people living in coastal areas feel an entitlement to a share of the common property and therefore resist attempts by government to limit participation or effort in the fishery – fishing is seen as a right, not a privilege; and (2) each fisherman is compelled to compete for a maximum share of the common resource to get as much as he can before the quota is caught by others.[8]

This statement is a long way from H. Scott Gordon's original formulation concerned with capturing the landlord's rent, and the herring gets redder (and ranker) the more it ages. Kirby's Point One refers to the fact that people in coastal areas often see fish for its use value for personal consumption, designated earlier as "subsistence production" – especially in Newfoundland and among native peoples as "food fisheries" – but this is not commercial fishing. The United Fishermen in British Columbia support the Native food fishery, as does virtually every other commercial user (more or less enthusiastically); the Newfoundland Fishermen's Union enthusiastically supports fishing for personal consumption in that province. But the traditional food entitlements of coastal people cannot serve as the justification for the problems of fisheries management! The second point is equally off base because it does not refer to common property at all but to the division of a *quota*, which is clearly state property, transformed and parcelled out as private property to designated commercial users. Moreover, it assumes that those working in the fishery are totally irrational – an assumption fortunately not yet proven. They certainly are no more irrational than commissioners and classical economists.

The notion that the fisheries are a common property resource is wrong-headed and historically questionable. The earliest fishers operated on charters issued by imperial states that fought one another for entitlement to fish on the Grand Bank. Fishing grounds have always been freely available on a commercial basis only to those with the means to capture them. This qualification is significant, particularly for all large-scale fishing. While the cost of entry into small-scale fishing was low, merchants were able to dominate participants through control over local markets and supplies, thus regulating entry. Large-scale fishing, which has increased in significance, has always been the preserve of major capital, which dominates labour through lay arrangements. In local situations small-scale fishers have regulated themselves as communities by means of lotteries for trap stages and a multitude of rights based upon custom and use that have ensured participants were regulated in their use of the resource. As fishers began to emerge from traditional forms of domination in the mid-1960s and early 1970s and were able to organize and expand their capacity (that is, exercise their property rights), the resource was transformed from common to state property through licensing schemes that limited entry to persons sanctioned by the state. But the way the state chose to exercise these rights was to turn them over to private hands, thus transforming the rights into private property. This is most directly evident in quota allocations to specific companies or organizations. The large-scale fishery has remained an integrated arm of the principal processing companies, and the essential marketing mechanisms have remained outside the fishers' control.

Relations of Production

Capitalist relations of production encompass virtually all commercial fishing in Canada. There are remnants of highly modified merchant capitalism whereby fishers sell to "middlemen" as is done by some West Coast trollers selling salmon to cash buyers or East Coast lobster fishers who sell to truckers, but for the overwhelming majority industrial production prevails. This is true

not only of marketing but also of boat-building, supplies, sources
of credit, and other necessities. While capitalist relations encompass commercial fishing, there are varying degrees of labour
process autonomy from the lowest, exemplified by trawler crews,
to the highest, among salmon trollers.

Appropriation relations occur through product, capital, and
labour markets while domination relations involve the organization
of the labour process. Both are social relations of production
involving exploitation. Trollers, who work alone, own their own
boats, and are free to sell on an open market, are in an
appropriation relationship with fish buyers but are not in a
domination relationship with either capital or labour (although
the state regulates how, when, and where they can fish, thus
having an important impact on the organization of their labour
process). The crew on virtually all large boats (draggers, scallopers,
seiners) are in both appropriation and domination relationships.
Based on the lay system, their payment depends upon the "price"
of fish (appropriation); their labour is directed by the skipper/
captain (domination). Shore workers and tender workers, whose
income is not based on the price of fish, are involved only in
a domination relationship. Virtually all others who work in fishing
are concerned about the price of fish; all fishers who do not work
alone are also concerned about the lay arrangement: that is, how
the value of the catch is divided between capital and labour and
among the labourers. The mystique of fish "prices" will be
discussed shortly.

In the social relations of production there is a distinction
between creating value and realizing value. Creating value involves
co-ordination and unity of the labour process and is expressed
as supervision. Realizing value involves control and exploitation
and is manifest as management. Small-boat fishers, whether they
nominally own their own boats or rent them, supervise themselves;
that is, they are autonomous in the way they organize their own
labour process for the purpose of creating value. Shore workers,
however, are excluded from supervising themselves and must
conform in their creation of value to the directions of supervisors,
as do crews on trawlers, often supplemented by invisible supervision through piece-work or incentive systems. The realization
of value is in the hands of management, which controls prices,
markets, development of equipment, and the rest. Management
has real economic ownership.

Small-boat fishers are like traditional craft workers in many respects – they own or control the tools of their trade and organize their own labour process – but in others they differ. The products of craft workers, with the formal subordination of labour, were the property of manufactory owners, and since the workers were organized under one roof they were subject to rationalization and a detailed division of labour that led to the real subordination of labour and loss of control over the labour process. Many small-boat fishers may not operate under formal subordination, but capital has achieved real subordination over them through control over the products of their labour and over the sources of capital, equipment, and supplies.

When fishers say they stay fishing because they love the "independence," they mean their independence with respect to their immediate labour process, of course, not their dependence on processors or banks. The work itself is long, hard, and dangerous and demands long hours devoted to repairs, maintenance, and rigging – a boat being "a hole in the sea into which you pour money" – but it also utilizes the various skills of fishers: knowledge of fish, catching techniques, navigation, mechanics, electronics. This last distinction does not apply to industrial fishers aboard trawlers or offshore scallopers, who are subject to a detailed division of labour and have limited discretion, being heavily supervised and directed in their work.

To contend that trawler crews are "co-adventurers" is a historical relic of contemporary convenience to capital, not in any sense a reflection of reality. Trawler crews lack either formal or real economic ownership of the means of production; they share in neither the privileges of ownership (as rentiers or capitalists) in terms of disposal of surplus value, nor do they control the labour power of others. They have none of the rights of property and all the obligations of labour.

Charles Steinberg has identified three legal barriers to unionization for Canadian fishers.[9] These are co-adventurer status, anti-combines law, and federal-provincial jurisdiction. Each one has been an impediment to collective bargaining rights at various times in different locations.

Co-adventurer status has caused the greatest difficulty in Nova Scotia trawler crews' attempts to organize. As Steinberg has convincingly contended: "The last reason to argue that 'sharemen' were 'co-adventurers' (in part because they had a capital investment in the form of dory compasses and bait tubs) disappeared with the dory and the schooner by the late 1940s."[10] Still, this has not prevented the erection of legal barriers. The Canadian Fishermen's Union won recognition based on the War Labour Board's 1944 certification (at Lunenburg Sea Products) but the recognition was invalidated by the Nova Scotia Supreme Court in 1947 (the Zwicker Decision) on the grounds that trawler crews were joint-adventurers rather than employees (who were under the board's jurisdiction). This "legal anachronism" was finally overcome after the share system was recognized as "an old incentive system" when the "Control Test" ("in whom rests the power to direct the work and the manner of doing it") was applied to trawler crews. Actually, it was the threat of organization of these crews by the militant United Fishermen and Allied Workers' Union that caused National Sea Products to extend recognition of the more moderate Canadian Brotherhood of Railway, Transport and General Workers' Union voluntarily in 1969. In 1971 the Nova Scotia Trade Union Act was passed, granting trawler crews the right to unionize after they had effectively done so, and in 1971 Newfoundland introduced legislation (not enacted until 1973) that also included inshore fishers. In 1982 New Brunswick recognized the right of inshore fishers to organize.

More significant on the West Coast have been the other barriers mentioned by Steinberg. Several times since the Second World War the right of fishers to bargain collectively has been challenged by the federal government using the Combines Investigation Act. Complicating this has been the issue of whether the fisheries are under federal or provincial labour jurisdiction, placing the United Fishermen in a Catch-22 situation that continues to leave West Coast fishers in a legal vacuum.

Recently, using "dependent contractor" provisions, inshore fishers have successfully argued their market dependence on processors, which has given them some leverage in securing provincial collective bargaining legislation in New Brunswick. The Kirby Commission supports similar legislation for Prince Edward Island, Nova Scotia, and, presumably, British Columbia. Dependent contractors are those who "bring to their work a substantial investment in the tools of their trade." To this is applied the criterion of "economic dependence" where the individual is "under an obligation to perform duties analogous to that of the employee."[11]

Rick Williams has put the matter succinctly, saying, "The issue of price [paid for fish] should never be separated from problems of control and structure in the industry."[12] The form of compensation is not determinant of the social relations of production. Price for fish is analogous to a type of piece-work, and there is no fundamental difference between time-wage and piece-wage systems. As D.F. Schloss noted in *Methods of Industrial Remuneration* as long ago as 1898, "In the practice of industry, whether a man be employed on a time-wage or on piece-wage, both the time occupied and the work done are, as a rule, taken into account ... time-wage very often has a piece-basis, and piece-wage has in practically all cases a time-basis."[13] For much too long the transparency of the labour-capital relationship has been obscured by labour legislation favouring capital and denying basic rights to labour. Price, for dependent commodity producers, can no longer be seen as simply a product market exchange but conceals a wage in compensation for labour power expended; that is, it is a labour market equivalent. Labour power is itself directed by capital to the extent that the quality and quantity of output are determined by capital for the producer. For fishers the key property relationship is not the relation to the boat, as is so often asserted, but the relationship between people in relation to the boat in terms of the expenditure of labour power and deriving the benefits from capital. For dependent commodity producers the boat is an elaborate tool, a necessary condition for the performance of labour. The key social relation is to the processor who buys the fish that the fishers produce with that tool in combination with their labour power. In the case of intermediate-scale fishers, such as those aboard seiners, the situation is similar except that the boat's share of the revenue from the catch is a type of rental for the use of the boat, which is owned either by the processing company or by someone else (who may also be the skipper).

The United Fishermen have struggled hardest for these principles, and they were successful in negotiating a share system for salmon seiners that survived the shift from table to drum seines in the early 1950s, which meant a drop in crew from seven to five, so that the labour share remained at seven-elevenths.[14] In the roe herring negotiations the United Fishermen have succeeded in negotiating a "labour rate" based on the amount paid to each crew member for each ton of herring caught. Clearly in both cases the exchange is for labour services compensated through various wage proxies.

Just as the illusion of prices must be broken to understand the dynamics of class within the fishery, so must the mystique of certification "legislation." An editorial in the *Fisherman* in 1970 stated it best: "Labor's rights were not won with the courts or in the courts, but in spite of the courts, in united struggle against unjust legislation. Against such strength, governments and courts alike are forced to bow."[15] As will be evident in the following chapters, this is not idle boasting. The United Fishermen sustained systematic attacks under combines legislation against the practice of minimum price agreements from 1958 until 1975, when Parliament declared a moratorium that exempted fishers, but they then found themselves attacked by the Restrictive Trade Practices Commission for restraint of trade by impeding the operation of the companies. In the meantime the Union had been before the federal and provincial courts innumerable times seeking certification for fishers; when the federal courts found them to be employees under "dependent contractor" provisions, it did not specify whose employees they were, saying that the question came under provincial jurisdiction. British Columbia legislation, in turn, has dependent contractor provisions, but they are not applicable to fishers. Mr. Justice McKay of the Supreme Court of British Columbia, in overturning an earlier decision by Mr. Justice Blond, ruled in 1979:

> The union represents three groups of "workers" – tendermen, shoreworkers and fishermen. With respect to the first two groups it is the certified bargaining agent under the B.C. Labor Code. It does not, however, enjoy a statutorily recognized bargaining status for the fishermen component of the union, although it has for many years been recognized as the *de facto* bargaining agent for its fishermen members.... Fishermen would certainly seem to be workmen in the sense that word is used in ordinary speech. One would have some difficulty in convincing a deck hand on a fishing boat that he is not a workman.[16]

This ruling officially recognized fishers as "workers," but they are still not certified under provincial law and continue to negotiate on the basis of strength rather than of legal authority.

The criterion of selling labour power for wages is not adequate to understand the class dynamics of fishing. Within the industry those closest to meeting this criterion are the shore workers, many of whom work on a combination of hourly wages and piece-rates or incentives (particularly on the East Coast). Among fishers, the closest are obviously trawlers crews on giant company-owned boats with fifteen to twenty workers and offshore scallop draggers. Traditionally trawler crews were paid by a lay system that divided the value of the catch between capital and labour according to a set formula. Today this has evolved into a sophisticated type of piece-rate system. Since 1975 trawler crews in Newfoundland have received a per diem which guarantees them a wage for each day at sea plus a share in the value of the catch (thus eliminating "busts" when fishers might receive nothing after a voyage). Trawler crews have no ownership in the means of production and are directed by the delegates of capital – the captain and his officers. Unquestionably they are proletarian by all conventional economic criteria, even though they have traditionally been designated by law as "co-adventurers." Politically and ideologically they have often struggled to form unions to represent them in negotiating the price of fish, benefits, and working conditions. With the formation of unions they have continued to struggle for a guaranteed wage.

Another set of fishers who own their own boats (at least nominally) or jointly with processors or operate them as charters or rentals, and who employ on a regular basis from five to seven crew (generally these are seiners or "nearshore" fishers) are not proletarian. They direct the immediate labour process of others and obtain benefits not only from their own labour (one crew share) but also from capital (the boat share). Typically, these skippers form themselves into associations or co-operatives. On the West Coast the crews on these boats belong to unions (the United Fishermen, the Native Brotherhood, or the Co-operative Fishermen's Guild) as they do in Newfoundland, but in the Maritimes these nearshore crews remain outside the union movement and tend to be members of associations such as l'Association Professionnelle des Pêcheurs du Nord-Est, to which skippers also belong (see page 124) or on their own like the Scotia-Fundy Seiners' Association (see Fundy Co-ordinator, page 134). Since their only revenue is derived from their crew share, they are clearly proletarian under the direction of the skipper. Politically and ideologically, however, there is considerable variation in their positions, derived in part from their close personal associations with the skippers.

Small owner-operator fishers are the most complex: inshore fishermen on the East Coast and gillnet and troller fishers on the West Coast. They are subject to various political and ideological tendencies as well as occupying heterogeneous economic locations. Although all of them direct their own immediate labour process, they differ significantly in their market locations. The most independent are the trollers on the West Coast and the inshore fishers around the Bay of Fundy; the least independent are the gillnetters on the West Coast and inshore fishers in the Gulf of St. Lawrence and Newfoundland.

One particularly problematic role is that of the "captain" (so called on large-scale boats) or "skipper" (the designation used on intermediate-scale boats). The position of the captain on a large-scale boat is clearly defined and has a long tradition that involves a high degree of autonomy when at sea and in command of the ship. On shore captains do the hiring of crew and at sea have complete authority over fishing operations. On large-scale vessels the captain is the company's representative and equivalent to a manager of an onshore operation. Problematic is the role of the skipper on the intermediate-scale boat. It is possible to differentiate skippers on the basis of whether or not they own the boat they direct, but this is not very reliable. As has been pointed out, the meaning of ownership becomes weakened by other claims plus the fact that formal ownership may be dispersed among several people and/or companies or held in partnership. In some cases skippers who also own their boats are small capitalists with total control over hiring and directing the labour process; in other cases they are no more than supervisors who act to co-ordinate the work of a crew. Even skippers who own their boats are certainly not perceived by crews as identical to the processors (or "real" capitalists). Skipper-owners are often perceived by the crews as engaged in a high-risk entrepreneurial activity and dependent upon the processors. This important distinction is reinforced by the practice of unions to negotiate annually with processors over the price of fish and to engage in frequent strikes but only rarely to negotiate with boat owners over share agreements for intermediate-scale boats. The dilemma of locating the skippers' role is best illustrated by their position within the two leading fishermen's unions. In the United Fishermen's Union (see page 91) the skippers on seiners (intermediate-scale boats) are *excluded* from union membership, as is anyone who regularly employs three or more persons. By contrast, the Newfoundland Fishermen's Union (see page 111) *includes* all skippers on intermediate-scale boats and everyone on trawlers up to the rank of captain. This difference is significant in the operations, practices, ideologies, and politics of these two powerful unions and will be important to keep in mind as their histories are traced to see how it came about and with what effects.

Social Categories

Shore workers can be divided into tender workers, who collect fish either at sea or on the docks, and plant workers, who process the fish. Plant workers can be either full- or part-time, depending upon whether they work in a year-round plant supplied by offshore fisheries or in a seasonal plant supplied by seasonal fisheries. Within the plants there tends to be a clear division of labour between men and women. Another important division is whether the plants are organized by a union or unorganized. Some shore worker unions are industrial unions integrated with fishers (the United Fishermen and the Newfoundland Fishermen) while others are distinct (the Prince Rupert Amalgamated Shore Workers' and Clerks' Union and the Canadian Seafood Workers' Union) or part of non-fishing unions (le Confédération des syndicats nationaux and the Retail, Wholesale, and Allied Workers Union). Implications of shore workers' unions for fishers' unions will be discussed in the following chapters.

Production units (boats) in Canadian fishing can be divided into three distinct categories of which each has different divisions of labour. Small-scale producers have a low division of labour and control over their immediate labour process. Intermediate-scale producers have a clear division between the skipper and crew but within the crew there is a low division of labour, often involving rotation (such as skiff operator, shore-man, cook, and so on on seiners); everyone is involved in all aspects of production and has equal shares. Large-scale producers have a clear division of labour involving captain, mate, engineer, bosun, cook, trawler crew and deckhands, who have unequal shares and payment. Whereas supervision is implicit in intermediate-scale production,

it is explicit in large-scale production. Each category can be
identified and operationalized in terms of specific types of fishing:

1. *Small-scale* (one to three hands)

Small-scale fishers are those working alone or in *de facto*
partnerships, occasionally employing a helper. On the East Coast
these would typically be called inshore fishers who trap lobster
or catch cod by line or herring by gillnet (or weirs), usually fishing
on a daily basis from their home ports in a 9- to 14-metre Cape
Islander or similar open boat. They tend to be concentrated mainly
in Newfoundland. In Quebec they would be referred to as "la
flotte artisanale." On the West Coast nearly all gillnetters and
trollers would be included here.

2. *Intermediate-scale* (four to ten hands)

On both coasts the most common fishers in the intermediate
category are purse seiners who fish for herring on both coasts,
for salmon on the West Coast, and for some groundfish and
mackerel on the East Coast. The longline fleet out of Newfoundland
is included, usually fishing with gillnets but also with traps, trawls,
or longlines about 60 to 80 kilometres from shore. Halibut
longliners would also be included on both coasts, and shrimp
boats, smaller scallopers, crab boats, or draggers on the East Coast.
These boats would typically be from 14 to 23 metres, with most
less than 20 metres. Fishers may go out daily from a home port
(as in southwestern Nova Scotia and the Gulf) or venture out
for over a week (as in northern Newfoundland and Quebec). This
mobile fleet most typically has a crew of five and sleeping capacity
in a fo'c's'le under the bow as well as an enclosed wheelhouse
with electronic equipment. The aft workdeck would be adapted
to the particular fishery, but usually it contains hydraulic equipment and a large hold. Unlike most small-scale boats, which are
fisher-owned, these tend to be both company- and skipper-owned;
often the processor has ownership shares in individual boats. In
Quebec these are referred to as "la flotte côtière." It is most
important to note that, in contrast to small-scale producers, there
is here a distinction between skipper and crew which creates
the possibility for a distinction between small capitalists and
labourers among direct producers. This distinction, it needs to
be stressed, is germane to understanding the internal class
dynamics of key organizations like the Newfoundland Fishermen's

Union as well as the class character of various co-operatives and associations such as the Prince Rupert Fishermen's Co-operative and Fundy Co-ordinator.

3. *Large-scale* (over ten hands)

Best known on the East Coast as trawlers and scallop draggers, these boats are called the offshore fleet, which fishes for groundfish or scallops. Virtually all are company-owned boats that can fish nearly year-round. They average about 45 metres in length and have about eighteen crew. Trips last from ten to twenty days. A stern trawler costs about $7 million to construct. Although on the East Coast there are fewer than 150 trawler-size vessels, they land almost half the volume of fish. Although less frequent on the West Coast, some large-scale boats are also used there for groundfish and halibut. In Quebec these are referred to as "la flotte hauteurière" or "la flotte de grand pêche." Large-scale producers are distinguished by a clear hierarchical division of labour and clearly differentiated roles.

Although on the East Coast these three categories would often be called the inshore, nearshore or mid-shore, and offshore fleets, these distance designations are deceptive and not very useful when applied to the West Coast. Nor are they even appropriate to the East Coast according to a recent study, which found that many medium-sized boats (defined as 36 to 65 feet, or 11 to 20 metres) regularly fished the offshore banks.[17] As categories they do capture fairly well the three types of fishing on Canada's seas. They represent real social and economic distinctions with meaningful political, ideological, and cultural consequences. It would not be useful, for example, to distinguish fleets by the species they hunt for; the three major species – salmon, herring, and cod – overlap in very significant ways in at least two of the three categories. Nor would it be useful to distinguish by area except in a very specific way, since the fleets compete for the same fish in overlapping areas and often sail from the same ports. The large-scale fleet obviously operates farther from port than the others, but these boats often catch fish that would be moving into the range of the other fleets or, in the cases of the Gulf of St. Lawrence and southwestern Nova Scotia banks fisheries, in the same area. Scale is the best criterion for distinguishing fleets, and the most appropriate indicators of scale are the number of hands, division of labour, size of the boat, and cost. By using scale it is possible to focus on class relations within the fishery in meaningful ways and begin to understand the nature of alliances and conflicts among fishers.

Small-scale fishers are not pre-industrial relics. On the West Coast, for example, the earliest small-scale commercial fishers were day labourers employed by the canneries; so-called "independent" fishers who owned their own boats appeared later when the canneries could be assured of a supply by means other than wage labour. Today's small-scale Newfoundland fishers are industrial fishers who sell to frozen fish factories that pick up their supplies in collector boats or transport trucks. They are not "independent" of the processor. Even salted cod are processed industrially, not in a domestic economy as was once the case under merchant capitalism.

Unionization has tended to be strongest among trawler crews and small-scale fishers (gillnetters on the West Coast and inshore fishers on the East Coast) who face industrial processors as their markets. Small-scale fishers whose markets are more diverse, such as trollers, have not been as forceful in drives to unionize, although political and cultural/ideological factors have at times made them union supporters. Intermediate-scale crew, especially seiners (the South-West Seiners but also l'Association Professionnelle des Pêcheurs du Nord-Est) have been successful financially, closer to the skipper, and sometimes less favourable than other sectors for unionization. Political and cultural/ideological factors on the West Coast and in Newfoundland, however, illustrate that these barriers can often be overcome and seine crews can be the union's foundation.

It is now time to chart the development of Canada's fisheries in the post-war era, following the emergence and interaction of key organizations representing the basic class actors in the industry. Some organizations change their class characters as they transform over time in the hectic world of the fishery. The struggle to survive is an interesting and revealing story containing many lessons for those seeking to organize resistance.

CHAPTER SIX

Formative Struggles and Consolidation: 1945 to 1969

The United Fishermen and Allied Workers' Union has set the tone for labour activity on the West Coast since its establishment in 1945, and the most formative of these disputes occurred in the 1950s and 1960s. In the following chapter the United Fishermen will appear as a major actor on the East Coast. This union has made itself the mark against which all other organizations in the industry must be measured.

In 1968 John Boyd reported to the Task Force on Labour Relations (the Woods Commission) that "the Pacific Coast Fishery is the only one with significant union organization and therefore is the only area in which the operation of [an] existing labour relations system can be studied and observed. The Atlantic Coast Fishery and the Inland Fishery are almost entirely unorganized, especially at the level of actual fishing operations."[1] While Boyd only slightly exaggerated weak union organization on the East Coast, his statement overlooked impressive developments in the co-operative movement.

Indeed, the co-operative movement was enjoying a period of expansion in the immediate post-war decades on both coasts. The formative periods of the United Maritime Fishermen's Co-operative and the Prince Rupert Fishermen's Co-operative will be key examples of how material conditions and political environment can affect the trajectory of organizations with similar ideological beginnings.

St. Francis Xavier Reaches Out

Almost omnipresent in the post-war period were co-op organizers from St. Francis Xavier University in Antigonish, Nova Scotia, led by Moses Michael Coady, the founding director of the Extension Department in 1928, until his retirement in 1952. The co-op program's influence was felt from Newfoundland to British Columbia but most directly in the Gulf of St. Lawrence inshore fisheries scattered along the Quebec, New Brunswick, and Nova Scotia coastlines. The movement grounded in this program reached communities engaged in farming, coal mining, and steel making as well as fishing. Its impact, however, was uneven; according to James Sacouman's account, "The magic of the Antigonish leadership and programme . . . [was] potent or impotent depending on the structural bases upon which it acted."[2]

A meeting in Canso, Nova Scotia, on the first of July, 1927, produced a resolution signed by forty Catholic priests from the diocese of Antigonish calling for "the formation of a province-wide union of the fishermen." The immediate result was a royal commission in August 1927. The MacLean Commission recommended that "fishermen be assisted to organize co-operatives and that an organizer be appointed to carry out the work." The report was filed in June 1928, and the federal government acted in August 1929, appointing Moses Coady as the organizer. Some of his efforts bore more fruit than others: "Organizational efforts in Lunenburg were almost futile because there was little contact with the deep-sea fishermen; but more especially because of the vigorous opposition from the large fish dealers of the place, who under no circumstances wanted to see the fishermen organized."[3] The same observation about southwestern Nova Scotia still has some validity today.

* * * * * *

The United Maritime Fishermen's Co-operative (UMF) *has a membership of about 2,700 inshore fishers, mainly in the Gulf of St. Lawrence. Its 1930 founding convention was in Halifax under the tutelage of the St. Francis Xavier University Extension Department. Initially* UMF *was an educational body of regional associations, but in 1934 the central entered marketing. From 1934 to 1961 there was a clear division: fishers fished,* local co-ops processed, and UMF provided supplies and markets for products. Each co-op was community based with, for example, sixty-seven co-op lobster canneries in 1942 (reduced to only four by 1975). After 1961 the central became involved in production and direct ownership, now controlling six facilities. After 1974 individual direct members were accepted in areas without local co-ops (like Prince Edward Island) and there are currently about 500 direct members and 2,200 more through twenty-nine member co-ops (nine of which have processing facilities). Representation in the central is through a delegate system.

Virtually all members are inshore fishers (thus catching only about half the year) and the central became involved in the purchase of several draggers to supplement the supply for their larger plants. This was an ill-fated strategy and UMF has been selling off the trawlers. There has been an on-going problem of membership loyalty with fishers only intermittently selling through the co-op. At the level of member co-ops there is a tendency to begin marketing directly and even drift away completely when they gain a certain size (such as the Lamèque Co-op, which left in 1981 as the largest individual co-op in the Maritimes and includes both inshore and mid-shore fishermen). Practices vary among the member co-ops. Moreover, UMF's areas of organization are the same as the Maritime Fishermen's Union (see page 126). While UMF officials have opposed the union, demanding exemption for co-op fishers, many co-op fishers belong to the union. The Maritime Fishermen's Union is currently winning the battle of wills (although the Union does not seek to weaken or destroy the UMF as a marketing agency because it is an important fish outlet for its members).

UMF has operated in the red during the 1980s but recently benefited from a federal government restructuring, which provided $6.5 million in preferred shares and forgave $2.5 million in loan interest payments. A new management team was installed in 1984 with François Babin replacing the highly respected but "old style" leader, Arthur LeBlanc.

* * * * * *

The founding convention of the United Maritime Fishermen's

Co-operative in 1930 gathered in a Halifax hall "200 delegates who represented all the fishermen except the Lunenburg deep-sea fishermen," according to the Co-op's documents. The first president, Chester MacCarthy, was a lawyer and the co-op manager of a Prince Edward Island lobster factory. He was soon followed by Burke McInerney (when MacCarthy broke away, taking the P.E.I. operations with him), who managed a fish plant in New Brunswick. A year later J. Howard Mackichan, an organizer from the St. Francis Xavier Extension Department, took over. The Co-op was sponsored by a grant of $5,000 from the federal Department of Fisheries. Gene Barrett has argued that the "MacLean Commission came up with recommendations which formally called for the establishment of a co-operative organization, assisted by the federal government and administered by a paid organizer ... to prevent the growth of working class sentiments and solidarity among fishermen."[4] This was a critical juncture, he argued, on a path destined to lead either to "protective" co-operativism or to unionism as practised on the West Coast. Government officials (aided by committed co-operators) guided fishers into the co-operative structure, postponing co-op–union confrontation until forty years later, when again it was to be forcefully repressed for another ten years.

Initially there were many small processing plants located in each community, and the Co-op's role was primarily educational. "Until 1934, business was not carried out by the UMF. Any supervision of marketing was on the regional basis and by the county associations. Beginning in 1934, the central office decided to go into marketing. From education to actions!"[5] The early years were difficult, but wartime conditions vastly improved fish markets and prices. Both of these collapsed in the post-war recession. According to a brief presented to the Royal Commission on Co-operatives by general manager J.H. Mackichan in 1945, closures were rampant and "whole fishing communities were thus left without an established marketing agency of any kind."[6] It was into this void that the United Maritime Fishermen stepped with vigour. Co-ops began with lobster canning but soon developed into general processing co-operatives for groundfish and herring. For marketing, especially in the complex export market, "the need became imperative of establishing a central cooperative marketing agency."[7]

Paralleling these developments was the establishment in 1939 of Pêcheurs Unis du Québec, forming a federation of thirty-one co-ops in that province, primarily located along the Gulf of St. Lawrence. The organization grew rapidly, increasing from eight branches and 1,503 members in 1939 to thirty-five branches and 3,019 members in 1944.[8] During those early years the two major co-op federations had close supportive relations both politically and commercially.

* * * * * *

Les Pêcheurs Unis du Québec *(PUQ) was founded as a co-operative central in 1939 with eight branches and 1,500 members, mainly on the Gaspé, Magdalen Islands, and north shore of the St. Lawrence. PUQ's beginnings were influenced by the Catholic co-operative tradition. In 1984 the federal government purchased the assets out of receivership for $15 million and now calls the operation Pêcheries Cartier. A $1.25-million restructuring grant in 1983 had not been enough to salvage the faltering organization. PUQ had about seven hundred members and six factories run by the co-op and owned by the federation with another seven marketing affiliates (all fishers' co-ops in Quebec are compelled to affiliate with a federation). Ten major plants employed 1,900 shore workers who were represented by Confédération des syndicats nationaux and Fédération des travailleurs du Québec. Membership in the co-op included captains of intermediate-scale boats, crew, and small-scale fishers but no shore workers. Small-scale fishers were in the numerical majority but intermediate-scale boats caught most of the fish.*

* * * * * *

During the 1940s the United Maritime Fishermen boasted some 4,500 members, virtually all small-scale fishers, and the organization was actively lobbying the federal government to establish a floor for fish prices as a result of motions passed at its annual meeting in 1944. In 1955 it demanded the extension of unemployment insurance to cover fishers.[9] Until 1961 the basic structure of the co-op federation remained the same, with local co-ops doing the processing and the central the marketing as well as providing fishers' supplies. Then a program of regionalization took place to rationalize the multitude of community co-ops, and the central organization became involved directly in production and the construction of regional plants. This move received official expression in the 1967 Committee on Structure report but was best expressed symbolically by the co-op's decision in 1968 to purchase two wooden draggers for the Alder Point Plant (to be named *James Tompkins* and *Moses Coady*) so supplies could extend the plant's operating capacity. In this way an inshore fishers' organization became directly involved in large-scale technology, an involvement that would haunt them. These and related developments suggested that managers rather than fishers had become the driving force of the co-op.

In fact, the United Maritime Fishermen was undergoing significant changes, drawn along by the pace set in the private market. According to its own documents,

> UMF Central was left with no other alternative but to become the proprietor of essential facilities. A partial list of these facilities include: the Central Lobster Cannery in Richibucto, New Brunswick; the Fresh and Frozen Fish Processing Co-operative Plant at Alder Point, Cape Breton; the Lobster Pounds at both Yarmouth, N.S., and Grand Manan, New Brunswick; the Fish Meal Plant at Lameque, New Brunswick; Supply Depots, and Lobster Assembling facilities in Newfoundland.[10]

Such facilities were built, financed, and administered by the central. Moreover, after 1974 a dual structure emerged when membership in the United Maritime Fishermen became possible without a membership through a local co-op.

The UMF Committee on Structure debated the issue of amalgamation with Pêcheurs Unis du Québec in 1965 but decided against it. Instead they chose a path of draggers and their own expansion program. The committee justified its actions based upon the financial and product markets open to fishers and member co-ops, aggravated by the lack of local talent:

> The chief drawback in obtaining financial assistance, whether from government or from financial agencies, is the limited qualifications of most of our co-operative managers and of the Boards of Directors who are responsible for the effectiveness of the investments involved. In many cases, because of lack

of business knowledge on the Board's part, the managers become the sole authority. They determine whether the co-operative shall be a business unto itself or an integral part of the movement, whether it shall market co-operatively or not.... Small, independent co-operatives can no longer hope to effectively compete against the new giants of the industry ... [thus the Committee recommends] all locals to be absorbed into ONE organization.[11]

Paternalism, benevolent as it may be, was becoming the order of the day. Despite appeals by the committee that strong contracts be established between members and the locals to ensure that all of the members' catch came to their locals and that, in turn, all locals worked exclusively through the central, neither goal was realized. There was no legal obligation to sell through the Co-op or even to be a member to sell to the Co-op. The major result of the restructuring was that only the weaker components of the United Maritime Fishermen were absorbed into the central, the stronger ones not being willing to surrender their independence. This is a problem that persists to the present.

Elsewhere in the Maritime Provinces the main activities involved the offshore fleet and its processing facilities, principally located in the Nova Scotia ports of Halifax, Lunenburg, and Canso. Some of that history has already been told and some is best saved until later, but it should be noted here that Nova Scotia labour relations were not as placid as commonly supposed. There was a "bitter spontaneous strike in 1938 that spread along the coast from Halifax and Lunenburg to other ports"; it was broken, as was a recognition strike by the Canadian Seamen's Union in 1945 (as a result of the Zwicker Decision overruling the War Labour Board).[12] Important for later events was the Canadian Fish Handlers' Union, which was affiliated as the shore workers' section of the Canadian Seamen's Union. Groups of workers from Lockeport, Halifax, and Lunenburg merged with locals of the Canadian Packing House Workers in the Cape Breton plants at Louisbourg, Glace Bay, and North Sydney in 1957 to form the Canadian Seafood Workers' Union (see page 106). Life would become considerably more lively when Homer Stevens came to call.

Newfoundland entered Confederation in 1949 and promptly passed a Labour Relations Act in 1950 that blocked collective bargaining for fishers. The act was reinforced by the Labour

Relations Board's refusal to recognize any group of fishers as employees until the dramatic reversal of 1970. There was some co-op activity on the Island, led by the United Maritime Fishermen. The Port au Port Fishermen's Association, formed on the west coast in 1963, in 1965 had 225 members whose catch of lobsters and salt cod was marketed through the Co-op, which had "advanced about $19,000 on credit to the Association in 1964." Generally, however, co-op activity was limited and not centrally directed. "All told, in 1965, just under 700 Newfoundland fishermen were marketing lobster co-operatively along the coast of western Newfoundland, and more than 1,000 sold salt cod through co-operatives. Many did not do so as members of registered co-operatives but as members of unregistered co-operative type organizations."[13] Organized representation for fishers was restricted to the Newfoundland Federation of Fishermen, a provincially sponsored association formed in 1951 that diminished rather than augmented fishers' strength.[14]

Union activity was also limited. The Canadian Food and Allied Workers' Union had entered Newfoundland in 1967, "having been awarded jurisdiction over unionization in the fishing industry by the Canadian Labour Congress (CLC). Six fish plants, with perhaps a thousand workers, had been organized previously as direct affiliates of the CLC, which were then duly absorbed by the CFAW."[15] Soon, indeed, this union would have about one hundred plants organized and be on the brink of merging with the fledgling Northern Fishermen's Union, which had recently brought together some inshore fishers along the St. Barbe coast and Bonavista Bay. As a result of their merger, Newfoundland fishing would never be the same.

The Stormy Pacific Coast

In British Columbia the United Fishermen and Allied Workers' Union had been formed in 1945 as the result of a merger between the Fish Cannery, Reduction Plant and Allied Workers' Union and the United Fishermen's Federal Union (see page 91). It has been the shore workers' section of the United Fishermen, with its formal bargaining rights within the industry, that has given the fishers their power to compel processors to negotiate minimum prices and working conditions. One year after the merger the net workers (who made and maintained nets) led a twenty-nine-day strike over pay and an eight-hour day. Noteworthy about the strike was that "the processors also agreed to sign a contract which, for the first time, covered white women and Chinese cannery workers." Fishers supported the strike, making it clear that "no fishermen could work on company boats or deliver fish to processors until all networker demands were met."[16] During the war the fishers' union had pressed for "equal pay for work of equal value" but the division of labour by gender and race, especially among shore workers, was staunchly reinforced by company employment practices. The initial strength of the shore workers had centred on white males in the reduction plants and cannery men (Chinese men having virtually disappeared because of lack of immigration). According to Alicja Muszynski, who has investigated these practices in detail, "the fact that women were unionized at all attests to the pressures they exerted to be included in negotiations and to the persistent and hard work of union leaders. Their commitment largely of an ideological and verbal nature during the war years, was, with the formation of the UFAWU translated into a specific programme of organization. In the following decades, women trade unionists became active in overcoming discrimination against women in the fishing industry."[17] As will be seen in Chapter Seven, however, the struggle for women's rights remained a difficult one for the union.

* * * * * *

The United Fishermen and Allied Workers' Union (UFAWU) *was formed in 1945 as a merger of earlier plant and fishers' unions and now has about 8,000 members. This powerful industrial union represents most gillnetters and seine crews in British Columbia, as well as tender workers and shore workers. UFAWU negotiates share agreements and working conditions with intermediate- and large-scale boat owners through the Vessel Owners' Association and minimum price agreements (including benefits) with the Fisheries' Association of British Columbia, which represents major processors and fish buyers. Talks with vessel owners are conducted intermittently while annual price agreements for herring and salmon are negotiated. Some trollers are members of the union, but for the most part trollers are non-aligned or members of the Pacific Trollers' Association (see page 96), a longstanding union opponent.*

UFAWU *makes it clear in its constitution and practice that it represents labour, not capital. Anyone regularly employing more than two people is not eligible for membership. In its fish price negotiations the union at times bargains alongside the Native Brotherhood (see page 93). The union has been involved in several serious conflicts, including an important break with fishermen and plant workers of the Prince Rupert Fishermen's Co-operative (see page 98) in 1967. In the late 1960s the* UFAWU *and its leadership under Homer Stevens made an organizational drive in the Maritimes; this failed but cleared the way for subsequent drives by other unions. The union became re-affiliated with the Canadian Labour Congress in 1972, nineteen years after it was expelled from the Trades and Labour Congress on charges of communist domination during the Cold War hysteria.*

Union fishers are not legally recognized in British Columbia so there is no regular check-off system. Thus the union has devised an effective "clearance" system that ensures that all crew on boats, other than from co-ops, belong to either the UFAWU *or Native Brotherhood and have paid their annual dues. This clearance is enforced by the refusal of shore workers to handle "hot" fish.*

* * * * * *

The whole period of the fifties and sixties was one when the United Fishermen were under attack from virtually every imaginable quarter. It should be understood, however, that the union was not simply being victimized; it was pursuing a most aggressive strategy to establish a presence within the industry and protect its members. As suggested earlier, the United Fishermen has succeeded in establishing itself as the standard. It has been at the centre, and all other major actors have had to define themselves in relation to it. Even the Prince Rupert Fishermen's Co-operative, which will receive a good deal of attention later in this chapter, had origins within the union, since the United Fishermen's Co-op (its predecessor) began as a branch of the United Fishermen's Federal Union. More important, the powerful Co-op had to define itself in relation to the Union during this formative period.

The first co-op to be born in the struggles with the Union was the British Columbia Fishermen's Independent Co-operative Association. Its founding members were fifty crew of eighteen draggers who delivered fish in Vancouver at the Campbell Avenue wharf, selling their catch by auction. Their co-op was formed in 1947 as a reaction to a Union strike over the price of cod.[18] The trawl fishery on the West Coast is far more specialized than that on the East, and most draggers are of only intermediate scale with crews ranging from three to five. The catch is sold fresh by auction at the docks, in addition to that sold by company-owned boats directly to the processors. According to A.V. Hill's account, "In 1947 the Union called a strike over the price of live-cod, and requested not only its members on the new company-owned draggers, but all other draggers as well to stop fishing ... the draggers promptly formed a co-op. Their speed shows that they had discussed the idea before."[19] This organization continues to operate, and even though it clashed with the Union in 1952 over the right to fish during general strikes, it is mostly outside the direct fire of the Union because the issues of salmon and herring prices and the wages of plant workers are not relevant to this early breakaway organization. Only trawlers that deliver fish to the processors remain within the Union's scope.

A more significant, and vicious, purging occurred in 1949 when the United Fishermen's Union was expelled from the Trades Union Congress for alleged communist leadership. Being outside the "house of labour" was to have much more than symbolic importance for the United Fishermen in the years to come (but more on that later).

* * * * * *

The Native Brotherhood of British Columbia *was formed in 1931 by coastal Indian fishers as a fraternal association. They were later joined by Natives from the Interior and up to 1969 spoke for all British Columbia Native people. At that time the Brotherhood and the Council of B.C. Indian Chiefs agreed that the Brotherhood should confine its activities to fishing-related concerns. The Native Brotherhood tends to serve as an umbrella for various activities. Related involvements are the Central Native Fishermen's Co-op (see page 141) and Port Simpson Fishermen's Co-op, which was formed in 1974 by seven bands and closed in 1984. Also related is the B.C. Native People's Credit Union, founded in 1972, with 700 members. Most*

recently the Native Brotherhood was instrumental in establishing the Northern Native Fishing Company which acquired
243 gillnet boats from the B.C. Packers' fleet using a federal
grant of $11.7 million. Besides these co-operative/corporate
activities, the Native Brotherhood negotiates the price of fish
with the processors, sometimes alongside the United Fishermen
and Allied Workers' Union (see page 91). It also operates as
an association for lobbying government, including membership
in the Western Fishermen's Federation.

The Native Brotherhood is a cultural/political organization
that acts at times in conflict and at times in concert with both
capital and labour, thus serving an important role in the West
Coast fishery. Various tendencies are discernible within the
Native Brotherhood. Membership includes Native people who
are intermediate-scale boat owners (mainly seiners), crew on
these boats, small-scale boat skippers (mainly gillnetters), some
shore workers and tender workers. Over the years much of
the Native Brotherhood leadership has been drawn from seiner
captains and it has been weakest in the area of representing
shore workers, where the Union has been strongest.

* * * * * *

Another important conflict in which the Union was to engage
during the 1950s (aside from those directly with the companies)
was with the Native Brotherhood. This indicated a tension that
has characterized the uneasy alliance throughout both organizations' histories. During this period the Native Brotherhood had
some 2,000 members, a third of whom were also members of
the United Fishermen and most of whom were fishers with less
representation among shore workers and tender workers (both
of these groups almost totally Union members). The Native Brotherhood's executive was empowered to act as bargaining agent for
the members. Natives constituted about a fifth of all commercial
fishers during this time but generally their numbers were in decline
both absolutely and relatively compared to those of white fishers.[20]
Stuart Jamieson's observation for the late 1950s is instructive in
this regard:

Displacement of Indian women from canning and processing
[because of greater concentration of plants in certain locations]

has further weakened the position of Indian fishermen, because much of their bargaining power rested on the companies' dependence on their womenfolk for canning labour.... As the position of native Indians generally in the fishing industry has become more marginal in recent years, the Native Brotherhood has declined in relative influence and bargaining power.[21]

Since 1936 Natives have attempted to establish some autonomous position within the fishing industry, initially through the Pacific Coast Native Fishermen's Association and then through the Native Brotherhood with which it merged. The Brotherhood, however, has not usually negotiated separately from the Union, operating on an oral understanding concerning recruitment and negotiation practices.

From the beginning of their uneasy alliance, the tensions have been as much philosophical as racial. While the Union's ideology is rooted in a militant, socialist understanding of the world, the Brotherhood has a strong religious background, especially among Protestants. "The religious foundation of the Brotherhood is symbolized by the fact that the leadership is drawn almost entirely from well-known Protestant families" and the official theme song of the Brotherhood is "Onward Christian Soldiers."[22] Initially the Brotherhood acted as a silent partner with the Union in signing virtually identical agreements with the processors, but during the strike-ridden and turbulent early 1950s the Brotherhood leaned toward support for more moderate positions. In 1952 this sentiment solidified when the Brotherhood decided not to join a Union-sponsored strike, but "they were forced to cease fishing anyway. The United Fisherman and Allied Workers' Union controls the personnel in the key links such as fish tenders and packers which are fully organized. During a strike they refuse to handle 'hot' fish and this soon renders strike-breaking ineffective."[23] Since that time the Native Brotherhood has continued with its uneasy alliance, sometimes signing separate but not significantly different agreements. The more typical practice, especially from the mid-1970s, has been to create parallel organizations outside the jurisdiction of the Union, which will be explored later.

The United Fishermen have been in conflict occasionally with the gear associations. Notable among others was the British Columbia Gillnetters' Association, formed in 1952 with an initial membership of 400, again in reaction to the Union's strike policy.

Membership in the Gillnetters' Association precluded membership in the Union. "The Association negotiated with the Fisheries Association on minimum salmon prices independently from the UFAWU in 1953 and 1954" but has not since been active in price negotiations.[24] Membership in the Gillnetters gradually declined to about forty members by the end of the period under discussion, although it continues to have some presence.

During this time the Union was under attack from many other quarters, including an aborted attack in 1953 by the Seamen's International Union, which "launched a program of declaring other trades unions to be communist-controlled; and then 'raiding' them."[25] The SIU attempt to marshal support from the B.C. Fishermen's Independent Co-operative failed. The only support for the union led by Hal Banks came from the tiny Deep Sea Fishermen's Union (which had only 200 members in 1953, declining to 120 in 1957 and 85 in 1966). This thorn in the United Fishermen's side would cause serious infection in 1967.

More significant was a series of attacks beginning in 1952 under the Combines Investigation Act, with further private suits launched in 1955, 1956, and 1958 and another major suit in 1960.[26] These and similar attacks in the courts will be discussed in later chapters, but it is worth noting in this respect the treatment the Union received at this time in the press. Western Fisheries, for example, in reporting on the Supreme Court ruling concerning the Restrictive Trade Practices Commission hearings when the Union demanded copies of evidence given by the companies and held by the courts, said: "The companies feel that some of the evidence given in private to the investigators would provide grist for the Communist propaganda mill which grinds out Red-line commentary each week through the offices of the UFAWU."[27] This makes clear the ideological environment surrounding the Union.

Two other major attacks of this period continue to have ramifications for the United Fishermen: the battles with the Pacific Trollers' Association and the Prince Rupert Fishermen's Co-operative.

* * * * * *

The Pacific Trollers' Association (PTA) is the strongest of the western gear/area associations, under the leadership of John

Sanderson and Al Meadows. It has formed the core leadership of the Western Fishermen's Federation and has been a regular opponent of the United Fishermen and Allied Workers' Union. The PTA was formed in 1956 with 50 members and currently has about 460 plus alliances with the smaller Gulf Trollers' Association and Northern Trollers' Association. Membership is open only to salmon troll boat owners or operators. Most members operate troll boats exclusively (as opposed to combination gillnet/troll boats) and consider themselves the most independent of all fishers. The Association represents both traditional ice trollers and the somewhat larger freezer trollers. Deckhands, who usually number only one for an ice troller and two or three for a freezer troller, are restricted to associate membership in the PTA. During strikes the PTA has run marketing operations for its members, such as during the three-week strike in 1975 when their salmon were sold in Seattle. This has led to charges of scab operations by the Union. Primarily the Association confines itself to lobbying concerning season, gear, and area restrictions but has also done some market research. There are various tendencies within the Association, which has wavered between being a strict association or a co-operative and even consideration of forming a union local.

* * * * * *

The Pacific Trollers' Association, founded in 1956 with a small membership, grew to nearly 900 members during the 1960s at the height of its strength. Trollers, it will be recalled, are the most independent owner-operators in the salmon fleet and tend to work alone or with a helper over an extended season. Major strikes were led by the Union in 1952, 1954, 1957, and again in 1959, each affecting at least 5,000 workers and lasting for significant periods.[28] Such strikes require the minimum support of two thirds of all union members before being authorized. The 1959 strike was the first "general strike" within the western fishing industry, taking place at the peak of the northern run and lasting for fifteen days. It was honoured by virtually all troll and trawl fishers on the coast, even those not directly involved in the dispute. All members of the Prince Rupert Co-op and the Pacific Trollers stayed in port. But the Union was then at its pinnacle of power; its position would soon come under attack as the Pacific Trollers challenged it in 1963 and the Co-op in 1967.

After the 1959 general strike the Pacific Trollers demanded that "PTA observers must sit on all future strike committees, and that before the trollers are asked to support a strike, a coast wide vote among PTA members be taken," and each local of the Association passed a resolution to the effect that a majority of its members must support a strike before it would be recognized.[29] In 1963, at the peak of the sockeye run, the Union called a twenty-one-day strike. This time the Pacific Trollers decided to pack their fish to Seattle, using skippers of sixteen halibut boats who obtained injunctions against the Union. This "scab packer service" as the Union called it became a focus for hostility. When the next major strike situation occurred in 1963 a confrontation developed in which the Pacific Trollers decided to slug it out, as Secretary-Treasurer Stan Stanton put it. After honouring the Union pickets for five days and being denied an easement from the Union, the Association decided to go fishing and sold 500,000 pounds of salmon (valued at $250,000) in Seattle.[30] Since then the Association has resorted to this strategy on other occasions. This action established the Pacific Trollers as an enemy of the Union but an adversary that had to be respected for its strength. The two have often come into conflict over some fundamental issues.

* * * * * *

The Prince Rupert Fishermen's Co-operative (PRFC) *was founded in 1939 with some assistance from St. Francis Xavier University's Extension Department, merging the North Island Trollers' Co-op (founded in 1934) with the Prince Rupert Fishermen's Co-operative Association (founded in 1931). Initially it only marketed troll-caught fish but in 1944 began to do processing. PRFC is a direct co-op with 1,450 members and does not serve as a central for other co-ops. There is a strict requirement to sell all production through the Co-op and generally only members' fish are bought (especially during strike situations). Currently there are 6 draggers, 25 seiners, 175 trollers, 134 gillnetters, and 138 combination boats fishing for the Co-op. Most (60 per cent) members do not live in Prince*

Rupert, but all sell through the Co-op, which has become the West Coast's second largest producer (behind only B.C. Packers). PRFC is a partial member of the Fisheries' Association of British Columbia for lobbying and marketing purposes but not for collective bargaining.

Since 1967 the Co-op has had its own unions. The Co-operative Fishermen's Guild (CFG) Local 80 of the Canadian Labour Congress was formed in 1970 following the decertification of the United Fishermen and Allied Workers' Union by converting the Deep Sea Fishermen's Union, which had been formed in 1913 for halibut fishery and had fewer than a hundred members in 1968. The Co-operative Fishermen's Guild includes crew on intermediate- and large-scale boats fishing for the PRFC. Its lay is negotiated with the Prince Rupert Vessel Owners' Association whose members own the large boats. It does not negotiate prices since these are set within the co-op structure; the Guild's members are simultaneously members of the Co-op. Initial payment is 70 per cent of the anticipated price with the balance paid when the product is sold. Another organization created out of the 1967 strike is the Prince Rupert Amalgamated Shore Workers' and Clerks' Union, also a direct CLC charter, representing shore workers after the United Fishermen and Allied Workers' Union was decertified.

* * * * * *

The most far-reaching confrontations centred around the Prince Rupert Fishermen's Co-operative. This Co-op had begun as an organization collecting fish from the trollers and selling them to local companies, not entering processing until 1944. Its growth was enhanced by the wartime economy and immediate post-war demand; its membership had risen to 3,290 by 1949, showing "increasing development in the gillnet and seine branches" with gillnetters on the Skeena River in 1945 and three seine boats in 1949.[31] During the early years its relations with the Union were most favourable. The *Annual Report* of 1951, for example, stated: "Wherever possible, the policy shall be to support organized labour."[32]

The Prince Rupert Co-op has a centralized organization, unlike

the federal structure of the United Maritime Fishermen's Co-
operative, and has a very close relationship with the credit union
movement which liberated the Co-op and its members from the
banks and the financial ties of the processors. Beginning in 1952
the Co-op ceased dealing with the banks, using the B.C. Central
Co-op system instead. Also in contrast to the eastern situation,
the Prince Rupert Co-op members are contractually bound to sell
their total production through the Co-op. This mandatory practice
is reinforced by a system of fines. The payment structure is based
on a first payment of two thirds of estimated value, a second
winter payment, and a final payment to close the account at the
end of the next year with share capital deducted from final
payments. Important to note is the type of fishers attracted to
the Co-op. As Boyd notes, "To be a member, a fisherman must
be financially independent or be able to obtain financing independently. He must be able to invest share capital in the co-
operative. These requirements tend to restrict membership to the
better fisherman who is in an independent financial position."[33]
The co-op structure on the West Coast attracts the more independent fishers and has helped them maintain independence from
both the processors and, as will be seen, the United Fishermen.

As early as 1952 the Prince Rupert Co-op developed a strike
policy and set up a special committee.[34] In 1957 there were ongoing
meetings with the United Fishermen over Co-op gillnetters fishing
during strikes against the companies.[35] The 1959 strike, however,
which was industry-wide, brought tensions to the fore. The *Annual
General Report* for 1959 stated: "This strike has more clearly shown
the true position of Cooperative fishermen during a strike from
a dispute over fish prices.... In the 1959 situation our employees
obtained agreements with terms less attractive than those offered
by our Association before the strike took place."[36] Relations were
deteriorating but mainly concentrated on the plant workers since
Co-op employees were offered higher wages than the settlement
the United Fishermen finally reached with the private processors.
By 1963 the Co-op had adopted a practice of paying higher wages
than the rest of the industry, and labour relations were being
handled through a Union–Co-op Coordinating Committee with
permanent delegates. According to A.V. Hill, a Co-op spokesman,
"The Committee worked for many years, and found solutions for
every mutual problem except one. But it wrestled with the
perennial strike question without ever solving it satisfactorily."[37]

The Union had a similar assessment:

> The Prince Rupert Fishermen's Co-op has been operating all
> week under a UFAWU agreement which provides shoreworkers
> and tendermen with the same wages and conditions operators
> have had before them for over a week.... Co-op fishermen –
> trollers and gillnetters – were back on the grounds immediately
> the two agreements were settled.
>
> Gillnetters voted by a large majority at a special meeting
> in Prince Rupert to contribute 10 per cent of the value of their
> catch to the central strike fund. Shoreworkers contribute 20
> per cent of their pay.[38]

All seemed to be under control. The Co-op could continue to
process fish and the Union could use the situation to pressure
the private processors on wages and prices.

All hell broke loose in 1967, bringing to a head a series of
festering pressures, including the Canadian Labour Congress's
opposition to the Fishermen's Union, tensions with vessel owners,
and, most important, the long-standing potential for conflict with
the Co-op as an employer of shore workers and a growing number
of crew on seiners. The bitterness from this watershed conflict
still colours relations on the West Coast.

In March 1967, the United Fishermen attempted to extend its
jurisdiction over the trawl fishery coast-wide by striking for the
first written share agreement. It quickly obtained such an agreement from the B.C. Fishermen's Independent Co-operative Association but was resisted by the Fishing Vessel Owners' Association.
According to Western Fisheries, "A total of 21 trawlers, plus the
60-boat halibut fleet, are involved in the dispute in Vancouver,
with another 30 longliners and draggers sitting idle in Prince
Rupert, where the strike has taken on ugly overtones.... Root
of the trouble is a jurisdictional clash between the old but tiny
Deep Sea Fishermen's Union and the strong, militant UFAWU over
who will represent the men on the draggers and longlining fishing
out of that port."[39] But that was only the appearance, a pretense
for a more fundamental struggle.

The Prince Rupert Fishermen's Co-op later claimed to have
"endeavoured to preserve its traditional neutrality" in disputes
over share agreements.[40] But "the crew members, who are also
co-operative members, of the beam trawl and longline vessels ...

saw no reason for the UFAWU to claim the right to represent them and stated they wished to be represented by the B.C. Deep Sea Fishermen's Union. The Co-operative was obliged insofar as possible to carry out its marketing contract with these members."

From the United Fishermen's perspective, the Fishing Vessel Owners' Association was rejecting terms accepted by the other trawl owners. Moreover,

> the issue has been complicated by alleged signing of a so-called agreement between the Prince Rupert Deep Sea Fishermen's Union and the Prince Rupert Vessel Owners Association. This agreement was announced on March 23, six days after UFAWU trawl crews had launched their coastwide strike.
>
> Prince Rupert vessel owners have also abrogated a memorandum of agreement signed with the UFAWU on April 30, 1966. . . . Following PRFVOA refusal to negotiate, longline vessels belonging to the Association members have been declared "unfair" by the UFAWU. Also declared "unfair" are trawl vessels belonging to the PRFVOA which fished beyond the trawl strike deadline and whose owners have refused to negotiate a trawl share agreement.
>
> Refusal by Prince Rupert Vessel Owners Association to negotiate has been paralleled by attempts to force UFAWU members into DSFU and cancellation by the DSFU of an agreement signed in April, 1959, by which both unions recognized the right of each other's members to sail on longline vessels under their respective jurisdictions . . . .
>
> DSFU actions during the current trawl strike demonstrate it is now willing to play the role of vessel owners' agent.[41]

It was after the Prince Rupert Vessel Owners' Association had changed the traditional understandings about lay divisions that the Union declared its boats "hot"; the Vessel Owners, however, pressured the Co-op to accept their fish. Initially the plant workers, at that time still United Fishermen's Union members, refused to handle the fish. The conflict then focused upon the Co-op's main plant where many workers eventually crossed the picket lines. The situation was further confused when the Deep Sea Fishermen's Union set "counter pickets" around B.C. Packers' plants to keep United Fishermen's Union plant workers out. The Deep Sea Fishermen's Union was simply trying to disrupt United Fishermen's activities; the United Fishermen were arguing that the Deep Sea Union had fallen under the influence of the Vessel Owners. As the animosity heightened, charges by the United Fishermen intensified against the rival union and its agent, Vince Dixon, contending:

> Domination of the Fishermen's Co-op by Prince Rupert Vessel Owners Association is an important factor in the dispute that has led to the Co-op plant being declared unfair by the UFAWU. . . . Five members of the 11 man board which directs the Co-op are big boat owners and members of the Association. . . . W. Dickens, a father of the Association member who owns the Sidette, is a sixth director. Another is a crew member of a big boat whose owner is a director and two more are crewmen on the Association boats.[42]

The United Fishermen's contention was that the board of the Co-op had been taken over by big-boat owners and their representatives, so that the small-scale fishers on trollers and gillnetters were represented by only three out of eleven members. The "neutrality" of the Co-op in the struggles between capital and labour was being challenged by the Fishermen's Union, and the Co-op itself was responding in such forceful terms as to create a situation where it exorcised itself of the grip of the powerful United Fishermen.

Plant workers who crossed the Union picket lines at the Co-op appealed to the British Columbia Labour Relations Board for decertification from the United Fishermen and applied to join the Deep Sea Fishermen's Union. The board agreed. This "new" union refused to accept forty of the United Fishermen shore workers with seniority who had continued to support the original union; the Co-op acceded to these demands and refused to re-employ the militant workers. It signed a new two-year contract with the Deep Sea Fishermen's Union.[43]

When the dust settled, and under the tutelage of the Canadian Labour Congress, a new structure was created. Shore workers at the Co-op were put into the Prince Rupert Amalgamated Shore Workers' and Clerks' Union as a direct charter Local 1702, and the Deep Sea Fishermen's Union became the Co-operative Fishermen's Guild as direct charter Local 80. The Guild represents the crew members on intermediate- and large-scale boats fishing for the Co-op and negotiates the lay arrangements with the Prince Rupert Vessel Owners' Association (whose sixty-five members own seiners and draggers). The Guild does not negotiate prices since they are said to be set within the co-operative structure, and its members are simultaneously Co-op members (with a good deal of overlapping among the executives of the Guild and the Co-op).

During the heat of the strike United Fishermen leaders rejected an injunction to call off the strike on the grounds that only a coast-wide vote of the membership was empowered to do so. Arising from the court case, two leaders, President H. Steve Stavenes and Secretary Homer Stevens, were jailed for a year for contempt of court and the Union was assessed damages of $107,000, which went to individual vessel owners in compensation for losses. The United Fishermen's Union was bruised but undaunted. It struck back by intensifying its resistance and, for the next period, shifted its attention to the East Coast.

CHAPTER SEVEN

The Canso Struggle and Newfoundland Recognition: 1970 to 1974

The way the Canadian Seafood Workers' Union president, Lawrence Wilneff, tells the story, Homer Stevens is "a little hard nosed; he just doesn't take 'no' for an answer." The story is one immortalized by Silver Donald Cameron in *The Education of Everett Richardson*.[1] The situation encountered by Stevens and the United Fishermen and Allied Workers' Union when they came to Nova Scotia differed considerably from the one they had experienced in British Columbia. As Con Mills, a Nova Scotia fisher and union organizer who worked on both coasts, said, in British Columbia "the union is like going to church, but it's a dirty word here; management there had to deal with the union and give it some respect, but not here." That was exactly what drew the United Fishermen east; they saw the mission to "organize the unorganized," as Homer Stevens put it, as part of the Union's mandate. They went east to organize the workers on both small- and large-scale boats, and they began by making alliances with the existing plant workers' union (which appeared unconcerned that the United Fishermen should raid it). After an exploratory attempt to organize some scallopers in southwestern Nova Scotia and trawler crew in Lunenburg, the United Fishermen decided to concentrate their main efforts in the Canso area. Lawrence Wilneff took United Fishermen's Jack Nichol around in 1969, introducing him to the local union officials and fishers, then did the same with Homer Stevens when he was released from jail after the Prince Rupert fiasco.

Action soon began in the Canso area. In February 1970, the

shore workers at National Sea Products struck, led by the 2,500-member Canadian Seafood Workers' Union in plants at Halifax, North Sydney, Lockeport, Louisbourg, and Lunenburg. The strike by 1,200 shore workers also effectively stopped thirty-three company trawlers employing 600 crew. It lasted for over two months, providing an important organizational opening for the United Fishermen. The groundwork was laid by Homer Stevens and other United Fishermen organizers during this period, and their alliance with the Canadian Seafood Workers paid off when that union continued to support the fishers of Canso in their bid for union recognition at Booth Fisheries during the spring of 1970. By the summer, however, matters became complicated as Albert Martell, president of Local 109 of the Seafood Workers, began to organize a campaign in opposition to the United Fishermen and called for intervention by the Nova Scotia Federation of Labour, even though he was not authorized to do so by either his own union headquarters or the local membership.[2]

* * * * * *

The Canadian Seafood Workers' Union (CSW) *has eighteen locals, eleven in Nova Scotia and seven in New Brunswick, representing about 4,540 plant workers in the summer and 2,500 year-round (60 per cent of whom are women). Formed in 1957 through a merger of the Canadian Fish Handlers and the United Fisheries Workers of Canada, the CSW is an affiliate of the Canadian Labour Congress and has a loose alliance with the Marine Workers and the Canadian Brotherhood of Railway, Transport and General Workers (see page 108). Its main negotiations are with National Sea Products, including joint negotiations for five Nova Scotia plants, and the Lamèque Co-op (see United Maritime Fishermen, page 84). CSW's activities in New Brunswick are run independently and there was a recent defection of two small plants led by the former provincial organizer to Le Syndicat Acadien, a nationalist organization. CSW is also under some threat from the Newfoundland Fishermen, Food and Allied Workers' Union (see page 111), which has gained a foothold in Petit-de-Grat and Canso where former CSW plants have been transferred to their jurisdiction. Historically, predecessors of CSW were involved in some important actions such as the 1952 organization of the National Sea plant* *in Lockeport and* CSW *itself in the strike in 1970 by 1,200 members against National Sea at five plants. Recently, however, membership has been diminished by the weak economy, and the Union has stagnated to the point where its autonomous future is threatened.*

* * * * * *

Attention shifted from local union politics to the national level. Recall that the United Fishermen had been expelled in 1949 from the "house of labour" and not readmitted. In the spring of 1970 Canadian Labour Congress President Donald MacDonald and the CLC executive proposed that "UFAWU should accept a generous offer of merger provided by the Canadian Food and Allied Workers Union. CFAW had offered to let UFAWU become an autonomous unit within its organization."[3] When the United Fishermen spurned the offer, the suitor turned to attack: "Canadian Food and Allied Workers, a division of the Amalgamated Meat Cutters and Butcher Workmen of North America, has launched a raid against the UFAWU at Petit-de-Grat, Nova Scotia."[4] The settlement of the eight-month Canso strike in the fall resulted in an interim agreement between the strike committee and the processor of an *ad hoc* nature but did not formally recognize the United Fishermen although it provided for minimum prices and a grievance procedure. Acadia Fisheries granted "voluntary recognition" to the Canadian Food and Allied Workers' Union, prompting Homer Stevens to say, "The raid by the Meat Cutters completely reverses assurances given by the CLC and Nova Scotia Federation of Labour during the strike that no affiliated union would interfere."[5] The question of jurisdiction under the Canadian Labour Congress, as will be seen in later instances, has more to do with power than with formality. The Canadian Food and Allied Workers claimed jurisdiction over the entire Atlantic fishing industry and took its mandate beyond superseding the United Fishermen to raid the Canadian Seafood Workers' local in Petit-de-Grat (even though the Seafood Workers were part of the CLC although at the time out of favour for supporting the United Fishermen). Moreover, the companies were far from neutral in these raids, with management at Acadia Fisheries approaching other unions to thwart the United Fishermen.[6]

* * * * * *

The Canadian Brotherhood of Railway, Transport and General Workers' Union (CBRT) *was founded in 1908 and represents about 35,000 workers in over 200 locals, about equally distributed in the public and private sectors. It was drawn into organizing some fish plants in Nova Scotia in 1968. Following the bitter strike in 1970-71, when the United Fishermen and Allied Workers' Union (see page 91) was rejected by the companies in the Canso Strait area, CBRT was accorded voluntary recognition for some trawler crew and scallopers by National Sea Products, Riverside Seafoods, and Nickerson's. By 1971 it represented most trawler crew and some scallopers in Nova Scotia. In 1982 the Newfoundland Fishermen, Food and Allied Workers' Union (see page 111) began organizing scallopers and trawler crew in Nova Scotia, following their earlier move into some plants. This pushed the otherwise complacent CBRT into attempting further organizational drives for scallopers and the Canadian Seafood Workers into alliance, but generally, the Newfoundland Union has been somewhat successful in gaining membership. Throughout these activities the Canadian Labour Congress has remained fairly detached while the more aggressive Newfoundland Union seems to have been making gains but encountering significant employer resistance, especially from scallop boat owners in southwestern Nova Scotia.*

* * * * * *

Parallel with the Canso strike, the Canadian Brotherhood of Railway, Transport and General Workers (CLC) was invited by the processors to organize the crews on National Sea Products' trawlers in Lunenburg. This followed a spontaneous strike by these trawler crews from the first of December, 1968, to the middle of January, 1969, inspired by the United Fishermen's organizational drive. The Brotherhood's negotiations were very quiet as National Sea Products offered voluntary recognition for a contract that, by the union's own admission, "was terrible ... not much really but a foot in the door." Also unionized by voluntary recognition were trawler crew and some scallopers at Riverport Seafoods and Nickerson's. Clearly these offers were extended because the companies feared the United Fishermen and the tactics (and tenacity) of Homer Stevens. By 1971 the Canadian Brotherhood had organized virtually all Nova Scotia trawler crew and some scallopers without really having to engage in recognition struggles. For the next decade this union serviced these members fairly comfortably with little innovation in succeeding contracts and with little motivation to extend themselves. Not until the Brotherhood was pressed by a source that would hardly have been expected at this early stage would real confrontation mark the unionization of crews on large-scale vessels in Nova Scotia.

Legislation governing trawler crew was passed in Nova Scotia after these voluntary recognitions occurred, legitimizing practices that had already been conceded by the companies when they granted bargaining rights to trawler crew. At a formal level, crew changed from joint adventurers to some type of ill-defined employees, yet the system of payment remained essentially identical, even after unionization under the Canadian Brotherhood and new legislation.

The lesser evil strategy of the processors had an impact that extended beyond Nova Scotia into Newfoundland, where the processors knew an organizational drive was imminent. They certainly did not want the United Fishermen; Homer Stevens later said, "We were breaking ice all the way, making a path" that the other unions followed. The Canadian Seafood Workers gave the idea of moving to Newfoundland some thought when National Sea Products took over a plant in St. John's in 1969-70. Lawrence Wilneff investigated but found that his union could not organize because the laws required unions to be affiliated in Newfoundland. His small independent union was confined to Nova Scotia and certainly could not expect assistance from the Canadian Labour Congress.

The United Fishermen's Canso strikers had been sent a telegram of support from Newfoundland by Father Des McGrath and the Northern Fishermen's Union, but at that time they were but a voice in the wilderness. The United Fishermen actually saw them only after the strike was over. The Northern Fishermen emerged alongside the Canadian Food and Allied Workers' Union. The two were soon to become the Newfoundland Fishermen, Food and Allied Workers' Union, an organization whose start was aided by the fears of the processors and the Newfoundland government that the "West Coast communists" might attack. As will be seen, however, once the Newfoundland Union got a footing it did a masterful job of organizing Newfoundland fishers and demonstrated that it too could be tenacious in its pursuit of its members' interests.

With 1,500 fishing outports and 6,000 miles of coastline, to say nothing of some of the most backward collective bargaining legislation in the country, Newfoundland did not seem ripe for organization of its fishing population. Nevertheless, in November 1969 a group of sixty-nine Port au Choix longline fishermen, aided by Father Desmond McGrath, each paid five dollars in voluntary dues "to investigate ways and means of self help."[7] These fishermen rejected the idea of a co-op and favoured a union. McGrath had been exposed to the co-op principles of the Antigonish movement at St. Francis Xavier University as a student, but the local fishermen had unfavourable memories of co-op failures in Newfoundland. In the summer and fall of 1969 some Placentia Bay fishers had brought a suit against the Electric Reduction Company of Canada for pollution damages in Placentia Bay that had closed fishing in the bay for several months. Richard Cashin, a St. John's lawyer, represented these fishers. Father McGrath contacted his former classmate to assist the Port au Choix fishers draft a constitution. Cashin studied the structure of the United Maritime Fishermen's Co-operative but ultimately based the constitution upon that of the United Fishermen and Allied Workers' Union. On May 2, 1970, the Northern Fishermen's Union was founded, its constitution providing coverage for fishermen and plant workers. These northern peninsula fishers soon set about negotiating fish prices with the companies and were joined by local plant workers.

Other pockets of labour organization already existed in the province's fishery. A local at Catalina, Port Union, and Bonavista, for example, "traces its origins back to the time of Sir William Coaker and the Fishermen's Protective Union, and it had a collective agreement in force in the 1930s, after Coaker had retired. In the 1950s, this local union became a direct charter of the Trades and Labor Congress and subsequently in 1956 a direct charter of the Canadian Labor Congress."[8] There was also an organization of plant workers called the Burin General Workers' Union, which led a two-week strike in 1954. This union expanded to include workers at Grand Bank in the 1950s, but during the 1960s unionization throughout Newfoundland declined under government-sponsored anti-union activity.

In 1967 the Canadian Labour Congress gave national jurisdiction over fisheries to the United Packinghouse Workers, and most Newfoundland CLC locals merged into that union which, in 1968, merged with the Amalgamated Meatcutters. In 1969 only eleven of a hundred fish plants in Newfoundland were organized, of which eight were organized under what was by then called the Canadian Food and Allied Workers' Union. According to Gordon Inglis, "organized plants were mostly large fresh freezing operations and union membership was about 1,700 – one-third of the total workforce in the processing sector."[9] As Inglis reports, CLC officials arranged meetings between the Canadian Food and Allied Workers' Union and the recently formed Northern Fishermen's Union, motivated by a concern that the Newfoundland fishers might merge with the dreaded United Fishermen. Meetings, in which McGrath and Cashin took part, over inclusion of shore, trawl, and inshore fishers were held in Toronto, then ratified during October 1970 in Chicago, prior to the Founding Convention in the spring of 1971. Inglis reports that the international union eventually paid over $500,000 for organizing, based upon the agreement that "the NFU would merge with the existing locals of the CFAWU in the province to form the Newfoundland Fishermen, Food and Allied Workers' Union, a provincial council of the CFAWU. The international provided an initial organizing subsidy of fifty thousand dollars and the promise of more."[10] One of the new union's first acts was to campaign for collective bargaining rights.

* * * * * *

The Newfoundland Fishermen, Food and Allied Workers' Union (NFFAWU) represents virtually all 10,000 "bona fide" small- and intermediate-scale fishers, 12,000 plant workers, and 1,050 trawler crew in Newfoundland plus some shore workers, trawler crew and scallopers in Nova Scotia. Formed in 1971 and recognized under a new provincial law especially designed for fishermen, NFFAWU combined the Northern Fishermen's Union which had been founded in 1969 by Port au Choix longliner skippers with the help of Father Desmond McGrath and lawyer Richard Cashin (both of whom had been classmates at St. Francis Xavier University along with Arthur LeBlanc, long-time head of the United Maritime Fishermen – see page 84) with the Canadian Food and Allied Workers' Union (CFAWU).

CFAWU *had been active in Newfoundland since 1967 as a branch of the Amalgamated Meat Cutters and Butcher Workmen of North America, which financed an organizing campaign under Canadian Labour Congress jurisdiction.*

For small- and intermediate-scale fishers NFFAWU *negotiates price agreements covering the various species and sizes of fish with the Fisheries' Association of Newfoundland and Labrador. For trawler crew, a combination of price of fish and per diem (since 1975) is negotiated. Trawler captains are not included in the Union but mates and chiefs are, even though, as their contract reads, they "are in fact ship's officers and responsible for exercise of certain management functions, which functions do not include the final authority to hire, fire, suspend, promote or demote." On intermediate-scale boats captains are also included in the Union whether they are owners or rent their boats. Shareworkers on small-scale boats are also included.*

Recently the Union formed the Labrador Fishermen's Union Shrimp Company, which holds two offshore shrimp licences and buys salmon on the Labrador coast. This organization combines features of a co-op and a NFFAWU *local but operates as a company. The Union has also been active in negotiating and administering over-the-side sales with foreign fleets for under-utilized species (squid and mackerel). Since 1981* NFFAWU *has been active in Nova Scotia, first taking charge of* CFAWU *locals in Petit-de-Grat plants and then actively organizing trawler crew and scallopers throughout Nova Scotia in direct competition with the Canadian Brotherhood of Railway, Transport and General Workers' Union (see page 108). Its name was changed to the United Food and Commercial Workers, 1252, Fishermen's Union in 1985.*

* * * * * *

Officially the Newfoundland Fishermen, Food and Allied Workers' Union was founded at a convention on April 28, 1971, as two locals (Local 1252 for plant and industrial workers and Local 465 for fishers) under a division of the Canadian Food and Allied Workers' Union, itself an international affiliate of the Amalgamated Meat Cutters and Butcher Workmen of North America. The founding and thus far the only president was Richard

Cashin. The founding convention made the following eligible for membership in the Newfoundland Union's fishers' section:

(a) The owner or part-owner of a vessel engaged in the fishery and actively pursuing the fishery.
(b) Any person who fishes with others for shares of the catch or wages.
(c) Any person below the rank of officer on a trawler, dragger or seiner.

The final category was later expanded to include officers below the rank of captain.

The reasons for the success of the Newfoundland Union are not self-evident. According to Richard Cashin the explanation can be found in the Union's ability to change the patronizing social/political attitudes toward the fishers by acting "collectively to counter-balance the other forces in society which have dictated to them what goes on." The fishery was ripe for organizing, according to Cashin, because of its recent concentration of processors and the tremendous gaps between the companies and the workers in a "feudal-like" system. Inshore fishers were locked into cartel-like prices; the system has now been changed to one of bargaining for prices and conditions of sale plus a health fund, workers' compensation, and a more sensible licensing policy as a result of the Union's efforts.

Part of the success must be attributed to substantial funding from the international union; another part can be found in the leadership qualities of McGrath and Cashin. Legislation passed by the provincial government helped but was really after the fact; by the time of the merger, nearly half the plant workers in the province had been organized, the Northern Fishermen's Union had nearly 2,000 members, and the companies were willing to grant recognition voluntarily for trawler crews to any union except the United Fishermen. The Newfoundland House of Assembly did not pass the law granting collective bargaining rights to inshore fishers until May 21, 1971; nevertheless, it was the first, and until the early 1980s the only, provincial government to pass such legislation. The Fishing Industry (Collective Bargaining) Act was not the gift it appeared to be. It was vague on the meaning of "fisherman" and "appropriate bargaining unit," leaving the Newfoundland Union to struggle for suitable definitions. Within the

Union these issues caused rifts. Some members wished to have a decentralized structure with greater local autonomy and control over funds. This group was led by Fred Locking, who had joined the Union as an international representative. The other tendency, led by Richard Cashin and Ray Greening, favoured centralized direction and pooled finances. The Annual Convention agreed with the pooled funds, and Fred Locking left to work for the Newfoundland Association of Public Employees.[11]

Why did the government concede what it did? Part of the explanation may rest with changes that were taking place within the industry. David Alexander reports that "in 1950 the fishing industry had been, for all practical purposes, wholly owned and controlled by Newfoundland [interests]; by 1970 probably over half of the catching and processing was controlled by non-resident firms," such as Booth Fisheries, National Sea Products, and B.C. Packers.[12] As fishing was being industrialized, it was coming increasingly under the control of outsiders. There was therefore an incentive for the government to recognize the Newfoundland Union so that Newfoundland interests would be represented in some way, even though that union had foreign affiliations. As the government sought new means to protect local interests, the Union appeared to be one such possibility. Thus the government removed barriers that had been erected earlier but were actually being eroded by the growing power of the Union.

The Newfoundland Union sought to be inclusive rather than exclusive. It was first of all a social movement that combined shore workers and fishers. Moreover, it included not only trawler crews but also small-scale fishers and a growing number of intermediate-scale fishers. In all instances everyone possible was included in the Union, such as the mates on the trawlers and the captains on the intermediate-scale boats. This practice was politically astute at the time and most pragmatic in that it eliminated a potential source of resistance. It has altered the nature of the Union somewhat and has had its effect on Union practices, as will be seen, but the most amazing feature has been the overall unity within the Union and the way the organization has handled potential rifts. The Newfoundland Union has managed to establish a kind of hegemony over the Newfoundland fishery; it has regularized conditions, actually "rationalizing" patterns of development and fitting well into the more industrial nature of the fishing companies. Serious conflicts have been present, but the

Union has generally brought to the industry a progressive direction that has helped Newfoundland society break some of its past paternalistic practices.

Two bench-mark strikes occurred in the Union's formative period: the Burgeo strike in 1971 and the trawler crews' strike of 1974-75, both of which helped to establish the Union as a force to be reckoned with in the province. Spencer Lake of Natlake, a plant jointly owned by National Sea Products and the Lake family, owner of Burgeo Fish Industries, proved to be the first opponent against whom the new union would earn its spurs. Lake's paternalistic statements provided the Union with lines it would use for decades. A familiar one was: "I am not anti-union, I just think that in certain circumstances unions are not practical. And this is one of them: isolated outports in Newfoundland. You haven't got the local leadership to run them intelligently, with all due respect to the people – I'm very fond of them."[13] The Union called upon its considerable resources when Lake refused to deal with fishers and union organizers. Immediately the Union made its presence felt locally, renting a store and some land upon which fishers built a stagehead for a salt fish operation:

> For the first few days while they waited for the salt and other equipment to arrive, they bought the fish and distributed it around to the hospital and private households to anyone who wanted it.
>
> As soon as they were ready they found a few of their number who remembered how to split and salt fish – they were in business. In spite of the fact that there had not been a salt fish operation on the south coast in over two decades their project went smoothly. At the request of the union the Canadian Saltfish Corporation sent in an inspector who declared the fish as good a quality as any being produced in the province.[14]

The Newfoundland Union may have been unconventional in its tactics, but this was an effective, visible sign to the community that it meant business. More conventional was a move to call upon their wider resources through their parent union in the United States. Virtually all cod entering the United States, including that from Burgeo, passes through the port of Gloucester, Massachusetts. The Union sent two representatives to establish an "information picket" when the *Caribou Reefer*, one of Lake's refrigerated cargo ships, arrived. The dockworkers of Gloucester, "like the majority of other workers there, are members of the Amalgamated Meat Cutters and Butcher Workermen of North America. They decided to honour the Burgeo picket line and refused to unload the ship."[15] The Union held out and eventually won what amounted to a recognition strike with all the ideological and political content needed to give it the momentum to organize the entire province.

The next major union victory arose from the 1974-75 trawler crews' strike, which gained recognition for trawler crews as company employees entitled to a per diem payment and finally ended the co-adventurer payment system in Newfoundland where income had been entirely determined by the catch of each voyage and the "price" of fish. This strike is the subject of a study by David Macdonald. Events were launched by an unlikely source: some 350 inshore fishers based from Port au Choix to Anchor Point began the first "legal" inshore fishers' strike in the East on the first of July 1974. At the same time Booth Fisheries broke off negotiations with trawler crews seeking their first contract, and the struggle spread to Burin on July 22, leading to the largest conflict in North American fishing history involving all the shore workers and fishers in the province.[16] The tie-up of trawler crews spread from Burin to St. John's, Burgeo, Marystown, Trepassey, Catalina, and Harbour Breton and lasted for six weeks, finally ending when the provincial government established a board of inquiry headed by Leslie Harris of Memorial University.

This inquiry produced the Harris Report and its famous Recommendation 8: "Trawlermen should negotiate with companies not the price of fish but rather the income level that will be attainable for full-time work." In addition to the changed method of payment, Harris recommended a major increase in the level of payment. Macdonald reports that "the companies involved refused to reach agreement on the basis of the board's report. Consequently, in January (1975) the trawlermen once again refused to sail unless the companies accepted the system of payment advocated in the report.... A settlement reached in March abolished the co-adventurer system, but provided less generous wage increases than those proposed by the board."[17] After nine months of dispute the trawler crews won a per diem of $20 a sea day plus a payment based upon the poundage of fish caught, increasing the average annual earnings for trawler crews on stern trawlers from $7,000 to $13,000 for 1975.[18] It was this gain that the Newfoundland Union would use as its ticket into the trawler fishery of Nova Scotia in the 1980s.

Although events on the West Coast in the early 1970s were not as exciting as those on the East, there were some notable developments. High on the scale of strangeness (in light of recent developments on the East Coast) were discussions of a merger between the United Fishermen and Allied Workers' Union and the Canadian Brotherhood of Railway, Transport and General Workers. Talks to this end had begun in 1968, authorized by United Fishermen convention delegates. The reasons, of course, were the continued exclusion of the United Fishermen from the Canadian Labour Congress and the fisheries membership of the Canadian Brotherhood on the East Coast.[19] The merger never materialized, but after nearly twenty years of suspension the United Fishermen was finally reinstated as an affiliate of the Canadian Labour Congress in 1972. But this was not until, as has been noted, a good deal of damage had been done to the United Fishermen's cause on both coasts.

The United Fishermen made one very significant gain in 1973: the end of discriminatory clauses in shore workers' agreements. Jack Nichol reported that after a week-long strike supported by fishers and tenderworkers, the milestone objective of equal pay for women was gained:

UFAWU cannery agreements were one of the most notorious examples of discrimination against women in employment. Two supplementary wage agreements, one colored blue and the other pink, set out wage conditions for men and women. The cannery women's supplement provided wages grossly inferior to those paid to men.

Female networker rates lagged 85 cents an hour behind the male networker rate. Generally, the same discrepancies existed in fresh fish agreements.[20]

The companies, of course, created the conditions, but this was the first time the Union had solidly demonstrated its determination to overcome these inequities.

Significant as these gains were, they did not end women's inequities. Rate discrimination based upon 400-hour versus 1,000-

hour rates (in terms of hours worked per season) depressed women's wages.[21] Not until the late 1970s was there an amalgamation of men's and women's seniority lists and finally a determination to eliminate the discriminatory pay categories.[22]

Tensions in relations with the Native Brotherhood surfaced again during this period. Natives were under particular pressure in the fishing industry as the companies began to withdraw the boats they rented. In 1971, B.C. Packers announced the elimination of 150 boats; "of these boats, 64 gillnetters out of a total of 125, and 17 seiners out of about 26, had been manned by Natives. Altogether, about 255 men were affected by this fleet cutback, 150 of whom were Natives."[23] Adding to the problem for Natives was a stricter enforcement of the Union's clearance program following the difficulties in Prince Rupert:

Basically, the clearance program requires the crew of each long-line, salmon, herring and trawl vessel to register the names of all crew members with the Union before sailing on the season's first trip. Each boat must clear with the number of crew members prescribed by the crew complement policy.

If any vessel clearing is in need of men, the "chances" must be filled by Union members. New members will not be considered while UFAWU members are registered and available for employment in the particular fishery in which the vessel will operate.[24]

Native Brotherhood members were hard hit by this more stringent policy. Although some were Union members, others, according to the *Native Voice*, "have strong religious scruples about joining a Union which was expelled from the Trades and Labour Congress of Canada for being Communist controlled since Communism is a bitter foe of Christianity."[25] And the differences were more than philosophical. Brotherhood president Guy Williams warned: "There is a feeling among Brotherhood members ... that Union organizers have been instructed to sign up as many Indian fishermen as possible." In 1970 the Brotherhood was reduced to only 900 dues-paying members, the life blood of its finances.[26]

Because of past experience in negotiating, the United Fishermen decided in 1973 to dissociate itself from the Native Brotherhood in its negotiations with the Fisheries Association and become the sole bargaining agent. This threatened the financial position of

the Native Brotherhood. On the other hand, the Native Brotherhood was attempting to establish a clearance policy different from
that of the Union. According to the Native Brotherhood, "The
hiring of crews on Native Indian fishboats is a hereditary one
and follows a practice set out by the ancestors of the present
day skippers. The policy is simply that the skippers from villages
have the right to hire a crew which will be beneficial to the
families concerned and the village as a whole."[27] This disparity
between union "hiring hall" practices and Native tradition had
behind it a conflict between Native skippers and union workers
that would not become clear until a later period when other Native
Brotherhood practices became more open.

Still another ongoing conflict during this period between the
United Fishermen and the Pacific Trollers' Association (see page
96) had a peculiar twist. As noted earlier, the United Fishermen
had organized only a small proportion of the troll fleet, and in
early 1972 an open meeting of trollers was called to try to open
avenues of discussion for a program of minimum price negotiations.
This was taken as an attack by the Pacific Trollers' Association
president, Larry Jones, who said that "the union would not in
any way be doing any negotiating on the association's behalf ...
the association would not work with the union on price negotiations."[28] The Union proceeded, attempting a tie-up of trollers
at the season opening on April 15, but did not get the required
two-thirds majority (claiming 61 per cent of those voting). The
Pacific Trollers viewed this action as a "raid" by the Union.[29] Taking
a page from the book of the Prince Rupert Co-op, the directors
of the Pacific Trollers decided to turn to the Canadian Labour
Congress and authorized a committee to carry out discussions
to "explore the advantages, disadvantages and possibilities of
affiliation with the CLC.... To this end they had two meetings
with CLC regional director Tom Gooderham, organizer Dick Larsen
and Prince Rupert agent Vince Dixon at the CLC Vancouver office."
The committee reported: "The CLC group understood our desires,
namely to protect ourselves from such activities of other organizations which might be harmful to us, to maintain as closely
as possible our mode of operating, our authority and our independence." A possible affiliation with the Deep Sea Fishermen's
Union or a direct charter were considered.[30] The directors rejected
the unionization path because as then president Joe Carcia put
it: "The PTA consists of approximately 550 independent business-

men, with a board of directors doing *their* business. . . . We don't want to be classed in the labour class and we don't want to have to fight anybody about it."[31]

This episode illustrates that within the Pacific Trollers there have been some tendencies toward unionism in terms of price negotiations, albeit of a defensive type seeking independence from the United Fishermen. Moreover, the Canadian Labour Congress, although willing to carry out talks, by this time was not willing to bend as far as it had earlier to accommodate anti-United Fishermen forces. It even had to retreat on some past decisions involving the Prince Rupert Co-op, as will be seen.

CHAPTER EIGHT

Struggles Continue and "New" Co-ops Appear: 1975 to 1979

Themes during the late 1970s on both coasts were labour's challenge to traditional co-operative forms and the emergence of new types of co-ops, often as a strategy to avoid unions. On the West Coast as new co-ops were being created to circumvent the United Fishermen's Union, the traditional Prince Rupert Co-op was experiencing unexpected resistance from its "house" union. On the East Coast the traditional United Maritime Fishermen's Co-op was challenged by a new force for unionization, the Maritime Fishermen's Union. A cornucopia of new associations and arrangements was created to deal with the variety of social relations that began to erupt. In Newfoundland the Union maintained its hegemony and extended it by taking matters into its own hands, including some production and marketing. It was a period of great activity, and the fishery generally experienced a boom before falling to pieces in the 1980s. It was a period when earlier tendencies became more distinct and solidified, causing some past tensions to break into open conflict.

Writing in 1945, Moses Michael Coady, founder of the United Maritime Fishermen and inspirer of the Canadian co-operative movement, said

> The techniques of running a co-operative business are exactly the same as those of a corporation. It gives the masses of the people the same intriguing lure for private enterprise that a joint stock company or corporation gives to old-time profit

business. The real distinction between co-operation and old-time business is that co-operation is private non-profit business and the latter is private profit business.[1]

Especially after its 1967 restructuring, the United Maritime Fishermen's Co-op came more and more to resemble other corporations in the fishery, not because profit was lacking (which was true) but because increasingly management became distant from the membership and the direct producers divorced from the leadership. A very complex structure of representation had developed:

> Each local co-operative association which is a shareholder or is affiliated with UMF is entitled to one voting delegate at all annual or special meetings of the Central; in addition, each local is entitled to one voting delegate per twenty fishermen members plus one voting delegate per $200,000 of business transacted with the Central the preceding year; the same formula applies to direct individual (fishermen) members within a zone. The maximum number of voting delegates credited to each local or zone is ten (10) regardless of the number of fishermen members and/or volume of business transacted with UMF Central.[2]

Such a delegate system is a complex mediation between the individual fisher member and management and/or policy making. The gulf between the ideal and the real was widening as the social aspects of the movement solidified (some would say mummified). The Co-op ceased to be the extension of the person who fished; it did not bring the fishers and their product closer to the consumer or their fellows as it once had. Membership loyalty became a serious problem as more and more members drifted away. The Co-op leadership, instead of coming closer to its membership, was attempting to run in a race where private capital set the pace. The managers said, "Our co-operative must centralize and amalgamate, because this is an age of amalgamation and centralization."[3] Yet by entering this race the United Maritime Fishermen lost what had been special to them.

Particularly noteworthy was the Co-op's failure even to address the issue of itself as an employer of labour, especially shore workers. Three of its major plants had become unionized: the 200 employees at Alder Point with the Retail, Wholesale and Allied Workers, the 150 employees at Chéticamp with the Canadian Brotherhood of Railway, Transport and General Workers, and the 1,000 employees at Lamèque joined the Canadian Seafood Workers. Each plant had a different method of payment, combining wages and some incentive systems. There was no broad policy covering labour relations (even though this was to be the "age of centralization"). Usually there was "labour peace" at the small, non-union community plants while the larger regional plants tended to be strike-prone. In many ways the United Maritime Fishermen was no different from commercial processors, even belonging to processor organizations such as the Seafood Producers' Association of Nova Scotia.

The operations of the United Maritime Fishermen are far from uniform. The Alder Point division, for example, works very much like a private company with central ownership, and the local manager says, "It's pretty hard to get a guy to sell here for a cent less when he can go to National Sea and get more. It's hard to get them to believe that cent will help the plant and sustain them in hard times." Very few of the fishers who sell here are members of the Co-op, and virtually none sell all their catch through this plant. At the Chéticamp Fishermen's Co-op, however, there are about eighty active members who run their co-op themselves. They are members of the United Maritime Fishermen only for marketing purposes; they are not "owned" by the organization. They were able to pay dividends during the late 1970s and maintained good relations with the plant workers, even to the point of discussing the possibility of their becoming Co-op members.

During the period in question there was an interesting clash between the United Maritime Fishermen and the Newfoundland Fishermen's Union involving a confrontation between old classmates Arthur LeBlanc and Richard Cashin. The issue was negotiations on the price of lobster, with the Co-op claiming that "fishermen cannot negotiate with themselves" and the Union claiming that the Co-op "appeared to be a co-op in name only and has operated in the same manner as any other fish company" in Newfoundland.[4] Resolution of this confrontation did not occur for some time.

More amicable relations exist with the fellow co-op Pêcheurs Unis du Québec. The 80-per-cent Acadian membership of the United Maritime Fishermen had drawn the two co-ops into some joint marketing ventures in the past and even into discussions of merging, but during the 1970s each was following its own chaotic path. Throughout the Gulf of St. Lawrence area were scattered many small co-operatives, some belonging to the co-op centrals and some drifting away. On the Magdalen Islands, La Coopérative Centrale des Pêcheurs des Îles de la Madeleine left the United Maritime Fishermen in 1974 to join Pêcheurs Unis du Québec. On the other hand, the Gros-Cap Co-op, established in the 1930s and operating a lobster and mackerel canning plant with perhaps fifty members, has studied the possibility of joining with one of the co-op centrals but thus far has found little value in the idea. Yet again, in 1976 the Quebec government and Pêcheurs Unis du Québec came together to establish Madelipeche when the U.S. owners of Gorton's decided to cease operations, thus leaving the province and Co-op operating three factories on the islands (creating a problem that came to a head during the massive restructuring of the 1980s). Some Quebec co-ops are large, unionized operations, resembling those of the United Maritime Fishermen's regional operations, while many others are very small, such as l'Association des Pêcheurs Côtiers de Grande-Vallée, which has only forty-six members (forty owners and six deck hands) who hand-line for cod and mackerel in their 6-metre boats and do not engage in any processing. The larger plants of Pêcheurs Unis du Québec, such as those at Newport in Gaspé and Rivière-au-Renard, are organized and have been subject to major labour strife. The strike in 1976 lasted from May 18 to July 5 and involved 464 workers and 14,490 days lost. More will be said later about the situation in Quebec, especially when the industry was restructured by the federal and provincial government.

* * * * * *

L'Association Professionnelle des Pêcheurs du Nord-Est (APPNE) is a strong grouping of intermediate-scale (semi-hauteurier) captains and crew centred in three ports in the Caraquet area of New Brunswick. These Acadian fishers, led by lawyer Gastien Godin, were formed into an association of both inshore and mid-shore boats in 1968 with the help of the St. Francis Xavier Extension Department. By 1978 it had evolved into an exclusively intermediate-scale organization as small-scale fishers were pushed toward the Maritime Fishermen's Union (see page 126). This left a mobile fleet of about 130 boats and 550 to 600 fishers (captains and crews averaging three to four) who *pursue groundfish, crab, shrimp, and herring.* APPNE *includes the entire New Brunswick crab and shrimp fleets and the Gulf Seiners (see Fundy Co-ordinator, page 134) who fish for herring. They are locally known as "Cadillac fishermen" in recognition of the lucrative times around 1980. More recently, times have tightened and* APPNE *is tending toward fish price negotiations through the use of "tie-ups for prices." Although ideologically opposed to striking themselves, they have passive support for the Maritime Fishermen's Union. Until 1984 they were strong members of the Eastern Fishermen's Federation (see page 152), but their lobbying influence has come more from their internal strength than from the umbrella organization.*

* * * * * *

Notable as a contrast to the two co-ops in the area is l'Association Professionnelle des Pêcheurs du Nord-Est (APPNE) based in Lamèque, New Brunswick. This Acadian association was set up in 1968, also with support from the St. Francis Xavier Extension Department, originally for both small- and intermediate-scale fishers. In 1978 APPNE became specialized in intermediate-scale fishing (leaving small-scale fishers to the Maritime Fishermen's Union, to be discussed shortly). Virtually all the vessels within the Association are fisher-owned. The four somewhat overlapping fleets fish for shrimp (100 members), crab (350 members), herring (100 members), and groundfish (150 members). Membership in the Association is extended to both captain and crew, each with the same membership status and voting rights but different fee structures (1 per cent of gross sales to a maximum of $500 per boat). There is a share arrangement of 40 per cent to the boat and 60 per cent to the crew. These are known as the Cadillac fishermen of the gulf with their mobile fleet of some 130 boats and a permanent office with a director, Gastien Godin, who is trained as a lawyer. The Gulf Seiners, which will be discussed later in connection with the Bay of Fundy herring seiners (see Fundy Co-ordinator, page 134), are also part of APPNE and have led the way in entering price negotiations, which are spreading throughout the Association. Generally, however, the Association attempts to walk a thin line between union-associated price negotiations and "market" prices. As such they have not opposed unionization for small-scale fishers but do not wish to be drawn into strikes themselves (even though they have, on occasion, participated in informal tie-ups for price).

* * * * * *

The Maritime Fishermen's Union (MFU) *was founded in Baie-Ste-Anne, New Brunswick, in 1977 after several years of struggle, mainly involving small-scale Acadian fishermen. In 1982 it gained bargaining rights in New Brunswick and in 1984 was certified in two areas of the province: the Caraquet Peninsula and the southeast. It has somewhat less strength in the Bay of Fundy area and has not gained bargaining rights in Nova Scotia or Prince Edward Island.* MFU *intends to negotiate the price of fish with the New Brunswick Fish Buyers' Bargaining Association and will ask the United Maritime Fishermen's Co-op (see page 84) to honour this negotiated price. Co-op management, especially at the Lamèque Co-op, was a major obstacle to recognition of this union, but the fishers themselves have supported the Union by overwhelming margins. Generally small-scale fishers on Prince Edward Island's west end and Nova Scotia's north coast have supported the* MFU; *those in southern Nova Scotia and the eastern Island have been more reluctant, tending to be more "independent" and preferring associations.*

The use of helpers constitutes a dilemma for the MFU. *Small-scale boat operators are eligible for membership in the Union and constitute the overwhelming majority, but they often work with helpers, depending upon the species caught and technique. Helpers are paid either a wage or on a lay. Wage workers are not eligible to be union members whereas those on lay arrangements are, the principle being that shareworkers have an equal interest in negotiating the price of fish.*

Thus far MFU *has not attempted to organize the crews on intermediate-scale boats, who are at present represented by l'Association Professionnelle des Pêcheurs du Nord-Est, although its constitution provides such a possibility. Its constitution also provides for organization of shore workers, but thus far* MFU *has been content to make alliances with the Canadian Seafood Workers (see page 106) regarding shore workers and the Newfoundland Fishermen, Food and Allied Workers (see page 111) regarding trawler crew.* MFU *has also become involved in over-the-side sales of gaspereau and mackerel in the gulf and gillnet herring in southwestern Nova Scotia, an important organizing breakthrough.*

* * * * * *

While there is no doubt that APPNE is "pour nos pêches acadiennes," as their motto expresses it, most Acadian fishermen are small-scale inshore fishers (at least a thousand of them on the gulf coast of New Brunswick) whose principal voice in the late 1970s was the Maritime Fishermen's Union (not to be confused with the United Maritime Fishermen, the co-op discussed earlier). Inshore fishers on the gulf had been represented by a series of associations such as the North Eastern or South Eastern New Brunswick Fishermen's associations and the United Maritime Fishermen's Co-op over the years, but, as the president of the Maritime Fishermen's Union puts it, "The co-ops' head office has taken the control away from the fishermen. . . . Instead of fighting to get inshore fishermen a bigger share of the stocks what the co-ops did was to get involved in the offshore fleet."[5] Gulf inshore fishers had demonstrated their opposition to seiners and draggers operating in "their" waters by burning a wharf at Caraquet in 1967 to protest seiners being brought from British Columbia and raising a major protest in 1979 to prevent seiners from unloading in Caraquet. The Maritime Fishermen's Union has been the organizational expression of these protests, recalling the Canso strike of 1970 that gained unionization for trawler crews but not recognition for inshore fishers.

The Maritime Fishermen's Union from the outset has presented the "fisherman as a worker," recognizing that there are two opposing views, which they characterize as follows:

First, there is the image of the inshore fisherman as a small independent businessman. This definition classifies the fisherman as someone who has only himself to blame if he is not successful, if he gets a pitiful price for his fish or if the fish stocks are decimated. The solution to the fisherman's problems, according to this view, is to follow the companies' lead and invest in bigger and more expensive equipment. . . .

The other view is one that identifies the fisherman as a worker: working long and hard to earn a living (which fluctuates between

$9,000 and $12,000 a year). This view sees the fisherman much more as an industrial worker, although recognizes that there are some differences between the two. . . .

The MFU is based on this second definition of fishermen.[6]

Its founding convention in March 1977 drew three hundred fishers who decided to make their domain Maritime-wide. The Union immediately demonstrated for collective bargaining legislation; in 1978 it was accepted into the New Brunswick Federation of Labour and soon afterward into the Canadian Labour Congress. In 1977-78 three locals were established in Nova Scotia (Guysborough, Northumberland, and Cape Breton), assisted by the Nova Scotia Federation of Labour and some financial aid from the Canadian Labour Congress. Two locals followed in 1978 on Prince Edward Island (Western and Eastern), supported by the Prince Edward Island Federation of Labour. Together with the two locals in New Brunswick (Northeast and Southeast), there were now seven. Initial expansion was too rapid for the Union's financial resources and organizers. It soon became evident that collective bargaining legislation would not come easily and resistance would be considerable, especially from the Maritime Fishermen's Co-op. Moreover, a great deal of political and ideological work would have to be done to educate fishers about the working-class perspective of the Union. While there was in Cape Breton a tradition of workers' struggles to call upon, in southern Nova Scotia and on Prince Edward Island there were long traditions of anti-union sentiment. The Union would find opposition from the Co-op leadership even though the membership supported the Union.

Even on Prince Edward Island, where there was overlap of Union and Co-op membership, the stronger rift occurred with Island Association members, as will become apparent in the 1980s. The Prince Edward Island Fishermen's Association, which is financed by the provincial government, has organized some minor boycotts of specific buyers and sought some improved prices, but overall it has opposed unionization.[7] Although at one time nearly all island fishermen were Association members, an emerging militancy was evident in some. The Union tapped into that militancy when it came from New Brunswick in 1977-78, signing about four hundred members. Poor organization and servicing because of limited resources and too little understanding of the local situation meant that the Union was to lose its momentum for a while on the island, resuming it again in the 1980s.

New Brunswick had to be the first battleground. The leaderships of the Union and the Co-op would first slug it out over which of the "two trains of thought" should prevail. In the skirmishes there would be "a lot of red-baiting," as Union organizers put it. The small-scale owner-operators formed the core of the Union's support, constituting about 95 per cent of the membership. There was some difference in the areas because of the local situations. In most places there were few employees hired to work on the boats, and they were hired on a weekly salary. In Cape Breton there were some shareworkers. Membership in the Union was confined to the owner-operators and shareworkers, casual hired labour being excluded. No specific rules were established regarding crew size because the largest boat in the Union was not over 14 metres long. The Union's constitution membership clauses read:

a) a self-employed commercial inshore fisherman, holding a permit to conduct commercial fishing and personally engaged in fishing;

b) a fisherman-helper, working for a self-employed commercial inshore fisherman, so long as part of his remuneration is paid on a share-of-production basis;

c) a person engaged or employed on fishing vessels of all types of which he is not the owner or the captain so long as part of his remuneration is paid on share-of-production basis; and

d) workers employed in fish processing plants.[8]

Clearly the Union had broader aspirations built into its constitution, even more evident in another clause on its goals, which reads: "By affiliating, amalgamating, merging or co-ordinating with any other organizations having objectives similar to those enumerated herein to the end that the Union may continue to grow in membership and ability to serve its members, provided that any amalgamation or merger shall be approved by a majority of two-thirds of the members of the Union in a referendum vote."[9] Point c would allow eventual association with the crew members of APPNE or even with unions representing crew on large-scale vessels (such as the Newfoundland Union) while point d was designed to include the Canadian Seafood Workers and unorganized plant workers.

Relations between the Maritime Fishermen's Union and the Canadian Seafood Workers' Union have been somewhat complex. Initially a Nova Scotia-based union with its strength in National

Sea Products plants, the Seafood Workers extended into New Brunswick in the early 1960s. The New Brunswick section of the Union has had a great deal of autonomy, especially with the rise of Acadian nationalism (including the breakaway of the small section called Le Syndicat Acadien led by Matilde Blanchard). The New Brunswick section (without Blanchard) has good relations with the Maritime Fishermen's Union and gave a three-thousand-dollar organizing donation to the Union, but the Nova Scotia section is less certain in its support because the Union has opposed trawler fishing in the gulf, and trawler production is what keeps shore workers going in Nova Scotia. In the 1980s a very complex set of relations between the Maritime Fishermen's Union, the Newfoundland Union, and the Seafood Workers' Union developed as talks of a merger and "one Atlantic union" for fishers and plant workers became a prospect.

More than any other region, the Gulf of St. Lawrence (exclusive of Newfoundland, where the Union is hegemonic) has bred a multitude of non-aligned area and/or species associations. This has been particularly true of Quebec and its Gaspé Peninsula. The following are a few examples: l'Association des Pêcheurs Côtiers de l'Anse à Valleau Gaspésie, Sector Rivière-au-Renard, is a thirty-member association of twenty owners and ten deckhands who make day trips in 6-metre boats, hand-lining and longlining and sometimes gillnetting for cod, herring, sole, and lobster (like the other associations listed here, they are not members of Pêcheurs Unis du Québec or the United Maritime Fishermen co-ops); l'Association des Pêcheurs de Crabe de Bascons Counties of Gaspé and Bonaventure has twenty members (ten owners and ten deck-hands) who catch crab in cages on trips lasting from one to two days using boats in the 15-metre range; l'Association des Pêcheurs Professionnelles Gaspésie de Shigawake et Port Daniel is a thirty-five-member association of boat owners fishing for lobster, cod, mackerel, and herring by longline, cage, gillnet, or driftnet, usually on two-day trips aboard 9-metre boats; l'Association des Pêcheurs de Crevettes de Matane, whose members fish for shrimp "from St. Michel to Newfoundland" aboard 20-metre trawl boats with crews of three on week-long trips, has eighty owner and crew members. In each of these instances the association was created to assist members in dealings with the federal Department of Fisheries and Oceans concerning various regulations and licensing practices; in other words, they are lobby groups. They try to give a voice to their members and protect their interests with the government. They seldom if ever negotiate the price of fish or work conditions and are not involved in marketing, which generally takes place through private corporations or a co-operative of which they are not effective members. It is important to note, however, that not all associations are as limited as these. L'Association Professionnelle des Pêcheurs du Nord-Est (see page 124), already mentioned, is an example of one that is strong and well organized. What follows will indicate that there are also others of importance.

One such group is the Fundy Weir Fishermen's Association, formed in 1973. The weir fishery on which it is based along the southeast coast of New Brunswick has existed for over a hundred years. The small herring are caught and kept alive in the weirs, where they clean themselves out before they are delivered to be packed as sardines (see Illustration 3, page 31). This association represents about two hundred people operating 250 weirs, each of which requires a licence, a site, and the weir itself. Fish are taken from the weir and pumped into company boats. The main buyer in Canada has been Connors Brothers of Blacks Harbour (part of the Weston empire), but other smaller buyers also exist, some of them in the United States.

During the war and in the immediate post-war economy, the high demand for sardines supported many plants in the area, but by the fifties and sixties the market slowed and the number of purse seiners competing for herring grew. The number of weirs declined from 600 in the 1940s to 250 by the 1970s. This was the situation when the Association was formed to lobby the Department of Fisheries and Oceans in an effort to save the weir operators in the face of declining stocks. At the same time the Association began talks with Connors Brothers over prices, intensifying negotiations when the herring seiners set up the Atlantic Herring Marketing Co-op in 1976 (see Fundy Co-ordinator, page 134). In 1978 the Association hired a full-time manager, Walter Kozak, who had been employed by Fisheries and Oceans. Since then the Association has been highly active, establishing a Catch Compensation Plan into which members pay 3 per cent of their catch. The Association itself is financed through organized sales to U.S. buyers and a levy on each hogshead (a unit of herring) sold. It has also instituted a group insurance plan. This obviously well-organized group of fishers has been effective in negotiating prices with a highly concentrated buyer in a specialized market:

90 per cent of sardines are caught by weir, the seiners catching the larger fish, and 85 to 90 per cent of the catch was sold to Connors Brothers over the 1978-81 period. Members sell to whom and when they wish, but the Association ensures price minimums, guaranteeing nothing to Connors except the conditions of sale.

The weir fishery is not without major problems, especially its vulnerability to the migration of fish because of the passive nature of the gear. With respect to the Maritime Fishermen's Union and its drive for collective bargaining the Association is fairly neutral as long as it can retain its autonomy. It says, "The position of our Association regarding Bargaining Legislation has been that we are not certain whether we need it, however, if there are fishermen's organizations in the province that would benefit by the legislation then as long as it does not commit us to anything we would work towards such legislation."[10] During the 1980s this association became an important voice in the Eastern Fishermen's Federation and had further involvement with herring sales in the Bay of Fundy. Most important to note is that this association effectively established price negotiations and union-like conditions for its members, not through legislation, but through its own organizational strength. It has formed a type of "quasi co-operative" of weir operators in relation to buyers and in many respects behaves like a union. It has responded to the material conditions of its environment in a pragmatic and (during this period at least) effective way for its members in what sometimes is a fairly lucrative fishery.

At one time the most powerful group in the Maritimes was the Nova Scotia Fishermen's Association in Yarmouth, founded in 1974 by a group of seiners to deal with the price and marketing of their catch. Originally it was aimed at all fishermen on the East Coast and was called the Atlantic Fishermen's Association. In 1977 the seiners formed the Atlantic Herring Fishermen's Marketing Co-op, which will be examined shortly, and broke away. The provincial government then provided the funding necessary for the Nova Scotia Fishermen's Association. This group had two sections, one for draggers and another for scallopers with quite distinct memberships. The draggers are boats under 20 metres (averaging 3.5 crew members per boat) and only the captain/owners belong to the Association. On the scallopers, however, everyone aboard the twenty large company-owned boats (fifteen crew per boat) are members. The scallopers have a fairly uniform pay arrangement in which the captains make a settlement when the boats come in to dock after a trip lasting up to twelve days. Each of the 325 members pays association dues of $125 a year. They have negotiated the share agreement and the price of fuel (which is deducted from the crew share) and even the price for scallops by means of a tie-up, thus refusing to go to sea. In the Scallop Sector captains are full members of the Association and are hired by the companies. They, in turn, hire the crews. Relations between the processor, the captain, and the crew are very close, with little interference between the boat owner and the captain, who has a high degree of autonomy. There is little crew turnover. Everyone shares alike in the catch except that the captain, mate, and engineer get an additional premium.

Aside from the membership of captains, how does the Scallop Sector differ from a union? Officials of the Association say that it is unlike a union because "we control it ourselves. We don't have a head office in Halifax, and theirs in Montreal and theirs in Chicago.... We're basically one small group able to control it ourselves. Our problems are peculiar to our area. We're more reasonable than a union would be. We don't want to be ripped off by the processors but we want them to survive.... If we were a union, we could be taken over." This fear of control from outside dominates the culture of southwestern Nova Scotia. Throughout the area there is strong parochialism and paternalism. Between the Scallop Sector and the two companies there is nothing on paper, only handshake agreements, and all is "understood."

Not so for the Dragger Sector, whose markets are much more dispersed. These crews catch groundfish (cod, haddock, and flounder) from three- or four-crew intermediate-scale boats fishing year round yet not in direct competition with the large-scale boats, which do not dock in the region. Basically all the boats have a 55/45 lay, but they differ in their deductions and the Association does not become involved in such matters. The dragger captain/owners pay a flat $500-per-boat fee for membership. They have tried to influence the price of fish through a tie-up but not really to negotiate the price of fish with the many small community-based processors. The organization has a defensive purpose, the organizers saying, "If we weren't there, we might have lost more," and "We don't win very often but we fight like bastards." The opponent in these remarks is not the processor but the government, and the battles are over issues of regulation and licensing.

Organizers say, "We don't want a union," but "we would like some systematic method for gathering dues from the freeloaders," and they repeat the same "outsider" arguments one hears from the Scallop Sector: "What we want is what we have. We want a little bit more, but we want to control it ourselves." Part of the reason is that this fishery has been better off financially than most and is closer to the U.S. fresh fish market, which the Association watches carefully. Late in the 1970s the Dragger Sector's "free-loader" problem was becoming epidemic, and there were only 115 paid members (although the Scallop Sector was healthy). Foreshadowing events of the 1980s, the president of the Association said: "One of the ways we have been able to keep the unions out is to have a good strong association." He was right.

* * * * * *

The Fundy Co-ordinator *is a creation of the Ministry of Fisheries and Oceans designed to market the herring catch of the Atlantic Herring Fishermen's Marketing Co-operative (AHFMC), which includes the owners of thirty-two herring seiners operating out of Yarmouth, the South-West Seiners' Association (SWSA) representing captains on fourteen herring seiners in Pubnico, and five of the eleven boats from the Gulf Seiners' Association (see APPNE, page 124) for over-the-side sales. Both AHFMC and SWSA represent capital exclusively on intermediate-scale boats while Scotia-Fundy Seiners' Association (SFSA) was formed in 1981 to represent the 125 crew members. SWSA was a breakaway from AHFMC (or "the Club" as it was known), and the original eleven captains who formed the association were later joined by three associate members. Of the fourteen boats, nine are individually owned, two by processors, and three jointly with processors. SWSA collectively buys supplies and materials, provides administrative services, and along with AHFMC nego-tiates the price of herring with the Seafood Producers' Asso-ciation of Nova Scotia. Since 1981 crew have sat in on the price negotiations, but their association does not regard itself as a union. All these associations were part of the Eastern Fishermen's Federation (see page 152) until the rift of 1983 concerning EFF's marketing involvement.*

* * * * * *

Also located in the same region and, as has been seen, having roots in the above association is the Atlantic Herring Fishermen's Marketing Co-op. Before B.C. Packers moved part of its seine fleet from the West Coast in 1964, the herring fishery had been a small-scale gillnet and weir fishery for over a hundred years. Then everything changed. The sixteen seiners from British Columbia, which left because a reduction fishery closed, came to the Gulf of St. Lawrence and the Bay of Fundy. In the same period the number of seiners operating in Newfoundland was rising from one in 1965 to fifty by 1969. These occasions sparked the dramatic protests by gillnetters in the gulf referred to earlier.[11] Before licensing was introduced there were over a hundred seiners on the East Coast, each valued at up to $2 million, with a collective capacity far exceeding the fish available. Fisheries and Oceans was held responsible for masterminding the expansion and began to "rationalize" the allocation of fish in what was to become the most transparently political fishery in the country.

In 1975 herring were captured by three main organized groups: the Fundy Weir Fishermen's Association, the group within the Atlantic Fishermen's Association, and the Bay of Fundy Purse Seiners' Association, formed by seiner captains from New Brunswick in 1972. Herring gillnetters were virtually unorganized.[12] In 1976 government-set quotas were introduced for the first time along with an organization to administer them. Initially quotas were based on the amount of each boat's past catch, number of crew members, and size of boat (in later years changed to an equal quota for all). It was during this year that "the Club" or Atlantic Herring Fishermen's Marketing Co-op was formed by twenty-seven seiner captains (out of a fleet of fifty-three boats) at the instigation of the government. As John Kearney relates the situation,

> a primary function of the AHFMC was to negotiate herring prices through collective bargaining with the processors and, by means of a radio dispatch system, to direct the seiners, while still at sea, to various fish plants to land their catch. In this way, the fishermen hoped to have a more orderly and price competitive method for marketing herring. To achieve this objective, the purse seine fishermen had first established, in consultation with the government advisors a system of sub-allocating the total fleet quota. These sub-allocations took the form of indi-

vidual (annual) boat quotas and weekly boat quotas.[13]

By 1979, the Co-op had forty-two member seiners selling to twenty or thirty plants.[14] The herring fishery had come under tight control and restrictions. It was a year-round fishery, beginning at the Bay of Fundy in October and November, then on to Caraquet and Sydney, to Newfoundland by early spring, returning to Sydney in the late spring, and going back to the Bay of Fundy for the summer. As the fishery became more restricted, being first barred from the Gulf of St. Lawrence in 1980 and then even further reduced by season-openings, it was increasingly evident that the seiners' fishing capacity would need to be reduced. Some life was restored to the fishery by over-the-side sales, negotiated by the government and administered by the Co-op. "Bay of Fundy seiners sold herring to Polish vessels in 1976, 1977 and 1978. The higher foreign prices helped support the fleet during the change over by Canadian processors from fish meal to food," the Canadian Fishing Report stated on the front page of its inaugural issue.[15] This was a practice that would expand greatly during the 1980s and become a focal point for much conflict (especially as the sales became a means for the government to dole out patronage).

Not all herring skippers were satisfied with the Atlantic Herring Fishermen's Marketing Co-op, and a group of nine broke away in 1976 to form the South-West Seiners Association, a holding company that purchased nine processor-owned boats, aided by a Resources Development Board loan and a $120,000 grant from Fisheries and Oceans.[16] They constructed a building in 1978-79 for repairs to boats and nets. As a group on their own, the South-West Seiners thought they would be able to make better deals for fuel and supplier discounts, but they continued to market their catch through the Co-op until 1979 under the quota system. The reasons for the split differ depending upon the teller of the story. According to Wayne Thorborne, president of South-West Seiners:

> Our main group first came together when ten of us bought our boats from the Sea Life Company, at the time Mr. LeBlanc (Minister F&O) and the rest of us were setting up the co-op. We were contracting fuel purchases together, and we had a seine loft and an office. We've got a building with ten acres, and engine repair men and net menders working for us; the whole thing amounts to an investment of $230,000 or $240,000.

We thought that the way the Co-op was going, we might do better to take the money we were putting into it and apply it to our own operation. We might be able to get into processing in a small way.

Compare this with the views of Dick Stewart, manager of the Atlantic Herring Fishermen's Marketing Co-op: "The reason for the split is a bit complicated. What really triggered it was two or three boats ... got into distributing fish. They made deals with several processors, outside of the Co-op, to sell to those processors only."[17] In some ways the South-West Seiners have developed co-operative principles with respect to catching fish, sometimes pooling their fish no matter who catches them, thus saving on fuel and effort. They take turns during the season, fishing for two weeks after a week ashore, because the quota restricts their overall catch and the buyers restrict the amount they can deliver daily. Crew shares remain the same whether or not they are fishing.

After a very turbulent first half of the decade, the second half of the 1970s was a time of consolidation and some innovative approaches to unionization for the Newfoundland Fishermen, Food and Allied Workers' Union. In the summer of 1978 the Newfoundland Union entered into an agreement with Ribno Stopanstro of Sofia, Bulgaria, to deliver 9.9 million kilograms of mackerel and 1.36 million kilograms of squid to its freezer trawlers. No Canadian companies were involved, the Union dealing directly with the Bulgarians. It was reported that in administering the sale, "the union will have a representative aboard each freezer trawler to check the weighing of fish, issue receipts to fishermen, and generally look out for the interests of the fishermen and the union.... Ribno will also be paying money to the union to cover such expenses as the wages of inspectors aboard the boats, the cost of unemployment insurance contributions and so on." This was a very bold move, motivated, Richard Cashin said, because "the companies have not shown any interest in the kind of planned marketing approach which the union has been advocating and which LeBlanc seems to favor, and secondly, squid and mackerel are species which fishermen had trouble selling last year." As to the issue of plant workers' jobs, they were assured that "the arrangements would not affect plant jobs through competition with existing squid markets by insisting on a clause which forbids the Bulgarians to sell any of the squid to Japan, where most of the Newfoundland companies sell their squid."[18]

There was more. In September 1978, a Soviet factory trawler, under contract to the Swedish company Joint Trawlers, arrived for the same kind of arrangement and the Union began scrambling to establish a distinct sales organization.[19] A third species was added when Fisheries and Oceans gave the Union a quota of 400 metric tonnes of herring, which they proceeded to sell for a record price.[20] According to Kevin Carroll, who was managing the sales for the Union, as the squid and mackerel were surplus to the capacity of the processing plants during the glut season, no shore workers were harmed.[21]

The Union's behaviour has been questioned, but the $500,000 gained plus the bonanza for fishers certainly strengthened the organization.[22] Nor did the Union stop there. In early 1979 "the union had incorporated Fishermen's Community Services Limited and has applied to register the Newfoundland Fishermen's Union Producers Co-operative Society as a certified cooperative."[23] The purpose of the Fishermen's Community Services is to provide its members with insurance and management counselling, including taxes, while the Co-op's task is to manage over-the-side sales. A further union activity was the Labrador Fishermen's Union Producers' Co-operative Society, created to hold two offshore shrimp licences for Union fishermen in Labrador.[24] Since it did not have the appropriate boats, the Co-op authorized negotiation of a charter with a group of Faeroese companies to use the licences in 1978-79, planning eventually to have boats crewed by Labrador fishermen. The structure of the organization changed somewhat as the Labrador Fishermen's Union Shrimp Company was formed:

> The fishermen's company is established on the co-operative principle of one man, one share, one vote.
>
> Every bona fide fisherman who is a member of the NFFAW on the coast of Labrador from L'Anse au Clair to Paradise River will be offered a share in the company ... the fishermen also made provision for shares to revert back to the company in the event a fisherman leaves the fishery for more than a year. . . . Anyone who has been a bona fide fisherman for more than 15 years will retain his share in the company for life.[25]

Utilizing the benefits from over-the-side sales and other ventures, the Union offered members to "pay half the cost of a health and welfare plan, the same as the companies do for the trawlermen and plant workers. The fishermen who chose to participate in the plan would then pay the other 50%."[26] Such activities have drawn the attention of various commentators who search for an explanation. David Close conjectures,

the Fishermen's Union is a relatively new organization, one not habituated to the routines of conventional trade union behaviour. This may render the union more disposed to unorthodox actions. Similarly, the fact that over 40 per cent of its members are independent commodity producers may have made setting up this selling co-operative a more plausible alternative than it would have been for a union with a more conventional membership.

Second, the political climate was right. The federal government could use the NFFAWU's initiative to show the merchants that aggressive marketing paid off. . . .[27]

Besides its own co-operative activities, the Union has given tacit approval to the Fogo Island Co-operative by not attempting to represent the fisher membership or the plant workers in this organization. Fogo Island Co-op, which stands as an island in a sea of Union hegemony, saw its membership expand from 127 in 1967 to 1,500 in 1983, of which 750 are fishers, 400 plant employees, and 350 members-at-large. Membership in the Co-op had been open to all Fogo Island residents over eighteen years of age but recently was restricted to fishers and job holders (after a minimum probationary period) because of pressures over a shrinking number of job positions available. A recent study by Roger Carter reports that "employees (plant workers and supervisory staff) were not permitted on the Board between 1974 and 1983" but currently one employee is permitted on the nine-member board dominated by fishers. Clearly Co-op members do not all have equal status. Moreover, Carter reports that fishers receive "the approximate union-negotiated fish prices but co-op employees are paid somewhat less than union scale." The wage question precipitated a wildcat strike by employees at the Joe Batt's Arm plant in 1981-82.[28] Thus far the Newfoundland Fishermen's Union has been content to allow the Fogo Island Co-op to continue unchallenged.

The late 1970s, however, were the peak of the Union's attractiveness. Organizing drives were a breeze. In Ramea, Newfoundland, for example, "trawlermen and plant workers organized themselves and acted almost unanimously in favor of joining the union fold. This marks the first time a local of any size has organized itself in this fashion" as 151 of 167 plant workers and 59 of 62 trawlermen signed cards. The Union would need all the reserves it could muster for the 1980s. In the meantime it was acting very much like a union by negotiating priority lists for full-time inshore fishers, requiring that "in each area a fishermen's committee will submit a list of the bona fide fishermen to the companies concerned, to enable the parties to ensure that these fishermen have the first opportunity to sell their catch to those companies they regularly supply, during periods of over-supply."[29] The Union was active in servicing its members, not forgetting about the inshore fishers who were most in need of protection (and least serviced by conventional union practices). Another form of "protection" was becoming more than an idea. The Union was beginning to focus on the differences in level and structure of payment between the trawler crews in Nova Scotia and those in Newfoundland. The *Union Forum* boldly stated in 1978: "The NFFAW feels it is very important that either there be one fishing industry union in Atlantic Canada, or else the other unions adopt a more militant stance so as to equal the settlements negotiated in Newfoundland. . . . The NFFAW has agreed to cooperate with the Maritime Fishermen's Union in their attempts to establish a strong union in the Maritimes."[30] The Newfoundland Union would entertain some very bold initiatives in the 1980s.

While unionization was making major gains on the East Coast, on the West Coast co-ops were being turned into tools for use against the union. By the mid-1970s the United Fishermen were again under attack from several different quarters: the gear associations (Pacific Trollers and Pacific Gillnetters); the Restrictive Trade Practices Commission, which, in pursuing a combines investigation, took files from both the Union and Native Brotherhood offices; and (ironically, under the circumstances) the Native Brotherhood itself. In 1975, Brotherhood officials were "observers" rather than delegates in United Fishermen's negotiations with the Fisheries' Association, although they did honour the strike that year.

Each side was attacking the other. The Union, through *The Fisherman*, said: "Even to qualify as a trade union, the Native Brotherhood would have to expel half its present executive because they are vessel owners, subordinate to the fishing monopoly and employers of their fellow Natives."[31] The Native Brotherhood, through the *Native Voice*, was equally aggressive, saying: "The past season's month long strike can be defined as being strictly an attempt by the Executive of the UFAWU to destroy and move the Native Brotherhood out of this industry."[32] The immediate issue was the inclusion of Native Brotherhood boat owners on the negotiating committee, but there was a more fundamental cause that suggests the differences between the two organizations are more than racial in origin and include basic class differences.

* * * * * *

The Central Native Fishermen's Co-operative (CNFC) *was organized in 1975 by Native seine captains who had been delivering to Millbanke Industries to keep the plant from closing. Edwin Newman, then a vice-president of the Native Brotherhood (see page 93), took over as president of* CNFC. *The new co-op was unusual in including as members boat owners, crew, shore workers, and administrative personnel. Decertification of the United Fishermen at the plants caused a serious rift between the Union and the Native Brotherhood. The Co-op's production was supplied by forty seine boats (about 200 members) plus forty trollers and ten gillnetters, most of which were crewed by Natives. After several strong years, 1981 and 1982 were disasters. In 1983 the shore facilities were operated by the Quality Fish Company at the insistence of the Royal Bank. By 1984* CNFC *ceased operations.*

* * * * * *

Following its decline in influence after the first half of the decade, the Native Brotherhood continued to hurt into the second half. Between 1977 and 1979 alone, 102 vessels left the Native fleet (53 gillnetters, 18 seiners, and 31 trollers) reducing the proportion of Natives in the fishery from 10.5 per cent to 8.8 per cent, a decline of almost a fifth in a short period.[33]

One survival strategy attempted by some Natives was formation of a co-operative. The Pacific North Coast Native Co-op (Prince Rupert) had been operating with funding from the province in the Port Simpson cannery on a small scale since 1969, employing 180 Native persons.[34] This co-op had originally been organized by seven band councils, but from the outset there was little membership loyalty among the Native fishers and few delivered all their fish. Although the fact that the Co-op received fish during strikes made it welcome to some fishers, it did not make it popular with the United Fishermen. The shore workers were Co-op members as well, thus side-stepping the issue of Union organization. At its peak in 1978 this co-op had twelve seiners and fifty gillnetters delivering fish and a maximum of 350 shore workers.

This experience inspired formation of another co-op, which was to become a major source of conflict between the Union and the Brotherhood. The Central Native Fishermen's Co-operative (see page 141) purchased the Millbanke Industries cannery (150 employees) at Shearwater, Bella Bella, in 1975 and a freezer plant (170 employees) at Ucluelet the next year. The first president was Edwin Newman, who resigned as the Native Brotherhood's first vice-president to take the position. Some of the workers aboard the boats and in the plants were not Natives but agreed to sign with the Native Brotherhood.[35] The impetus for the Co-op had come from twenty-two seine skippers who helped underwrite the start-up costs. The fleet grew to forty seiners and forty trollers plus ten gillnetters. "Profit-sharing" programs were developed for all Co-op members and the membership was to cover labour both on the boats and in the plants.

There was immediately confusion about labour practices and the right to fish during strikes. Even the *Native Voice* expressed concern:

We therefore must respect the decisions of the Central Native Fishermen's Co-operative and the Pacific North Coast Native Co-operative to form their own companies. However, we believe that if they want to opt out of the present tie-ups which threatens all other fishermen's livelihood, they must clarify their new status in the fishing industry, whereby they are exempt from further tie-ups.

The present confused situation relative to new co-ops and Brotherhood and UFAWU membership only gives Mr. Stevens a further excuse in his annual attempts to destroy the Brother-hood.[36]

For its part, the Union renewed its attacks, pointing to boat-owning members of the Brotherhood who were on the executive and identifying the Central Native Fishermen's Co-op as yet another attack on the Union.[37] Ultimately the Union laid charges of labour code violations against the Native Brotherhood, the Pacific North Coast Native Co-op, and the Central Native Fishermen's Co-op for interfering with the Union and against the Fisheries' Association of British Columbia for taking advantage of the situation.[38] The Central Native Co-op attempted to oust the Union from the Native plants where it had been certified and continued to fish during strikes, particularly the five-week strike in 1975 that launched the Co-op's career. According to Co-op officials, the "Brotherhood told the Union to get the hell out – stop picketing – and let us operate." By the time the British Columbia Labour Relations Board hearings were over, the Union was to win the legal point but lose the battle. Although the board ruled in favour of the Union concerning successor status at the Co-op plant, a vote was quickly held to decertify the Union at the plant.[39] Some of the board's findings are important, however, for understanding the position of labour within a co-op:

> The L.R.B. decision ruled that 310 members of the C.N.F.C. must actually be considered employees and rejected the argu-ment that as members of the co-operative they cannot be union members. . . . In ruling that the workers are still employees, the L.R.B. noted that the workers are still doing their jobs in much the same manner and similar direction as when they were not members of the co-operative.
> The ruling also said the co-operative has represented itself to various government bodies as the employer of the shore-workers and it added that the management sets the basic wage and may discipline or discharge workers.[40]

A new era in relations between the Brotherhood and the Union had been launched, even if the Brotherhood had an arms-length relationship with the co-ops. In the 1980s that pattern would persist but in an even more difficult environment.

It was not only Natives who were using the quasi co-op strategy to circumvent the Union. Another entity was Quality Fish, about which more later. Interestingly, both Quality Fish (with a half-million-dollar debenture held by Nozaki Trading) and the Central Native Fishermen's Co-op (with a $2.9-million debenture held by Marubeni) were heavily indebted to Japanese companies.[41] They were to become exceptionally close in the 1980s.

Another familiar line of attack appeared during the 1975 strike when the Pacific Gillnetters' Association re-emerged after over twenty years' dormancy. The Association's constitution forbade applicants to have membership in any trade union.[42] After the strike the Gillnetters were charged before the Labour Relations Board, which found that "PGA members laid careful plans to handle their fish in the event of a strike ... PGA directors admitted that the association had contracts with two small fish companies. PGA members agreed the contracts had been signed to provide an outlet for scab production."[43] The Gillnetters' Association has had little influence within the industry since the 1975 strike but does represent a tendency even among users of this gear type to favour entrepreneurial activity more aptly belonging to the Pacific Trollers' Association (see page 96).

In the late 1970s the Pacific Trollers continued as a significant organization but were joined by the Northern Trollers' Association in 1977. This was a regional group from Prince Rupert with 130 members north of Cape Caution. Like the Pacific Trollers, this group included only vessel owners, but most were Prince Rupert Co-op members as well. In 1979 yet another area group was added to these gear associations with the hundred-member Gulf Trollers' Association centred in the Gulf of Georgia area.

The Prince Rupert Co-op was having its own internal problems. In the mid-1970s when the management locked out shore workers, the Co-operative Fishermen's Guild was accused of scabbing its fish during the lockout. The Prince Rupert Amalgamated Shore Workers' and Clerks' Union was locked out for seven weeks in 1978, bringing to a head difficulties that had been building for the previous four years. In a move that should not have been very surprising at one level but was quite shocking at another, the board of the Co-op moved to compensate the vessel owners for lost sales. The report of the Annual General Meeting for 1978 explained:

Several of our members' vessels (those with multi-man crews) refrained from fishing during the major portion of the "lockout". The direct loss of income to fishermen on these vessels was crippling. In order to minimize the irreparable damage to those members and to assure that those vessels will continue as viable commercial fishing ventures within the Association, modest monetary payments have been made to them to be divided between the crews and skippers, in accordance with the standard share agreement.[44]

Despite the fancy language, there could be little doubt about what happened. After the bitter seven-week strike, the longest shore-worker dispute on the West Coast, during which the Guild supported the management that had locked out five hundred of their "fellow" union members, some Guild fishers continued to sell their fish. In 1976 and 1977 the Prince Rupert Fishermen's Co-op had urged its members to join the Co-op Fishermen's Guild.[45] The Guild, it will be recalled, included within its ranks not only crew but also boat owners who have marketing contracts with the Co-op. Subsequently the British Columbia Federation of Labour launched an investigation of the Co-operative Fishermen's Guild and its business agent, Sid Dickens. The investigation revealed payments of $30,000 to each of fifteen seine boats in "compensation" for losses during the lockout and recommended that the Guild's charter be lifted "on the grounds that the organization represents only a small minority of co-op board members."[46] The Guild's actions would become even more virulently anti-labour in the 1980s.

Co-op shore workers certainly took a path radically different from that of the Guild, but that might have been expected, given the overlap between Guild and Co-op membership and the exclusion of shore workers (a hoary co-op problem). The second half of the decade was complicated. The powerful Prince Rupert Co-op brought a labour conflict upon itself that spiralled into major proportions. The Central Native Co-op, in its desire to escape the United Fishermen's Union, drove the wedge between the Union and the Brotherhood even deeper. Ahead, the 1980s would put all organizations under tremendous stress as the boom years retreated and a deep recession took a heavy toll.

CHAPTER NINE

Crisis, Restructuring, and Realignment: The 1980s

The 1980s have been a time of great social change for the fisheries during a restructuring of the corporate world and a realignment of fishermen's organizations. No corner of the industry has been left untouched. The Maritime Fishermen's Union has become a major force, not only in New Brunswick but in the very heart of anti-union territory, southwestern Nova Scotia. The Newfoundland Fishermen, Food and Allied Workers' Union has also extended into Nova Scotia and become involved in some major confrontations. A new grouping of "independents," the Eastern Fishermen's Federation, was created with exceedingly generous federal funding but, after riding a brief crest, its wave broke. In the corporate sector the federal government created two giant processing entities, one public, the other private, in Newfoundland and Nova Scotia respectively, and in Quebec both levels of government became owners of processing plants. On the West Coast processors were also restructured and the federal government intervened. Despite a major rift with the Native Brotherhood and another bitter confrontation at the Prince Rupert Fishermen's Co-op, an amazing degree of solidarity was exhibited by the fractious Western organizations beset by several crises.

At the end of the 1970s few observers thought the Maritime Fishermen's Union (see page 126) could survive. In the summer of 1981 the New Brunswick legislature passed Bill 94, a long-awaited fisheries act, but it was an empty proclamation. With the assistance of the New Brunswick Federation of Labour and the Union's persistence, however, a new piece of legislation was passed in April 1982. Bill 25 gave the Union enough strength to test the waters. These proved to be most friendly on the part of the fishers, but a few processor-led obstacles remained to be overcome. After a ten-year struggle the Union was officially recognized, but the battle with the co-op managers still had to be concluded. During the initial certification process, when a board was convened to decide whether co-op fishermen should be included in the bargaining unit, the Lamèque Co-op disrupted the proceedings by offering board member Kim d'Entremont (of the New Brunswick Fish Packers) a job. Consequently, the sitting board was dissolved and five new members were appointed, thus delaying by another year the Union's bargaining.

Ray Larkin, the lawyer for the Maritime Fishermen's Union, has described the New Brunswick legislation as a measure granting the "fishermen the right to organize themselves into a union and the right to collective bargaining with the buyers of their fish. The new law creates the Fishing Industry Board with wide powers to promote collective bargaining.... Fishermen can strike or tie up. The buyers can refuse to buy fish. The Act calls all of these actions boycotts. The fear of a boycott is one of the prime motivations on both the union and buyers to settle."[1] The province is divided into three areas: Bay of Fundy, northeastern New Brunswick, and southeastern New Brunswick. Fishers are defined as owner-operators and shareworkers. Votes require a majority of at least 60 per cent of the area's fishers. Keeping co-op fishers in the bargaining units was crucial since, as discussed earlier, the Union and the United Maritime Fishermen's Co-op draw on the same small-scale fishers; there has been a major ideological difference between them concerning politically perceived "dependent" or "independent" commodity producer relations. The Union's arguments presented to the Fisheries Industry Relations Board are as follows:

1. The Union is as beneficial to the coop members as the other fishermen. The income, methods, and species fished by the coop fishermen are identical to the other inshore fishermen ...

2. On the points [the Union] wanted to negotiate, the Lameque coop wasn't different than other buyers.... If the Lameque

factory workers could belong to the CSAW union, why couldn't
Lameque inshore fishermen belong to the MFU?

3. One of the coop's favorite arguments was that the fishermen
couldn't negotiate with themselves since the inshore fishermen
are also members of the coop. But ... coop executives do the
managing and they have more power than the individual
members. . . .

4. The coop's final argument was that, in the end, the coop
wasn't a buyer. There were claiming to be nothing more than
an agency that was putting fish on the market ... [but] once
the fish was in the hands of the coop, it belonged to them
and the fishermen couldn't very well take it back. The fish
belonged to the proper legal entity, which is the coop, and
no longer to the individual members.[2]

The board ruled in the Union's favour. In 1984 certification votes
were held. On the Caraquet Peninsula 480 fishers were certified,
and on the southeastern coast 585, causing the New Brunswick
Fish Buyers' Bargaining Association to be assembled.[3] According
to Gilles Theriault, president of the Union, 95 per cent of the
fishers who signed were skippers.[4] The species for which prices
were to be negotiated included lobster, herring, mackerel, groundfish, scallops, salmon, gaspereau, and smelt. The average turnout
for votes in the three areas was 86 per cent and the average vote
in favour of certification was 75 per cent. That was overwhelming
support.[5] Each local was to operate autonomously; therefore
disputes in one did not need to force another to follow. There
were, however, some further impediments as contract discussions
still had to settle on "a formula for the deduction of union dues,
accreditation of the fish buyers association, and the question of
whether the fish buyers can alter the price of fish while contract
negotiations are underway."[6] The Union was able to negotiate
a price for herring but could not get a lobster agreement for the
1984 season, although it appeared that one would be obtained
for 1985 based on a formula tied to the Boston market price.[7]

Success for the Maritime Fishermen's Union has been slower
on Prince Edward Island. In the winter of 1981 the Union pressed
for an inquiry into collective bargaining rights, which it obtained
in the form of the Weeks Commission. The commission "recommended that collective bargaining rights for inshore fishermen

should no longer be denied them" but also recommended binding arbitration, exemption for co-ops, provision for a province-wide bargaining unit (which the Union refers to as the "Island Michelin Bill"), and that helpers on boats be excluded from membership.[8] The Union did not support these recommendations, yet the provincial government chose to put the issue to a plebiscite. The Union boycotted the plebiscite, which resulted in 554 opposed to "union-type bargaining" and 299 in favour from 1,322 ballots distributed (only 64 per cent returned). The Union claimed that 95 per cent of its 450 members refused to vote.[9] The situation on the island remains unclear at the time of writing. At its fourth Annual Convention, the Prince Edward Island Fishermen's Association, the Union's main local opposition, voted "overwhelmingly in favour of going to the government for a 'Fisheries Act' that would make legal the mandatory check-off of dues from all Island fishermen. This will in essence force fishermen to either become an association member, join the MFU or opt out altogether."[10] Obviously the Association, like the Union, has been troubled by dues collections and the present uncertainty. It claims 800 to 900 members (of whom 300 were at the convention), but these are concentrated in the east end of the island while the Union's strength is in the west end, where its Local 5 annual meeting attracted only thirty-five members.[11]

Most crucial to the Maritime Fishermen's future is its progress in Nova Scotia, an organizing job that will require large sums and encounter strong resistance from many quarters. The Union devised a three-year plan and asked the Newfoundland Fishermen's Union for support. It received this in the form of $50,000 a year for three years. The Maritime Fishermen debated whether they were mortgaging themselves to "Cashin" but they decided there was nothing to lose since even failure would open the way for the Newfoundland Fishermen to come into the Nova Scotia inshore fishery. That union, in fact, had already begun moving into the trawler sector. Neither union would have much difficulty in the Cape Breton area; the test would come in southwestern Nova Scotia, and the contest would require hiring many organizers, borrowing, and seeking out additional sources of funding.

The Maritime Fishermen's Union had been very cautious about taking government funding, fearing that it would come under control just as other organizations were dominated by the government (the Eastern Fishermen's Federation, for example: see page

152). In typical Fisheries and Oceans fashion, the Union was offered a squid allocation of 2,000 metric tonnes, which it cautiously accepted on the condition that "this allocation not affect in any way the squid market for inshore fishermen" and that the money be used to organize a pension and health insurance fund "for dues paying members of the MFU."[12] Sad to say, it was reported in the next issue of MFU that "there was no squid to be caught this year."[13] This venture did, however, mark the beginning of the Union's marketing career. The next summer over-the-side sales organized by the Union sold 1,926 metric tonnes of gaspereau and mackerel to Joint Trawlers for $560,000. The project, authorized by the federal government, lasted eight weeks and involved over two hundred fishers.[14] Fish was accepted from all inshore fishers; non-union fishers were asked to pay dues as recognition for the Union's work in securing the sales.[15]

The Union's next move was more dramatic. For a long time small-scale fishers had opposed seiners in the Gulf of St. Lawrence because they were depleting the herring stocks. Harsh confrontations have included the burning of wharves used by seiners. At the seventh Annual Conference in 1983 the Union resolved "that the mobile herring seiner fleet be banned from all fishing in Canadian waters" and further demanded "the prohibition of the gillnet herring fishery for boats 50 feet and over."[16] This was significant given the Union's move at the end of the year into southwestern Nova Scotia, the heart of the herring seiners' territory, and even more boldly, its approach to Fundy Co-ordinator (see page 134).

In March 1983 the Union established Local 9 in southwestern Nova Scotia and by April had challenged the cut announced by Fisheries and Oceans in the gillnet herring quota for over-the-side sales. It managed to get the quota raised from the original 1,000 metric tonnes to 2,500 by the time sales closed. Fundy Co-ordinator was compelled to co-operate, and the Union made access to the Soviet trawlers easier for the gillnetters and hired a radio-operator to direct their deliveries, overall assisting forty union boats.[17] The next year the Union formally applied to manage over-the-side sales for the herring gillnetters, also asking for a higher quota and a ban on seiners at the Trinity Ledge spawning grounds during the month of September. They were successful and signed a contract with J. Marr Seafoods from England to sell 4,000 metric tonnes of gillnetted herring to the Soviet ships at $170 per tonne (the same price that the seiners received). Also made available were mesh bags, each holding a tonne of herring, to ease unloading of gillnetters onto the factory ships. The Union was able to recruit over a hundred Yarmouth-area gillnetters. There remains significant resistance from some non-union gillnetters (especially twenty-eight from the Yarmouth Bar area), even though the Union has agreed to handle herring from non-union gillnetters. Prices for over-the-side sales rose by $10 to $180 a tonne in 1985, with 2,500 tonnes allocated to the Union gillnetters and 8,000 tonnes to the seiners through Fundy Co-ordinator. In addition the Union gillnetters were allocated 1,500 tonnes and the seiners 8,000 tonnes to sell to processors who would resell the fish in semi-processed form to the Soviets: the processors thus had "a piece of the action" for the first time.[18] This whole project has been an important demonstration by the Union, obviously significant for attracting members (and gaining revenue) but most important, to establish a presence. The gillnetters would have little chance of running the entire herring over-the-side sales, but the Union has shown, for the first time, that it can be effectively keyed into these lucrative sales.

The Maritime Fishermen's Union has also proven itself in dealing with the perennial problem of licence limitation. It pioneered the way not only for local fishermen in the Northumberland Strait inshore zone – where Fisheries and Oceans had grappled unsuccessfully with the thorny problem for years – but for all fishermen's unions. The Maritime Fishermen resolved, at its sixth convention in January 1982, to develop a one licence policy for the area with the objectives of giving priority to persons dependent upon the fishery, maximizing the numbers able "to make a decent living," stopping the constant rise in the number of fishers, and, finally, refraining from putting undue pressure on either the fish stocks or the fishers. From these objectives were developed the criteria for a "Bona Fide Fisherman," defined as either a person who holds a Class A lobster licence or a licensed individual, with equipment, who had made at least 75 per cent of his/her income for the last two years by fishing or whose fish had a landed value of over $10,000. Persons who met these conditions received a Bona Fide Fishing Permit whereas others were considered part time, and only bona fide fishers were entitled to new limited-entry licences, transfers, and priority status for government programs and subsidies. Other features of note are that the person, not the boat, is licensed, and the boat can be sold independent of the licence. A licensed fisher must be aboard the boat when it is fishing, and the fisher is not compelled to "use or lose" the licence. New entrants are judged by a board of fishers, and they must serve an apprenticeship of two years as crew members before being eligible.[19] Fishers were the architects of their own plan, which promised to reduce the number of participants by a third over the next decade.

Even though the future certainly looks brighter for the Maritime Fishermen's Union midway through the decade that it did at the beginning, the situation remains complex. There are still a number of unions for trawler crews and plant workers in the Atlantic region; l'Association Professionnelle des Pêcheurs du Nord-Est (see page 124) remains a powerful force among Acadian skippers and crews of intermediate-scale boats.

Thus far the Union has been unable to obtain a Rand-formula or compulsory check-off for dues in New Brunswick (although there have been some negotiations for a joint recognition deal with the revamped United Maritime Fishermen's Co-operative, which would provide the Union with funds in return for services to Co-op fishermen, such as representation on various boards.

In 1985 the Union was still very much in debt. It nevertheless remains aggressive, contemplating an Atlantic fishermen's union that would take in Quebec, beginning with the Magdalen Islands, and Newfoundland in addition to the Maritime Provinces. The ninth Annual Convention "gave the executive of the Union a mandate to explore long term solutions" including "the feasibility of amalgamating or merging with another Union."[20] There is still opposition. The matter of the southwest Nova Scotia seiners is still unresolved, although the Union is faring quite well. Also in Nova Scotia the Eastern Fishermen's Federation, which had spearheaded Union opposition, is still a force to be reckoned with.

* * * * * *

The Eastern Fishermen's Federation (EFF) *was formed in 1979 as an umbrella organization at the behest of then Minister of Fisheries Roméo LeBlanc, with a squid allocation of 2,000 tonnes (valued at $1 million). Federal initiative initially brought together six fishers' associations, then thirteen by 1980, rising to a high of about twenty-five in 1982. Core support came* from Nova Scotia and Prince Edward Island associations. Funding allowed the hiring of an executive director, Allan Billard (a former provincial and federal fisheries department employee, most recently from CBC Maritimes fisheries broadcasts), and a staff of about four. EFF was designed primarily as a lobbying group meant to give one voice to the diverse Atlantic groups. When it became involved in some fish marketing and over-the-side sales to foreign fleets, its growing strength was eventually undermined.

Although eligibility was open to any fishers' organization with one hundred or more members (and even that criterion was flexible), membership came primarily from small- and intermediate-scale boat owners. At one time there were one crew association (Scotia-Fundy Seiners), several combining both captains and crew (Nova Scotia Fishermen's Association, Scallop Sector, and l'Association Professionnelle des Pêcheurs du Nord-Est – see page 124), a small co-operative (Cape Sable Island Fishermen's Co-op) and a large co-operative (United Maritime Fishermen–see page 84). Attempts had been made earlier to form similar umbrella groups. The Atlantic Fishermen's Association in 1975 tried to bring together fifteen Nova Scotia fishers' associations, and the Prince Edward Island Fishermen's Association called a meeting in 1976 that included six Nova Scotia groups. It took substantial federal funding and ministerial persuasion to finally accomplish the task. Recently, however, the loose alliance has been shaken.

Internal conflicts diminished the credibility of the EFF considerably. Two significant seiner groups withdrew in 1982 (the Atlantic Herring Fishermen's Marketing Co-operative and the South-West Seiners – see Fundy Co-ordinator, page 134), as did the important United Maritime Fishermen in 1983 and the influential Association Professionnelle des Pêcheurs du Nord-Est in 1984. Conflicts were linked to EFF's involvement in over-the-side sales and processor-like activities plus the rising strength of the Maritime Fishermen's Union (see page 126), which has been its constant opponent.

EFF's remaining strength is among small-scale boat owners in Prince Edward Island and Nova Scotia with New Brunswick support now confined to the Fundy shore. It has only weak

*representation in Quebec (mainly on the Magdalen Islands)
and none in Newfoundland.*

* * * * * *

As mentioned in the previous chapter, the Atlantic Fishermen's
Association in 1975 had attempted to draw together regional
fishing groups, using funds from the province of Nova Scotia,
but failed. The next year the Prince Edward Island Fishermen's
Association called a meeting of groups (including six from Nova
Scotia) to discuss federation, but little emerged from that effort.
In 1979 the Eastern Fishermen's Federation was initially formed
as a "loose umbrella" for six Nova Scotia groups, expanding to
thirteen, some of them outside the province, by 1980, and to
seventeen by 1981; it was a new contender. Allan Billard was
recruited as the director from the Fishermen's Broadcast of CBC
Maritimes, having formerly worked for federal and provincial
fisheries departments.[21]

The Federation was a product of Fisheries Minister Roméo
LeBlanc's wish to have one voice speaking on behalf of Maritime
fishers at consultative committees. A substantial squid allocation
payment made possible the hiring of the director and staff and
paid for a central office in Halifax. One of the early members
was the United Maritime Fishermen's Co-operative, represented
by Arthur LeBlanc, who has said: "The Minister asked that we
participate and I have no objections so long as the EFF stays within
the parameters it was intended to serve and that is to be the
voice of the fishermen from the point of view of legislation. But
as soon as they become involved (well, now in the over-the-side
sales, that's half bad) in marketing, that's the end of that because
that's not their mandate." It was, in fact, the United Maritime
Fishermen's Co-op that "negotiated squid sales with the Japanese
on some good terms for the EFF, as seed money." Allan Billard
agrees that it was the minister who asked the groups to form
the Federation. The presence of the Co-op, he thinks, gave a
processor's point of view within the Federation so that they had
a window on that world. The Federation contends, however, that
the Co-op should be seen as a fishers' organization that processes
fish rather than a processor with fishing capacity, hence its
eligibility for membership in the EFF.

There are fundamental ideological differences between the Federation and the Maritime Fishermen's Union. The Federation claims that "fishermen do not want to be considered labourers," and their member groups dismiss the need for a union. The Federation's early years were primarily consumed with lobbying and internal organizing, with only limited involvement with negotiations for the price of squid for some member associations and local processors. Later it made some mackerel, gaspereau, and herring price agreements with foreign interests and investigated markets for some of its members. Primarily its role was to identify fishers' problems and take them to the government for a hearing and, in return, interpret the government's problems to the fishers. Some of the member groups were formed in order to associate with the Federation, lured by free travel expenses and advice, but most have their own agendas and run their internal affairs (although autonomy varies greatly).

As long as the Federation remained fairly low key and local in its concerns, providing advice and helping the associations make representations to the Kirby Commission, it was "safe." Opposition to the offshore fleet's expansion and to legislation allowing unionization were issues that satisfied both small- and intermediate-scale members. Over-the-side sales, however, irritated some members yet were demanded by others. In 1982 the Federation sold mackerel and gaspereau to the AMFAL Group from Halifax and J. Marr Seafoods; then in 1983 the Federation officials got into hot water when they undertook over-the-side sales of herring for gillnetters in response to competition from the Maritime Fishermen's Union. Federation staff were working with the Fundy Co-ordinator to assist the gillnetters. In so doing, the Federation came under criticism from the Seafood Producers' Association of Nova Scotia,[22] especially when the EFF recommended forming a Crown corporation to sell under-utilized fish species.[23] More significant, however, was the withdrawal of the Atlantic Herring Fishermen's Marketing Co-op and the South-West Seiners from the Federation because it "can't possibly be running around representing all those diverse interests." The Federation director "had moved into our business of over-the-side sales, representing he had more authority than he did" to help the gillnetters.[24]

Attacks on the EFF intensified in the next two years, partially as a result of internal changes in the member associations. Gains made by the Maritime Fishermen's Union in New Brunswick were reflected in the posture of the United Maritime Fishermen's Co-op. The Co-op's 1983 Annual Meeting passed a resolution recommending withdrawal from the Federation; members of the Maritime Fishermen's Union were behind the motion.[25] The situation at the Co-op was even more complex, as will be discussed shortly.

One strong remaining Federation member is the Fundy Weir Fishermen's Association, which has suffered a devastating setback in the 1980s. Fish stocks for weir herring declined by over 70 per cent in four years from the normal level of 25,000 tonnes to only 7,500 tonnes in 1984, the lowest level on record. Seiners were blamed for the depletion of the stocks.[26] Meanwhile, another strong EFF member, l'Association Professionnelle des Pêcheurs du Nord-Est, dropped out when the Federation took a stand against seiners catching mackerel.[27] It will be recalled that this association included the Gulf Seiners in its membership (see page 124). The Federation, much weakened by defections, was by the summer of 1984 left with a few groups on the Fundy shore of New Brunswick, five in Prince Edward Island (although they could all be regarded as branches of the Prince Edward Island Fishermen's Association), a small representation in Quebec, and none at all in Newfoundland; the only remaining stronghold was in Nova Scotia, where the seiner groups had defected. The once 3,000-member-strong Nova Scotia Fishermen's Association (Dragger Sector) had folded after ten years when only thirty-eight boats with 158 crew had paid their 1983 membership. The Scallop Sector, representing large-scale boats from Yarmouth and Saulnierville, remains, but the collapse of the Dragger Sector leaves small- and intermediate-scale draggers open to unionization.

In October 1981 a group of crew members on herring seiners in the Fundy area had come together to form the Scotia-Fundy Seiners' Association. They crew boats represented in the Fundy Co-ordinator and wished to have some influence on the government's decisions about stocks, quotas, and (in a more minor way) conditions on the boats and prices. The first meeting drew 90 people; the association quickly took shape with 125 members, drawing the line at expanding beyond members of the Atlantic Herring Fishermen's Marketing Co-op and the South-West Seiners after the Eastern Fishermen's Federation advised them, "You have a nice group there . . . just your group has quite a bit of credibility so stay with your own group." The Association has attempted to avoid getting involved with lay arrangements even though the payment systems vary, leaving such decisions "up to the skippers." This Association does not favour collective bargaining legislation and wants no part of unions as the "crew and skippers are very friendly here"; most boats are said to be owner-operated, the skippers "relatives or guys next door," and there is little turnover among the crew. To the Association the "fishing industry is all politics, run by government," and what they want is a voice where it really counts – in government decision making. Faced with declining quotas, they wish "some representation on working groups, management meetings and all meetings with Federal Fisheries in Halifax pertaining to the herring seine fishery." The leaders say, concerning the Maritime Fishermen's Union, "We don't even want to hear the name; that's a group we oppose – we feel they are having altogether too much say in the Gulf area," and concerning Cashin's union, "He doesn't want to come around here. He wouldn't have much success here."

In their blanket opposition to unions the Scotia-Fundy Seiners are not alone. The skippers on the boats they crew are equally adamant. Brad Titus, general manager of the Atlantic Herring Fishermen's Marketing Co-op, says, "We don't want a union. We don't want to have a bunch of people coming in here and trying to tell us what to do." Seldon d'Entremont, president of the Scotia-Fundy Seiners, echoes these views, saying: "Nobody around here [Pubnico] wants them. We don't want them to put us ashore in a strike over prices.... I've never liked ... [unions] and I think there are a lot of people like me. To say unions on this side of the province is a bad word."[28] These same sentiments were presented previously by the Nova Scotia Fishermen's Association concerning opposition to unions by people in the Yarmouth, Digby, and Shelburne areas. It should be recalled that this attitude was encountered by the Maritime Fishermen's Union when it came to organize the gillnetters for over the side sales.

It is difficult to argue with the officials from the Scotia-Fundy Seiners when they say the fishery is predominantly political. Daily bread for these people is dependent on a herring quota set by government with sales to two markets: over-the-side (or direct) and domestic processors. The price for direct sales in 1982 was $305 a metric tonne; exactly the same fish sold to domestic processors for only $125 a metric tonne, after difficult bargaining. Sales were allowed by the Minister of Fisheries on condition that the seine groups market together through Fundy Co-ordinator.[29] Appearances suggest that permission to sell over the side is pure patronage, handed out to keep the most active groups quiet and in line. From its beginning in 1977 with a market of a few Portuguese trawlers, the over-the-side sales program in the Bay of Fundy has become an annual ritual, with eight foreign trawler/purchasers in 1982 and twelve government observers. Each boat, each interest group, and the distribution of direct versus domestic sales were carefully measured out, the bonus price from the direct sales subsidizing the impossibly low domestic price. In 1983 the domestic price remained at $125 but the direct price fell to $240, and exactly half the quota was allocated to each group. But a crisis was at hand when the total quota was halved from 1982. Each interest group now needed to scramble even harder for its share. The marketing arrangements of the Fundy Co-ordinator began falling to pieces as groups split away. A former backroom practice then came out in the open: conspiracies between seiners and domestic processors to "hide quota" by underreporting deliveries.[30] By 1984 the bottom fell out of the domestic market, where the official price was listed at $113.50 but many skippers sold for less; the price of direct sales declined to $170. Cheating became rampant, as the Sou'Wester reported:

> Dwindling herring stocks in southwestern Nova Scotia also saw quotas being slashed, but there was again a problem in the reporting of fish landings by the purse seine fleet.
> The DFO attempted to use documents found in a raid of the offices of the Atlantic Herring Fishermen's Marketing Co-op to try and get an idea of just how much fish was landed, but the court ruled the raid illegal and ordered the return of the documents to the co-op.[31]

The government's solution to the situation was to restore "order" by reducing the sixty-three-vessel purse seine fleet "by at least some 20 to 25 vessels so that the remainder can be viable."[32] It became clear just how independent these seiners were and who has been benefiting: "It is estimated that 65 to 75 per cent of the herring seine vessels are partially or wholly owned or controlled (through loans) by processing companies. Ten vessels are owned outright." The proposal by the South-West Seiners and Atlantic Herring Fishermen's Marketing Co-operative is now to manage an "enterprise quota system" and a five-year buy-back of vessels using a landings charge. All is not what it seems in the "free enterprise" region of southwestern Nova Scotia. Unions, it will be seen, can crack the façade, but the struggle is a challenging one.

Some developments at the United Maritime Fishermen's Co-operative (see page 84) have been anticipated. Co-op management opposed the Maritime Fishermen's Union, as did the Eastern Fishermen's Federation, and in New Brunswick that opposition was headed by the Lamèque Co-op, the largest component of the UMF central, which itself had become more independent by the early 1980s. In spite of its common opposition to the Maritime Fishermen's Union, the UMF management had always feared a possible move by the Eastern Fishermen's Federation into marketing. In the end it was Co-op members' support for the Union and their opposition to the Federation that caused the UMF to withdraw from the EFF. Co-op management had always claimed fishers would have to "make a choice" between the Union and the Co-op, but once the Union had signed up a vast majority of Co-op members, a truce was declared. The Union, which had not wanted the Co-op to fail because it is an important alternative outlet for fish, offered the Co-op the minimum prices, which would be negotiated with the "private" processors.

The United Maritime Fishermen had entered the decade in financial trouble, incurring a loss of nearly $3 million in 1981. Delegates to the fifty-second Annual Meeting in 1982 were told that two of its three draggers were being sold and the third had already been sold.[33] In 1983 the Co-op closed one plant and negotiated a $6.5-million loan guarantee from the federal Department of Industry, Trade and Commerce. The Antigonish movement, which had sought to introduce social change in stagnant rural areas through adult education, collective action, and morality reinforced by papal encyclicals, was spent. Its early efforts to mobilize people to create practical institutions to take some command of their own lives were no longer evident. The United Maritime Fishermen, as a corporate institution, was on the point of bankruptcy by April 1984. To save it, the Department of Regional Industrial Expansion was persuaded to restructure its $6.5-million long-term bank debt while the federal government bought $6.5 million in Co-op preferred shares and forgave $2.5 million in loan interest. A new "management team" led by François Babin, who replaced Arthur LeBlanc, was installed at the Annual Meeting in March 1984. At that time the Co-op launched a new program to try to improve communications with fishers and persuade them to bring their deliveries back to the Co-op.[34]

Another traditional organization in the Maritimes, the Canadian Seafood and Allied Workers' Union (formerly the Canadian Seafood Workers Union – see page 106), was threatened in this period. The Seafood Workers had never been very strong (as a Union official said, "organized labour is so unorganized" in the Maritimes). There are even variations within the contracts negotiated in common for the five plants of National Sea Products. In the Lunenburg local, for example, there is opposition to seniority for call-ins so that unless there is a half-day's work for the whole gang (of about four hundred) no one is called, while in Halifax the management can call half a gang; yet in North Sydney the seniority list is so strictly followed that the top person must be called first regardless of the job to be done. The Union president says, "I don't think you could have five countries any more different than the way things are in those five plants in the same company [National Sea]," where the contracts depend upon the whims of each local. This local "autonomy" means that the policies developed at union conventions are hard to implement. Moreover, the New Brunswick section "operates like another world altogether."

Threatened by the arrival of the Newfoundland Fishermen, Food and Allied Workers on the scene, the Seafood Workers have strengthened their ties with the Canadian Brotherhood of Railway, Transport and General Workers' Union. According to a Seafood Workers official, "We had delegates up to the Day of Protest in Ottawa and on the way back the Newfoundland delegates, on the same plane, were saying, 'It's the fishermen now, but you guys are next.' Cashin has the money – they have six or eight people here organizing the fishermen – it's hard for us to play that sort of game." A comparison of CBRTGW contracts with those of the Newfoundland Union indicates much stronger language in NFFAWU agreements concerning working conditions, safety, plant committees, maternity leaves, and control over incentives. The Seafood Workers have some reason to be concerned. Petit-de-Grat and Canso, once their locals, are now part of the Newfoundland Union, having earlier joined its parent, the Canadian Food and Commercial Workers' Union. Canso had left the Seafood Workers after the 1970 strike, but Petit-de-Grat did not leave until 1980 when, according to the same Union official, "Cashin came in and effected a settlement of fishermen, and the plant workers thought, 'Here's the second coming of Christ,' and changed from a Nova Scotia local to Newfoundland."

In the near future the relationship between the Seafood Workers and the Maritime Fishermen's Union will have to be resolved in New Brunswick, where ties have become close between the plant workers and the fishers. In Nova Scotia the fate of the Seafood Workers depends upon that of its ally, the Canadian Brotherhood, and whether the CBRTGW can survive in the trawler fishery, given the hegemony of the Newfoundland Union.

The Canadian Brotherhood (see page 108) represented about a thousand trawler crew in Nova Scotia in 1981 along with a large number of other groups, most of them hospital workers. The trawler crews all belonged to one local, but the Union had different contracts with each employer; and there had not been a strike prior to the entry of the Newfoundland Union. "Raiding" began in December 1981, when the Newfoundland Union entered the province on the grounds that a large number of trawler crew had appealed to it, even though the Canadian Labour Congress had sanctioned the Canadian Brotherhood's jurisdiction. Canadian Brotherhood officials said the invaders were making "wild promises" and "were just looking for power"; the Newfoundland Union, they said, was always on strike whereas "we would rather work for $5 an hour and have a job than $10 and not have one ... that's what's been happening in Newfoundland." The Canadian Brotherhood saw itself as "more realistic" about wage demands and had a philosophy much like that of the Canadian Seafood Workers. There was a twist, however.

In June of 1982, headquarters of the 38,500-member Canadian Brotherhood entered an alliance (within the Canadian Labour Congress) with the United Fishermen and Allied Workers' Union (7,500 members) and three other unions, the Shipyard General Workers' Federation of British Columbia (3,000 members), the International Longshoremen and Warehousemen's Union (3,000 members) and the Maritime Marine Workers' Federation of Nova Scotia (4,000 members). The resulting collectivity is called the Alliance of Canadian Transport and Maritime Unions. This indicates that the national and regional union offices need not be identical in their approaches.

The Newfoundland Fishermen's toe-hold in Nova Scotia was restructured in September 1981 when Local 1252 was merged with Local 309 of the United Food and Commercial Workers in Petit-de-Grat. Local 309 had some 290 members, made up of 200 plant workers with Richmond Fisheries, 70 trawler crew with Richmond Trawlers, and 20 salt fish plant workers with Isle Madame Fishermen's Co-op. The Petit-de-Grat plant, originally owned by Booth Fisheries, had been the site of the 1970 trawler crew strike. The workers joined the Canadian Food and Allied Workers in 1971, subsequently becoming Local 309 of the United Food and Commercial Workers as the name changed.[35] Some of the six hundred trawler crew represented in Nova Scotia by the CBRTGW had indicated to the Newfoundland Union that they wished to bolt.[36] On the Newfoundland side, Richard Cashin thought the Nova Scotia deep-sea fishers were ripe for organizing; moreover, CBRTGW's negotiations were hurting his bargaining in Newfoundland. The decision to move, therefore, was "not necessarily out of evangelism or idealism but out of a practical protection of what we have done," he said.

The Newfoundland Union's campaign concentrated its attacks on "the feudalistic co-adventure arrangements" in Nova Scotia. Trawler crew belonging to the CBRTGW had rejected a contract offer in December 1981 and again by 54 per cent in May 1982, while the Newfoundland Union claimed to have signed up 66 per cent of the fishers involved in the disputes at National Sea Products' ports in Lunenburg, Halifax, and Louisbourg. Simultaneously the Newfoundland Union signed 250 deep-sea scallopers fishing for Nickerson's out of Riverport. During the changeover period some tension was apparent as demonstrated by a dozen Canadian Brotherhood members who picketed their own union offices on Barrington Street in Halifax with signs reading "CBRT a Railway Union, Railroading Fishermen" and "Two Sweethearts, CBRT and National Sea."

As would be expected, the Canadian Brotherhood appealed to the Canadian Labour Congress for a ruling. It was upheld in CBRTGW's favour, but Richard Cashin ignored it, telling the press that "the CLC jurisdiction ruling is an in-house matter and has no bearing on the legality of what we are doing."[37] Pressing ahead, the Newfoundland Union distributed pamphlets to Nova Scotia trawler crew describing per diems of $33 a sea day (paid on landing), an additional $4 for trip-off pay, and an additional rate per pound of fish (paid before the next sailing). Nova Scotia negotiations were based upon a traditional lay calculated as the value of the species multiplied by volume, split 37 per cent to the crew's gross stock and divided by the number of crew members (with a "broker" minimum per trip); the Newfoundland payments were the per diem plus a lay (albeit based on a reduced percentage). Another issue was job security and seniority for members. Much was made of the practice of not paying for fish that spoiled because of a plant malfunction, whereas in Newfoundland the catch is no longer the crew's responsibility after the trawler docks. Furthermore, the CBRTGW's bargaining abilities were questioned, the point at issue being a 2½-cent-a-pound subsidy that all trawl-caught fish received from the federal government in 1975. The Newfoundland Union had insisted the 2½ cents be added onto the price negotiations, clear of conditions; in Nova Scotia, where the CBRTGW did not take a similar position, the price dropped when the subsidy was withdrawn.[38]

When the dust had settled, the Newfoundland Union prevailed, but it had not ousted the CBRTGW completely. By the spring of 1983 the Newfoundland Union was representing about three quarters of all deep-sea (large-scale) crew, including those on trawlers and scallopers. All told there were eighty trawlers in Newfoundland (twelve belonging to National Sea), the seven trawlers already organized at Petit-de-Grat, and a gain from the CBRTGW of 230 trawler crew at Nickerson's in Canso and 250 scallopers at Riverport. The CBRTGW still had 350 trawler crew working for National Sea throughout Nova Scotia and added 180 scallopers employed by Scotia Trawlers and Adams and Knickle in Lunenburg. The Newfoundland Union now represented 700 large-scale boat crew in Nova Scotia compared to the CBRTGW's 530.[39]

As will be seen, there remained "recognition" struggles for the Newfoundland Fishermen's Union in Nova Scotia, particularly for their scallopers, but the Union had made a significant impact on the conduct of the industry. One example was an arbitration case in which a company was found liable for a trawler captain's actions at sea. The significance of the finding is that it emphasizes that "Nova Scotia trawlermen are not 'co-adventurers' but employees who are paid on piecework, and that the company has a responsibility to them just as any other employer has to its employees." The case involved the responsibility for 95,000

pounds of haddock brought in by the *Marjorie Colbourne* to Canso
Seafoods and subsequently dumped.

> When the vessel got into some small haddock, the captain
> phoned ashore and the company advised him they had a market
> for it. The captain went ahead and caught the haddock, but
> the crew questioned this at the time because the haddock was
> so small.
>
> They brought it in and all the haddock was rejected and
> dumped. It turned out that the captain had given the company
> false information when he phoned ashore, telling them the
> haddock was larger than it actually was.
>
> The question was whether or not the company was responsible
> for the captain's actions – in other words, whether or not they
> had to pay the crew for the fish that was lost.
>
> The company argued, based on the "co-adventurer" system,
> that they had no liability for the captain's actions. During the
> course of the arbitration, however, they admitted that crew
> members on the trawlers are in fact employees of the company.
>
> The Union's argument, based on the legal doctrine of fairness,
> was that the company was liable because the crew members
> have no control over the captain, who is the extension of the
> management aboard the boat.
>
> The arbitrator ruled that the company was liable and ordered
> them to pay the crew for the fish that was lost.[40]

Trawler captains in Nova Scotia appeared to exercise a great
deal of autonomy and even engaged in a type of strike action
in January 1980. The issue then was the quota for trawlers, and
the captains were acting "on behalf of the entire offshore fishery"
with tacit support from the companies.[41] The action obtained the
concession of a haddock quota of 4,600 additional tonnes from
Fisheries and Oceans. National Sea was particularly concerned
about access to fish by trawlers because the company had just
taken delivery of six new trawlers, three from Japan and three
from Halifax Industries. Over half of the company's fish was
supplied by its own trawler fleet, and it was concerned that the
share of the groundfish catch landed by trawlers had declined
from a peak of 57 per cent in 1973 to 43 per cent in 1981. But,
as the Kirby Commission pointed out, "if redfish is excluded, the
trawler share has changed relatively little over the past decade."

The decrease in redfish resulted from a decline in the gulf stocks and weak markets, not quota restrictions. "The dependence of trawlers on the Gulf in the early 1970s was not based on the cod fishery, but rather on redfish" since 70 per cent of the gulf catch for the trawler fleet was redfish.[42]

These facts did not prevent the companies (and trawler captains) from blaming their crisis on exclusion by the government from the Gulf fishery. One means to solve the crisis, widely supported by fishing groups (including the Maritime Fishermen's Union, the Eastern Fishermen's Federation, and the Newfoundland Fishermen's Union) was to buy all the trawlers from the processors, thus injecting needed capital into the companies, and to create a separate holding company in which fishers could have a voice. The "idea of a 'separate fleet' got no serious consideration from the Kirby group."[43]

The Newfoundland Union's membership peaked in 1980 with over 10,000 inshore fishers, 1,050 trawler crew, and 12,000 shore workers during the height of the season. The heart of the year-round fishery in Newfoundland is the Burin Peninsula, where there are trawler-fed, year-round plants in Marystown, Fortune, and Grand Bank. Various plants have different incentive systems for cutters, who process fish. Those at Fishery Products in Marystown, for example, have a group plan (five cutters to a group), inherited from the time when the plant was owned by Atlantic Fish, that pays for fish cut at a rate above average requirements. Management proposed changing to a system for individuals that imposed penalties for defects. Until the late 1970s the Union had taken little interest. Then there were some "mixed feelings about these plans, which exist in some plants but not in others, with some in the union feeling plant workers should be paid simply on the basis of a day's pay for a day's work."[44] Fishery Products was beginning to alter its payment system to a standard set at its Burin, Catalina, and Trepassey plants, where a $22.50 ceiling was set for 133-per-cent performance (that is, 133 per cent of the established average daily cut). Such schemes were not covered by the Union's contracts yet were increasingly becoming negotiation issues.[45]

Union bargaining began to get difficult in 1980 after several consecutive years of wage increases. The focus had been primarily on trawler crews' incomes and plant workers' wages; less attention was paid to the small- and intermediate-scale fishers who, accord-

ing to Union estimates, were averaging annual earnings of $8,000
to $9,000 from fishing but were beginning to be pinched by rising
operating costs (interest rates and fuel), especially as costly
longliners became more common.

In 1980, the companies decided to announce fish prices on
their own and, at the urging of the Fisheries Association of
Newfoundland and Labrador, to stop deducting union dues. In
response to this challenge the Union decided as a tactic to boycott
the Fishery Products plants at St. Anthony and Port au Choix
(areas where fishers could salt their fish). The other companies,
however, generally supported Fishery Products and locked out
fishers throughout the province.[46] Plant workers too had been
without contracts and decided to strike the five Fishery Products
plants supplied by trawlers in July 1980. At the same time National
Sea Products locked out its workers in the St. John's plant. The
issues for negotiation were "wages, the incentive plan, rates of
production and hours of work."[47] When later in the month the
Union stepped up the pressure, the entire membership of the
Fisheries Association shut down all the remaining seventy-five
plants. The Union remained solid, with all sectors in support,
but the message from the companies was clearly that they had
less and less to give. The governments were saying the same,
and Premier Brian Peckford made his famous statement that he
"would rather have 10,000 fishermen making $5,000 each than
5,000 making $10,000 each." To this Richard Cashin replied that
that was possible only if the same principle were applied to
teaching (Peckford's original profession) by "putting three people
in each classroom and paying them $7,000 each."

The Newfoundland Union was still able to demonstrate its
strength and was successful in winning from the province a
workers' compensation scheme for fishers that designated the fish
buyer as the employer. Previously workers' compensation had
applied only "when at least three sharesmen fish with the skipper.
The skipper needed a separate plan. . . . The system posed a
problem when, in family operations, no one knew who was the
skipper-employer."[48] This gain was significant since it extended
coverage to all fishers, whether shareworker or skipper, and
premiums were paid by the fish buyer, not the skipper. Skippers,
it will be recalled, are union members in Newfoundland in vessels
up to the level of trawler. This development officially recognized
not only the responsibility of skippers to report accidents and

undertake safety procedures (making them analogous to super-visors) but also the employer-like responsibilities of fish buyers.[49]

The unionization of small-scale fishers received another impor-tant boost in 1982 when, for the first time in Newfoundland, a collective agreement was the basis for the winning of a grievance. Article 4.04 of the agreement reads: "All fish shall be receipted at time of purchase. Where deductions from gross weight are made, the company shall bear the onus of demonstrating if called upon the justification for weigh back." Nine fishers selling to the Nickerson chain were subsequently paid in full after the company notified them they would be paid only 1½ cents a pound (the price for offal).[50] The Union was making other gains for small-scale fishers, particularly regarding the price of lobster.

The first real negotiations on lobster prices had occurred in May 1978, but the price was not controlled as for other species.[51] Buyers, including the United Maritime Fishermen's Co-op, refused to negotiate. Similar problems occurred with salmon prices, where many small buyers like to play the field on price and the number of part-time fishers is high. Union fishers are not compelled by agreement to sell lobsters or salmon to local companies as they must other species. In the 1980s, however, the Union became increasingly interested in negotiating prices for these two species as part of their broader "bona fide fisherman" program. In 1983 the Union was finally successful in negotiating the price of lobster with two buyers "who have agreed to deduct union dues and to pay fishermen 70 per cent of the Boston market price for their lobster." The Union, of course, encouraged its members to sell to these buyers.[52] In 1984 the Union and the United Maritime Fishermen's Co-operative finally came to an agreement about deducting union dues for direct-purchase lobster from Union fishermen in Newfoundland.

For some time the Union had been attempting to address small-scale fishers' problems by controlling moonlighters, that is, part-time fishers who have other jobs. This should not be confused with fishing for domestic use, which the Union supports as long as it is done without fixed gear. In Newfoundland there are over 27,000 licensed fishers but only about 12,000 full-timers. Part-timers block the grounds and flood the markets when times are good and at the peak of the season. From the Union's perspective, a full-time fisher is one whose "primary source of income" is derived "from the fishery during the fishing season," which can vary from area to area. Therefore only full-timers should be granted the restricted licences and receive priority by government policies.

In an area such as St. Anthony, the season can be as short as twelve weeks, and in Port aux Basques as long as forty-five weeks. Guidelines are set by the Union membership in each local area, and bona fide lists are drawn up to give members the first crack at sales to the plants during the glut periods and to allow them to be eligible for health and welfare plans. There is an appeal committee for dissatisfied fishers. The eligibility rules, according to Earle McCurdy, the Union's secretary-treasurer, have the following provisions:

– that a person fish the full season in his local area.

– that he have no other full-time employment.

– there is no automatic disqualifying of someone who works at another job after the fishing season ends.

– an old-age pensioner can get on the list, if he was regularly engaged in the fishery at the time of his retirement.

– someone who fished squid but little or no groundfish will not make the list.

– those who fish exclusively lobster or salmon will not make the list.

– although a cod trap or longliner operator may use non-bona fide fishermen as helpers, those persons don't become eligible for union membership or the fishermen's list.[53]

Union by-laws restrict membership to bona fide fishers (with exceptions for illness, boat damage, and the like). The initial round produced 270 lists covering 375 fishing communities and over 8,500 bona fide fishers, with the numbers approaching 12,000 by the mid-1980s.

The Union itself was undergoing some internal restructuring as delegates to its convention approved the change to one local (1252) that absorbed the Provincial Council and Local 465 that had been created at the 1971 inception.[54] Over-the-side sales by the Union to the Portuguese and Joint Trawlers continued into the 1980s, but in 1983 the Union shifted these sales to the Canadian Saltfish Corporation, a Crown corporation, although it retained administration on the vessels.[55] Some restructuring took place in the Labrador shrimp operations as well when the Labrador Fishermen's Union Shrimp Company became "essentially the

Labrador branch" of the Union although it held two offshore shrimp licences. The company "is supposed to use the profits from those licences to improve the lot of the fishermen along the south Labrador coast.... In the winter of 1982-83 the LFUSC decided to start buying salmon itself. It arranged a deal with a Scandinavian processor to put freezer boats in two places along the coast and collect salmon."[56]

The harshest restructuring was not within the Union but among the fish buyers. The fishery was in a state of crisis. By August 1981, eighteen processing plants and trawler operations were closed down in Atlantic Canada, mainly those of National Sea and Nickerson's, throwing four thousand people out of work.[57] The reasons were primarily financial, the result of high fuel costs, high interest rates, and soft markets. The industry was in need of reorganization, and at risk were 129 trawlers, 45 processing plants, and a debt of over $300 million, held principally by the Bank of Nova Scotia (over $200 million), the Province of Nova Scotia (over $40 million), and the Province of Newfoundland ($30 million).[58]

Although the stakes were high in financial terms, they were equally high for the local communities. At Grand Bank, a community of four thousand, for example, the plant was closed in August 1981, and the Lake Group attempted to transfer ten trawlers from there to another plant. The citizens of the town refused to let them be moved, establishing a constant watch with the fire siren to sound the alert in the event the company tried to move the ships. An early-morning police siren, sounded in response to a traffic accident, sent five hundred people to the wharf.[59] Gallant efforts like that at Grand Bank were repeated throughout the region, but attacks were becoming too widespread. Of Newfoundland's twelve trawler-fed plants, only half were operating normally by 1983 (Trepassey, St. John's, Fortune, Catalina, and Burgeo) while Fishery Products was attempting to close Burin, Harbour Breton was in trouble, Ramea was in receivership, and the Lake Group was trying to close Grand Bank and make Fermeuse into an inshore operation. Gaultois was temporarily closed. In the Maritime Provinces Nickerson's closed its plants at Lismore, Nova Scotia, Georgetown, Prince Edward Island, and Grand Manan, New Brunswick. Nickerson's large Riverport plant had burned down.[60] It was into this desperate scene that the Kirby

Commission stepped, eventually orchestrating the most massive corporate restructuring in the industry's history.

Kirby's assumptions, like those of so many government commissions, focused on the attitudes of the participants in the industry. The report states: "A recognition of this mutual interdependence and its practical translation into a more tolerant attitude in relations between fishermen and processors is one of the first requirements of a more successful industry. The problem cannot be resolved by government policy. Its resolution will require a fundamental change in attitude on the part of fishermen and processor alike."[61]

The real problem is to explain the material conditions that give rise to attitudes (ideologies, perspectives, interests), not simply to assume that the primary requirement is a will for people's attitudes to change. The Kirby Commission did not entirely subscribe to its own platitudes. It concluded that the industry's malaise did not arise from its basic resource, for the volume and the value of production had risen steadily following institution of the 200-mile limit: "The catch in 1981 reached 779,000 t., up from 470,000 t. in 1976. The landed value of that catch was $264 million, up from $94 million in 1976."[62] The solution, Kirby decided, was twofold: the trawler/processor complex, devoted to large-scale production and needing even larger-scale capital, required "rationalizing" and an infusion of funds (including help with marketing); on the other hand, the number of small- and intermediate-scale fishers needed to be reduced. The only difference between the Kirby recommendations and most other official assessments was their grandeur.

Kirby's census of fishers produced important social indicators regarding the number of fishers on the Atlantic coast (23,434 active full-timers plus 4,369 part-timers equivalent to full-time), the regional variations in income and length of season, the importance of work in the processing plants to complement fishing incomes, and markets and financial conditions.[63] Much more important than the formal report were the behind-the-scenes dealings that accompanied the financial restructuring of the entire processing industry. The difference in outcome for Newfoundland, which ended up with a state-owned corporation, and the Maritime Provinces, which received a private company, should be regarded as an indicator of the relative strength of the fishermen's organizations in each location and the capacity of local private capital in each setting. In Newfoundland the Union was a strong political force vis-à-vis the federal and provincial governments and helped resist plant closures in a visible way that did not occur in the Maritimes.

In Newfoundland the Union certainly did not get all it wanted, but it did influence the outcome of the restructuring. The Union had demanded a fishermen's bank, worker participation in management, quotas allocated by ports rather than by companies, separation of the harvesting and processing sectors in the offshore fishery, and the establishment of a "single-desk" fish products marketing agency by extending the mandate of the Canadian Saltfish Corporation. Basically all this boiled down to a proposal for federal nationalization of the trawlers, provincial ownership of plants, and the establishment of a national marketing structure. Richard Cashin's assessment was, "I think one way out of the dilemma is to separate the trawler fleet from the processing companies.... It can be done by a crown corporation, owned and operated by government to supply plants; or by a holding company with part of its mandate being to phase in ownership of the deep-sea fishermen."[64]

According to the Kirby Commission, the move to nationalize the Newfoundland processors was "pragmatic, not philosophical" since, as reported in a *Globe and Mail* editorial, "three Newfoundland fish-processing plants – Fisheries Products Ltd., the Lake Group and John Penney and Sons Ltd. – owe $85-million more than the value of their combined assets."[65] Early in 1984 the new company, called Fisheries Products International, was formed. Ownership was 60 per cent federal, 25 per cent provincial, and 12 per cent Bank of Nova Scotia (with 3 per cent set aside for employees). The company's foundation rested on a $75.3 million investment by the federal government, $34 million from Newfoundland, and $44 million in debt turned into equity by the Bank of Nova Scotia. The company has thirty-two plants and 17,000 workers. Management is required to consult with both levels of government before the company's business plan can be approved by the board.[66]

Lest the motivation be unclear, Kirby said of the new corporation: "Government and the bank have simply become the buyers of last resort, a possibility we had foreseen from the beginning if no private investors could be found."[67] There is little danger that the new company will depart in a direction radically different from that of private capital, given such board members as William James (Chief Executive Officer of Falconbridge Nickel Mines), Frank Stronach (Chief Executive Officer of Magna International), J. Howard Hawke (Chief Executive Officer of Bache Securities), and Paul Desmarais (Chief Executive of Power Corporation). Prominent Newfoundland businessmen on the board include James Greene, Victor Young, and Andrew Crosbie.[68]

On the eve of the restructuring in Newfoundland the Newfoundland Fishermen's Union was offered a "social compact." To this Richard Cashin responded:

If social compact means a way in which to depress wages to workers and prices to fishermen, then this Union will have no part of it. If, however, social compact includes the preservation of the rights currently enjoyed by fishermen and workers, including adequate wage and price increases for the future, then our Union stands ready and willing to negotiate with both levels of government a new partnership in the fishing industry.[69]

The compact would soon turn out to be Cashin's first interpretation.

By October of 1984, the Union struck Fisheries Products International, closing "all the FPI's larger plants, putting some 4,000 plant workers out of work as well.... Wages, working conditions, and union security are the key issues in the dispute."[70] Support was solid with 98 per cent of the 630 trawler crew who voted still favouring a strike in July. They had been without a contract since September 1982, and when the company offered one, the *Financial Post* reported that it "made no mention of the $33 per diem trawlermen now receive in addition to their share of the catch. Instead, the company proposed a minimum settlement of $330 per trip, which would come off the catch value.... Fishery Products' proposal would have taken chiefs and mates out of the union, required a Christmas sailing, and reduced turnaround times from 48 hours to 36 hours, leaving trawler crews one night home after a trip which usually lasts 10 days."[71]

The Union adopted a "Unity 84" campaign based upon the issues pertaining to trawler crews, the fact that plant workers were making only five cents an hour over their January 1982 rates (and there were also proposals by the employer to alter fifteen of twenty-two contract clauses), and the prices of fish paid small-scale fishers, which had failed to rise over the last five years.[72]

Cashin claimed that the new company had "taken the most provocative approach to collective bargaining by any major employer since the Burgeo situation in 1971.... It's all the more strange when one realizes that this is a restructured company controlled by the federal and provincial governments.... Ironically, the FPI committee the Union met with was more or less the same group that negotiated our last contracts four years ago."[73]

In the settlement following a tough six-month strike the Union achieved some gains in pension plans, wage levels, and shore leave schedules, but most fundamentally it did not lose many of the rights the company was attempting to retract.[74] It was at this point that the Union changed its name to the United Food and Commercial Workers, 1252, Fishermen's Union – reduced for normal usage to the "Fishermen's Union." The Union also decided, for the first time, as a result of their strike experience with the new company, to back the New Democratic Party in the next provincial election.[75]

While the strike in Newfoundland was under way, the Union was engaged in what amounted to a recognition strike among the scallopers in southwestern Nova Scotia. The Fishermen's Union had obtained certification for 150 large-scale scallopers on seven draggers belonging to Pierce Fisheries of Lunenburg and one each belonging to Lawrence Enterprises and L&R Trawlers. All of these were previously unorganized.[76] Later they were joined by 250 unorganized Riverport scallopers and 240 former Canadian Brotherhood trawler crew from Nickerson's. In April 1984, a strike by 150 scallopers began; John Boland, a Fishermen's Union representative, said, "This is probably the first legal strike by fishermen in Lunenburg, or Nova Scotia for that matter.... It's almost a feudal-type of system here. They [the fish companies] do not want to see that control go but we have got to break the system in this town."[77] The Union was demanding an insurance plan, vacation pay, and a twenty-month contract; the companies were demanding a cut in the crew's lay from 60 to 55 per cent. The resources of the Union were utilized as strikers were paid $65 a week plus $10 a dependent.[78] The companies were intransigent, but after eight months the Fishermen's Union won a Nova Scotia Labour Relations Board ruling against Pierce Fisheries as "guilty of unfair labour practices."[79] The following month a settlement was reached with a thirty-month agreement ratified by a 70-per-cent vote. The scallopers retained their 60-per-cent split and gained vacation pay, job security, and cost-sharing for medical and insurance plans. First contracts were also quickly negotiated for 200 scallopers in Riverport and 200 draggers in Canso.[80] The Fishermen's Union was back on a roll as 750 food-processing workers from Prince Edward Island joined the Union in 1984 together with 32 employees of Canso Sea Products at Larrys River, Nova Scotia, and workers at New Harbour, Whitehead, and Canso feeding stations.[81]

Fishers in Nova Scotia had acquired a new militancy. There had been mass demonstrations in the past, such as the destruction of property at Shelburne in April 1977 to protest against offshore lobster fishing. The most hostile confrontation, however, occurred in the spring of 1983 in Pubnico when fishers demonstrated against the Department of Fisheries and Oceans about the number of lobster traps fishers were allowed. Although regulations regarding these numbers had existed since 1968, they had not been effectively enforced. When rigorous enforcement practices, including a new tag system and checks of set gear, were put in effect, there was widespread confiscation of traps. About a hundred fishers attacked two Fisheries and Oceans boats and thirteen were charged.

There was also, as in Newfoundland, a significant corporate restructuring in Nova Scotia. It began with National Sea Products taking over Nickerson's (reversing an earlier deal) and the selling of marginal Nickerson interests. After a great deal of corporate manoeuvring, 47 per cent of the revamped National Sea was held by private investors that included Scotia Investments (Jodrey family), Ilesview Investments (Morrow family), and Empire Company (Sobey family), 20 per cent by the federal government, and 14 per cent by the Bank of Nova Scotia; there was also a common float of 19 per cent. In addition, the Toronto-Dominion Bank held $75 million in preferred shares. As might be expected, the Eastern Fishermen's Federation applauded a "private deal" while the Maritime Fishermen's Union called it a "sophisticated bailout." As the facts became public it was clear that both were right; in the final arrangement, Scotia Investments held 47 per cent and the federal government and the Bank of Nova Scotia held 34 per cent jointly. The federal government provided the bulk of the financing; "in return for 65 per cent of the financing of the new National Sea, the governments involved will end up with four seats on what is expected to be a 13-seat board of directors."[82] The president, William Morrow, remained at the helm, and Scotia

Investments turned out to be the legal expression of all three families – Jodrey, Sobey, and Morrow.[83] Thus the new National Sea was a combination of all the old major actors (minus the Nickersons) with a great deal more public money, but there was little public accountability in return. The new company can expect a more unified labour movement to be banging at its door in the near future.

As a result of the restructuring, some advances were also made in co-operation among unions. The Fishermen's Union held meetings with the Canadian Seafood Workers' Union and the Maritime Fishermen's Union. Both these unions had observers at a United Food and Commercial Workers' meeting of locals from the three Maritime provinces in Halifax at the end of 1983.[84]

The fishery in Quebec resembles the small- and intermediate-scale aspects of the Maritimes fishery. There are about 5,000 full- and part-time fishers concentrated on the Gaspé, the North Shore, and the Magdalen Islands. In 1922 Ottawa ceded authority over this fishery to Quebec under "an informal arrangement," but in 1981 the federal government reclaimed authority for boats longer than 10.6 metres (which was about 80 per cent of the fleet) and in 1983, at the urging of the Kirby Commission, it asserted complete control even though the Quebec government insisted on continuing to issue licences.[85] The principal organization of the Quebec fisheries has been Les Pêcheurs Unis (see page 87), which is a co-op operating like the United Maritime Fishermen. During the 1980s Pêcheurs Unis and its member co-ops suffered severely in their levels of production, debt, and marketing, and the management came under regular attack by the members for being too centralized.[86] By 1982 the co-op was reduced to only 535 member fishers, together with another 193 independents who sold to six plants employing some 2,000 workers. The co-op was being kept afloat by a $1.25-million federal grant.[87] The indications were that the co-op had indeed distanced itself from the fishers and also the shore employees. Its headquarters were located in Montreal, where the majority of marketing took place, far from the eastern Quebec membership, and the member co-ops were only loosely federated.

Plant workers represented by the union called Le Confédération des syndicats nationaux (CSN) had struck five of the plants for a month in 1982, bringing to the surface tensions between co-op workers and the management, with plant workers being scape-goated for the failure to meet costs. Financial difficulties also weakened the relationship between the central and the member co-ops.[88] The most unifying factor within the co-op management had been common opposition to the CSN union during the 1982 strike when, after beginning in one or two factories, the rest of the CSN-represented plants were locked out because of slowdowns. By the end of the strike the entire co-op complex was on the brink of bankruptcy, and the CSN was blaming the co-op itself for poor management because of the evident poor productivity, market dependence, and failure to expand into large-scale fishing. It also criticized the co-op for its failure to adhere to co-op principles with respect to share capital and membership loyalty.

By 1983 restructuring of the entire co-op arrangement was overdue. Unfortunately, there was little order in the reorganization. The Minister of Agriculture and Fisheries of Quebec provided a grant of $484,000 to three regional co-ops to buy the Pêcheurs Unis plants in Newport, Rivière-au-Renard, and Rivière au Tonnerre and promised another bank loan of $910,000 under a plan whereby the plant workers would contribute 3 per cent of their wages and the fishers 5 per cent of their catch as investments.[89] But despite all this and another federal contribution of $1.25 million for restructuring, the situation was still not improving. In October of 1983 the federal government offered to buy Pêcheurs Unis, but the province wanted fishers and plant workers to buy the operation with an arrangement whereby plant workers were to invest $500 each and contribute 3 per cent of salaries, accompanied by a wage freeze, and fishers would contribute $5,000 plus 5 per cent of income.[90] The Quebec government had taken over 49 per cent of the Madelipeche operation to be run by the Pêcheurs Unis after Gorton's (a U.S. company) closed its doors, and the province also provided $2.6 million for a shrimp boat (Lumaaq) to go with another operated by the company.[91]

Going from bad to worse, Pêcheurs Unis declared bankruptcy in January 1984, forced by Madelipeche's seizure of assets for $2 million worth of fish. By this time, the provincial fisheries department owned 85 per cent of Madelipeche. In February of 1984 the Department of Fisheries and Oceans finally purchased the assets of Pêcheurs Unis at a cost of $15 million to recover the company from receivership.[92] The name was changed to Pêcheries Cartier. In total the federal government put up $30 million to pay creditors and provide for further investments. Thus by 1985 there were two government-owned fish companies in Quebec, Pêcheries Cartier, holding most of the plants of Pêcheurs Unis, and Madelipeche Incorporated of Quebec, which continued to expand in 1985 by purchasing the assets of National Sea Products on the Magdalen Islands for $2.5 million and investing $3.5 million in plant modernization.[93]

Throughout the Atlantic fishery by the mid-point of the 1980s restructuring had produced a new set of actors. In Quebec the long-time confusion continued about whether a co-op had even existed. In the Maritimes the United Maritime Fishermen were attempting to rebuild a co-op structure, but here too there was little resemblance to traditional co-op arrangements. The Atlantic industry was dominated by two processor giants: Fisheries Products International and National Sea Products, both heavily financed by the state yet one public and the other private (although it was difficult to tell which was which). For the first time ever the labour movement in the fisheries appeared on the verge of creating an Atlantic fisheries union, led by the efforts of the Fishermen's Union in Newfoundland and the Maritime Fishermen's Union. Such a transition would not be simple, but much of the opposition had been weakened in the first half of the 1980s so that the prospect was a real one.

The three themes of crisis, restructuring, and realignment were also bearing heavily on the Western fisheries. Crisis stimulated attempts at unified positions by organizations that in other times had been bitter rivals, their differences now at least partially submerged. Not all internecine conflicts were abandoned during the 1980s, however, and there continued to be major labour confrontations, especially within the co-ops. There was also a different kind of conflict between the United Fishermen and the Native Brotherhood. The West Coast too had its obligatory official fisheries commission, but Peter Pearse did not have nearly the impact of Michael Kirby, except that his proposals helped cement an opposition.

The Eastern Fishermen's Federation (see page 152) was active at the beginning of the decade in bringing groups from across the country together in convention.[94] One outcome of these meetings was formation of the Western Fishermen's Federation in January 1982 under the leadership of the Pacific Trollers'

Association. The Federation's aim was to secure the kind of funding its eastern counterpart enjoyed.[95] The nine other founding members besides the Pacific Trollers were the Prince Rupert Fishermen's Guild, the Native Brotherhood, the Gulf Trollers' Association, the Northern Trollers' Association, the Abalone Harvesters' Association, the Pacific Coast Salmon Seiners' Association, the Deep Sea Trawlers' Association, the Fishing Vessel Owners' Association, and the Pacific Gillnetters' Association. Notable for its absence was the United Fishermen. In the view of its organizer, John Sanderson (an officer of the Pacific Trollers), the Federation was intended to represent "fishermen-owners."[96] The Federation never really got off the ground; by April the United Fisherman were adamant that they would not join, and all the seiner groups withdrew because of the statements attributed to the Federation on gear allocations.[97] It revived to some extent late in the year and again early in 1983 when two well-attended meetings in Victoria resulted in a proposal for a Pacific fisheries council of twelve members. The council proposed to represent interest groups "made up of five basic sectors. These are the commercial fishery, the employed workers in the industry (both on shore and at sea), the processors, the native Indian fisheries, and the sports fishery. Each segment of the industry deserves equal consideration and therefore each should have an equal voice in consultative councils."[98]

In November 1983, both coastal federations had a meeting in Ottawa to discuss the possibility of a national organization for lobbying. The meeting was to be the peak of influence for each. As has been seen, the Eastern Fishermen's Federation began to crumble at this time; so did its Western counterpart. In February 1984, the powerful Fishing Vessel Owners' Association withdrew in disagreement with a statement by the Pacific Trollers' president, John Sanderson, about gear allocations. The United Fishermen again rejected membership at their thirty-seventh Annual Convention, and the Federation itself voted to "disassociate the federation from any public statements of its member organizations."[99]

The Pacific Coast Salmon Seiners' Association (PCSSA), which included crew, skippers, and owners, had been founded in 1978 to maintain the seiners' share of the salmon allocation. The members thought they needed their own organization to communicate with government for that purpose, arguing that seiner interests were not adequately represented by either the United Fishermen or the Brotherhood. The Seiners' Association did not require members to renounce membership in other organizations.[100] Its core of support was naturally the seine vessel owners, and it was most like the Vessel Owners' Association in its actions. Here was a classic case of association for lobbying government because other gear types were already formed for that purpose. As an official said, "We wouldn't need PCSSA were it not for other groups like the Pacific Trollers and Pacific Gillnetters."

The Pacific Gillnetters' Association continued to exist in the 1980s with some two hundred members, but it was basically a spent force. More influential, as its activities in the Western Fishermen's Federation indicate, was the Pacific Trollers' Association (see page 96). Despite earlier flirtations with unionization, the Trollers remain the classic "independent" fishermen. Nevertheless their behaviour in the 1980s indicated that they could be militantly independent yet conciliatory towards other gear groups. In the early 1980s the Association executive was burned by too readily accepting restrictions proposed by the Department of Fisheries and Oceans against the wishes of most trollers. The executive learned to be more militant when an *ad hoc* group called the United Trollers was formed and threatened PTA territory. The Pacific Trollers tried to build bridges between the users of various gear types and other area associations, such as the Gulf Trollers and the Northern Trollers, who were invited to sit on the PTA board in 1982. The Pacific Trollers even attempted to form some alliances with the United Fishermen, inviting Union members to open association meetings. In part this new behaviour can be explained by some changes in the material conditions of trollers during this time. Trollers had developed techniques for catching sockeye that contributed to a greater share of their traditional coho and spring salmon catches, yet the prices they received were not the premiums they had come to expect. In fact, their prices fell toward the minimum price for all salmon negotiated by the United Fishermen.[101] There was also a tendency toward freezer trollers, which are somewhat larger than ice trollers and thus cost more and use more labour.

By the mid-1980s the Pacific Trollers were unclear in their directions. One tendency was toward union-like activities to increase prices; the other was to try to expand markets with co-op-like activities with a mandate in 1983 to seek new buyers,[102] a strategy intensified in 1984 through their own pilot marketing operation and invitations to companies to respond.[103] The Trollers were also involved in a new group "to defend the rights of commercial fishermen in the negotiations on Native Land Claims and the commercialization of the Indian food fishery. The purpose of the group is to take action both politically and in the courts to ensure that non-native commercial fishermen do not lose their rights to catch fish."[104] This organization was obviously not popular with the Native Brotherhood, which was becoming increasingly isolated within the industry.

Native fishermen were, in fact, under considerable pressure at the beginning of the decade as the number of rental boats decreased; Natives had operated about 60 per cent of all rentals. The food fishery was also under attack; "D.F.O. Raids Sting Natives," the *Native Voice* put it when 138 people ("all but one Indian") were charged with the "illegal sale of fish" following a four-month undercover investigation.[105] Between 1977 and 1982 there had been a joint Native Brotherhood/United Fishermen bargaining committee on prices, but in 1983 separate talks were again the order of the day. This time the Fisheries Association refused to continue talks with the Brotherhood while negotiations with the United Fishermen were under way.[106]

Barbs were still being hurled between the Union and the Brotherhood. At issue was Native involvement in the B.C. Packers' gillnet fleet. The Union viewed the deal as a corporate bailout; for the Brotherhood it was a means to maintain a presence in the fishery. Both were right.

After B.C. Packers purchased the Canadian Fish Company's assets, including about 125 gillnet rental boats, it sought to dump its entire 275-boat rental fleet. The fleet was once required to ensure a supply of fish, but within a less competitive market this strategy was no longer necessary, and the cash was much more attractive. When negotiations between B.C. Packers, the Brotherhood, and government departments began, the United Fishermen opposed the sale on the ground that other fishermen needed access to the fleet and that the sale was a government subsidy filtered through the Native groups into the coffers of B.C. Packers. Nevertheless the deal went through; the Native Brotherhood and tribal councils formed the Northern Native Fishermen's Company to acquire 243 gillnetters. The company is owned jointly by the Nishga, North Coast, and Gitksan Carrier tribal councils.[107]

The Union's opinion was expressed by the *Fisherman*: "The federal government announced June 10 it will give B.C. Packers $11,730,000 for 243 vessels of its rental fleet as part of a 10-year, $24 million program to establish a Northern Native Fishing Corporation."[108] Actually B.C. Packers received "only" $8.7 million; the other $3 million was designated for vessel maintenance. According to the Pearse Report, "The corporation intends to retain title to the licences, and to lease the licences and sell the boats to Indian fishermen, most of whom have hitherto operated the vessels under company rental arrangements."[109] By 1984 the fleet was reduced to 204 actual vessels because many were in ill repair (although the company still holds 252 licences) and 49 had been sold to Natives, all of whom had to be approved by the company board "based on the individual's background, financial situation and production records. The buyer is required to pay 15 per cent down. The company obtains and guarantees a bank loan on the purchaser's behalf for 35 per cent of the price and finances the remaining 50 per cent under a second mortgage." The selling price is about $65,000. According to John Wytenbroek, the manager of the Native corporation, "I don't want to sell all the boats. We should always maintain 30 or 40 rentals [although] that is not necessarily the opinion of the directors."[110]

From a corporate perspective, the fish-catching business was a losing proposition. The West Coast fleet was reported to have lost $70 million in 1983 and was burdened with tremendous over-capacity.[111] This situation had been anticipated by Galen Weston, head of George Weston Limited, owner of B.C. Packers, who spoke of a "strong belief in the efficiency of the owner-operator" while using the proceeds from the sale to finance Weston's further expansion in grocery wholesaling and fish processing. According to reports, the Native fleet will continue to supply B.C. Packers, which is also going to sell its seiner fleet as soon as possible.[112]

The United Fishermen is still the core labour organization on the West Coast. It has continued to represent nearly all the non-co-op shore workers, arranging strong contracts based on seniority principles and no piece-work. It had standing committees on fisheries regulations, safety and navigational aids, and the environment, a women's committee and an Indian Rights Committee. Politically it has endorsed the New Democratic Party federally and provincially. It is the only West Coast organization capable of dealing internally with conflicts among different gear users.[113]

Most important, it has the capacity to exert pressure on and command respect from its adversaries while effectively representing fishermen. In 1980, for example, the Union declared the Pacific Seiners' Association "to be incompatible with the ideals and principles of our industrial union" on the ground that the Association is "dominated by vessel owners who receive special bonuses and work hand and glove with the companies."[114]

In one arena the Union was finally relieved from attack: the Combines Branch dropped the action it had begun in 1975. The *Fisherman* reported: "After more than eight years of dragging the union through hearings and court battles, the Restrictive Trades Practices Commission has announced it is closing the file."[115] The Union, however, is still not formally recognized by the state as the bargaining agent for British Columbia fishermen.

Although it continued to take a hard line, the Union was attempting to be conciliatory toward certain groups, particularly Native people. The thirty-seventh Annual Convention in 1982 debated a policy paper entitled "Aboriginal rights, title, land claims and the search for unity," and it was adopted.[116]

During the 1982 strike the Union took a less rigid stand against the Pacific Trollers' Association: "In a major policy shift, the committee exercised its authority approved by the convention, to declare troll catches of sockeye, pinks and chums to be unfair production during the strike. Trollers were allowed to continue fishing for springs and coho, provided they delivered to the U.S."[117]

The Union continued to represent the majority of fish workers on the West Coast; in 1983 its membership was 3,000 fishers, 3,500 shore workers, and 350 tender workers. As a union it continued to service its members effectively, gaining dental care coverage in 1984 from the thirty-six-year-old Welfare Fund that is financed by company contributions negotiated annually and open to fishermen and tendermen members of the Union, the Native Brotherhood, and the Fishing Vessel Owners' Association.[118] Strikes in the mid-1980s were strongly supported by membership votes and tended to be of a shorter duration than formerly. In 1984 a four-day strike gained a two-year fish contract that was accepted by 67 per cent of the members (79 per cent having rejected an earlier offer) accompanied by an 80-per-cent vote by shore workers.[119]

At mid-decade the Union was considering one interesting possibility. Reflecting the financially difficult times and developing class fraction alliances, seiner skippers were taking a closer look at the Union, especially since crisis times had reduced or eliminated bonus payments. It had always been a Union rule that when a boat had two owners, one had to be a Union member to prevent circumvention of the Union by dividing shares. Otherwise owners were barred. At the 1984 convention, however, a new direction was suggested:

> Should owners of large fishing vessels be allowed to join the UFAWU? Union convention delegates decided no Feb. 1, but agreed the question is a tough one that should be reviewed by the incoming General Executive Board ... delegates were swayed by the reasoning of union president Jack Nichol, who pointed out that the distinction is based on a very real difference between vessel owners and crews. "There is a hell of a difference between the man who owns the boat and the man on deck ... vessel owners often are involved in a special relationship with the company that generates bonuses, under-the-table payments and an economic pressure to take a pro-company line...." The incoming board will review the situation to see if concepts such as a vessel owners' local – a practice used by the longshoremen's union to organize foremen – could help resolve the matter.[120]

Even if skippers were granted membership in the United Fishermen in some fashion, this most proletarian union is in no way led by capital. Its traditions, ideologies, and practices have consistently supported the cause of labour in a way that is not true of any other West Coast organization, all of which have tended to be mixed in their alliances between capital and labour or to be purely representative of capital. This recent turn of events for the United Fishermen should be read as the proletarianization of seine boat skippers rather than as a change in the Union's direction.

For much longer than it has been conventional wisdom, the United Fishermen has advocated a limited entry policy for the fisheries, adoption of a "bona-fide fisherman" definition, and a waiting list for non-transferable licences as they become available. Since at least 1957 the Union has supported licence limitation but has been opposed by "independent" fishers and corporate interests. An indication of the vehemence with which the Union stand was attacked is indicated in a *Western Fisheries* column of 1957: "The UFAWU suggests a limitation of fishing licences, a politically poisonous policy for any government, and an idea which will find little favor with adherents of competitive enterprise."[121] In the mid-1960s the Union launched a systematic campaign advocating limitation and regularization of new licences with priority to go to Native fishermen and sons of fishermen. The Fisheries Association strongly opposed the plan, as did the Prince Rupert Fishermen's Co-op, which continued to think of the fishers as entrepreneurs.[122] To its credit, the Pacific Trollers' Association was also an advocate of licence limitation as early as 1961, although it was motivated in part by the encroachment of gillnetters into trolling and a desire for single gear licences.[123]

When licence limitation was finally introduced through the Davis Plan in 1968 it was in a form opposed by the Union because the scheme made the vessel, not the fisher, the unit of licensing. This was the plan supported by the Fisheries' Association because it made vessel ownership the method for determining the right to fish; the Union's plan would have made the person the unit to be licensed, and licences would not have been transferable. Capital controlled labour, a relationship the Davis Plan reinforced. The census taken when the plan was introduced revealed the extent of direct company control of gillnetters and seiners. The companies owned 172 seiners and 569 gillnetters outright but also had conditional sales agreements with another 670 gillnetters and 7 seiners and held mortgages on 81 seiners and 293 gillnetters.[124] Union fears that the companies would expand their control under the new licensing scheme were well founded, but control over fishers was based not on direct ownership alone. It is widely conceded that the program failed; fishing capacity, instead of being contained, increased markedly because only the weakest producers sold their licensed boats; the strongest intensified their catching capacity. Many of them consolidated their gillnet licences into much more efficient seiners. The stakes spiralled as the licence itself took on an exceptionally high value so that entry was restricted only to those who could afford the cost (and all too often burdened with debt to the processors and banks those who thought they could). Numerous commissions, most notably those conducted by Sol Sinclair, investigated the problems of licensing throughout the 1970s to little purpose as the state seemed paralysed.

It took the crisis of the 1980s and the Pearse Commission to bring the issues to a head, but even then there was no clear resolution. Pearse's recommendations would have led to a self-fulfilling prophecy of competition among fishermen who would have to bid for the right of access to the resources and then pay a royalty for each fish caught. This scheme was solidly opposed by virtually every sector except corporate capital. Pearse's rationale was naïve to the real forces within the industry; he argued:

> The economic problem does not arise from the expansion of fishing power as such but from the unnecessary cost of too much labour and capital employed in fishing.... Economic rationalization of the fleet calls for measures to ensure that no more labour and capital will be expended in fishing than is required to harvest the catch, so that costs will not be excessive. This must be the primary objective of a licensing policy and the main criterion for evaluating its success.[125]

Pearse assumed that there was an identity of interest between capital (of all kinds) and labour, an assumption at variance with the politics of the real world and bound to arouse opposition.

Pearse's royalty scheme was an idea he had been advocating since 1973 on the West Coast Fleet Development Committee (and it is of interest that the United Fishermen had been alone at that time in voicing opposition to this "double taxation" on fishers.)[126] Pearse's contention has been that royalties are a way of both limiting access and paying "economic rents" to the public owners of the resource. His assumption, however, that fishers are like forestry or mining companies who can pay royalties (and pass them on as part of their cost of doing business) misrepresents the fact that fishers are captives of fish buyers and do not capture resource rents. They are simply conduits between the resource and the buyers who, in turn, have the economic clout to capture rents. The plan was never adopted, although its announcement served to bring together some otherwise diverse interests.

Indeed, developments in the West Coast fishery during the 1980s can best be explained not by the Pearse Commission but by the economic crisis that its existence reflected. It was the crisis that restructured the industry.

As we have seen, several co-ops had been created to evade both the United Fishermen and the large processors. Notable were the Central Native Fishermen's Co-op (see page 141) and the Quality Fish Company, which created a quasi co-op of plant workers, tender workers, skippers, and crew in 1980. Its structure was a co-op for production but a private company for marketing. Both these new style co-ops, which included as members, in at least a nominal way, all parties, were heavily in debt. As mentioned earlier, in 1980 the Central Native Fishermen's Co-op owed $2.9 million in debentures to Marubeni of Japan and Quality Fish $500,000 in debentures to Nozaki Trading of Japan.[127] They were also indebted to Canadian banks.

The structure of the Quality Fish operation was a form of labour contract with a production co-op designed to circumvent the United Fishermen. According to *Canadian Fishing Report*,

> Quality [management] began thinking of a way to avoid strikes and shutdowns without going the entire co-op route of ownership by members.
>
> In May [1980] the company began operating in conjunction with a "co-op" formed by plant workers, tendermen, captains and crew.
>
> Besides the captains and crew of 20 or so vessels the company owns or partially owns, some fishermen aboard 12 or so independent vessels selling to Quality have joined. Quality employs some 70 plant workers in the salmon season and up to 300 in the herring season. . . .
>
> The "Co-operative" consists of three categories of members, who are fishermen, tendermen, or shoreworkers. Membership is open to anyone working in these jobs on application plus purchase of at least one share of the capital stock of the Co-operative. . . .
>
> In conjunction with the Company, the Co-operative enters into agreements with owners of fishing and packing vessels whereby they deliver to the Co-operative all of their seafood produce for handling and processing; products then go from Co-operative to Company for marketing. . . .
>
> The Co-operative agrees that the Company shall have the right to limit the quantity of fish and shall be sole judge of grade and quality. The Company agrees to use its best efforts to get the highest available market price for all fish products. The Company keeps title to all products at all times.[128]

When, during the early 1980s, the Central Native Fishermen's Co-op experienced a financial crisis, its creditor, the Royal Bank, forced it "to hook up with Quality Fish Co-operative. The bank refused to extend Central Native more credit without a government guarantee of repayment." The arrangement called for Quality Fish to run the Central Native plant at Bella Bella and CNFC boats to deliver their catch to either Quality Fish-run plant.[129]

By 1984 the Central Native Fishermen's Co-op had ceased operations, as had the Port Simpson Fishermen's Co-op.[130] Quality Fish withdrew from its agreement with Central Native, and CNFC fishers were left unpaid for about $2 million in catch, although the Royal Bank (owed $500,000) managed to recover most of its money.[131] Following the bankruptcy of CNFC, Quality Fish leased the facilities of the Central Native operation, but the fishers were outside that agreement.

There were other corporate restructurings under way. Cassiar Packing (which was jointly owned by Ewen MacMillan and Marubeni, the Japanese company) went into receivership in 1983, owing the Royal Bank $13 million.[132] Ocean Fisheries purchased Royal Fisheries (Cassiar's Prince Rupert subsidiary) and two Cassiar plants from the receiver for $4.4 million; the company's plants at Rice Mill Road and Skeena River remained closed in 1984.

At the Prince Rupert Fishermen's Co-op practices were looking increasingly less co-operative and more corporate. In 1980 the Co-op bought 40 per cent of a fish processing plant in Cleveland, Ohio, called Dolphin Seafoods and purchased part of the freezer trawler *Callistratus*. Its membership was still substantial, with 1,400 fisher members working from about 500 boats. Relations with the "house" unions began to sour, however, as the sweetheart deal with the Co-operative Fishermen's Guild, Local 80, finally fell to pieces:

The Canadian Labor Congress seized control of the Co-operative Fishermen's Guild Oct. 22 and ordered the freezer-trawler *Callistratus* to tie up until 15 processing workers from the boat are reinstated and paid back wages.

The extraordinary move, which sees Guild president Sid Dickens dismissed and all powers of the Guild executive transferred to CLC representative Bill Smalley, was provoked by clear cut defiance of CLC demands that the *Callistratus* owners settle with the 15 workers. . . .

Smalley, who learned that Dickens himself had advised the vessel to unload in direct defiance of the CLC, applied to Congress headquarters in Ottawa for trusteeship. . . .

Dickens' son is a shareholder in the vessel, as are two brothers
of the Guild secretary Paddy Greene.[133]

PRFC relations with its other union, the Amalgamated Shoreworkers' and Clerks' Union, Local 1674, which had been conflict
ridden in the late 1970s, continued to be difficult in the 1980s.
The Co-op attempted to impose wage freezes in 1982, which the
Union rejected; 121 members were laid off in a form of lockout.
The B.C. Labour Relations Board ruled in June 1982 against the
Co-op's practices as unfair intimidation. Generally, the Co-op was
moving in the direction of hostile labour-management relations,
clearly so with shore workers and less so with crew members,
although there were still PRFC members who believed in traditional
co-op principles and were attempting to stem the tide by returning
to those principles. During the crisis of the 1980s, however, the
Co-op's behaviour resembled the survival mode of corporate
processors, and it participated very little in the fishers' alliances
that were being formed.

The most significant of these was the Fishermen's Survival
Coalition, which took shape in December 1983 under the sponsorship of the United Fishermen, with 250 delegates "including
representatives from all the fishermen's organizations and individuals from all gear types." From the initial meetings a steering
committee was formed from members of the United Fishermen,
the Fishing Vessel Owners' Association, the Pacific Coast Salmon
Seiners' Association, and the Pacific Trollers' Association, with
agreement that the Native Brotherhood should be represented.[134]
The coalition sent a delegation to Ottawa in early February, 1984,
with a great show of unity among traditionally rival groups. The
notable exception was the Native Brotherhood, which at the same
time sent a letter to the Fisheries minister saying that "the Native
Brotherhood of B.C. does not support the Fishermen's Survival
Coalition, primarily because their lobby intends to oppose any
greater allocation of salmon to Indian people."[135] The coalition
continued to meet throughout 1984 and at the end of the year
held its second Fishermen's Survival Conference, still representing
the original major participants at a meeting of 150 delegates. The
conference endorsed criteria for administering a government-
sponsored boat buy-back program.[136]

The precise nature of that program remains unclear at the time
of writing. The Trudeau government had promised $100 million

for a scheme to reduce the fleet by about one third, but it was conditional upon agreements with the banks and the vessel owners and a system of vessel quotas and royalty fees.[137] This scheme developed as far as a proposed Pacific Fisheries Restructuring Act, which aimed to reduce capacity by 35 to 40 per cent and was estimated to cost as much as $200 million,[138] but the election victory of the Conservatives in 1984 intervened, and a new agenda is yet to be implemented. By the summer of 1985 the advisory process was "in danger of disintegration," according to Jack Nichol, president of the United Fishermen's Union and one of the co-chairs of the Minister's Advisory Committee, as the Pacific Trollers' Association and the Brotherhood withdrew (the NBBC had withdrawn, then rejoined the MAC earlier).[139]

Clearly a new era had arrived throughout Canada's fisheries. Capital had become much more consolidated, but so too had labour, and the ambiguous status of many fishermen was giving way to fairly clear class positions. The crisis had accelerated a restructuring of both capital and labour and led to a realignment of the combatants for the years ahead.

CHAPTER TEN
Class Struggle Does Matter

Various conclusions can be drawn from this study. Associations within the fishery tend to be formed with the lobbying of governments as their main object and often are actually created by the state, or at least by state policies, to mediate between the members and the state or respond to state policies. Association members tend to be the most "independent" fishers and act like small capitalists. Unions tend to be formed with capital as their main object of struggle (hence their stress on selling the labour power of their membership) and take shape as capital concentrates and brings workers together, separating them from individual production practices. Co-operatives tend to be formed when capital fails to satisfy market requirements. Co-operatives often give an illusion of being outside the capital and labour dynamic, yet that fundamental relationship is germane to the co-operative form, with members seeking "independence" often at the expense of either crew or process workers. These types of organizations are useful labels and categories, but this study has made it clear that the social relations and practices of each type of organization can vary considerably according to its political and ideological context.

Context is, in fact, an important consideration for understanding the concrete practices of participants in the fishery. It is important to explore appearances so as to understand that control of an immediate labour process need not correspond to broader control (or lack of it) over financing, supplies, markets, or state policies. What may appear to be entrepreneurs haggling over the price of fish are often industrial unionists negotiating a wage rate. Contextual factors compel or induce participants to act in particular ways.

Fishers in Canada today are not highly individualistic "vestiges" engaging in free market relations. Most fishing labour is socialized labour and most fishers participate in an industrial capitalist economy. Although the timing has been somewhat different on the two coasts, merchant relations having been slowest to disappear in Newfoundland and industrial relations quickest to erupt in British Columbia (where fisheries were at an early stage attached to canning rather than to the salt fish trade), by the mid-1980s the coastal fisheries have become uniformly corporate-dominated and are becoming highly unionized. Other significant forces have been explored throughout this study, but they must respond to this dominant tendency.

Fishers are far from being homogeneous. The captains of large-scale trawlers are managers performing the capitalist requirements of surveillance and control. Trawler crews are industrial workers performing only the obligations of labour. Skippers of intermediate-scale boats occupy the most volatile positions. To the extent that they are dominated by large capital they are pressed into an alliance with the more proletarian elements, only acting as supervisors of the immediate labour process. To the extent that they can engage in entrepreneurial activity they create quasi co-operatives to handle the marketing of their fish. When this occurs the skippers tend to become separate from the crews on their boats and act like small capital. Crews on the intermediate-scale boats may be drawn under the hegemony of the union (as is clearly the case on the West Coast) or that of small capital (as tends to occur in southwestern Nova Scotia). In another instance, the Newfoundland Fishermen's Union operates under a combination of practices wherein skippers on intermediate-scale boats have influenced the Union to engage in co-operative-like activities while the Union itself continues to engage in proletarian practices vis-à-vis large capital.

Small-scale fishers have increasingly tended toward proletarian practices throughout the industry in Canada. There are some important pockets of "small business" ideology and practice, but the dominant tendency among fish workers is towards unionization, as the Newfoundland Fishermen's Union has illustrated most thoroughly. So too as the Maritime Fishermen's Union has gathered momentum it has challenged the traditional hegemony of a "small business" ideology among Maritimes small-scale fishers. Given this variety of class structure, practice, and ideology within Canada's fishery it is not reasonable to make generalizations about the "interests" of Canada's fishers.

As has been argued, on the West Coast the United Fishermen and Allied Workers' Union sets the tone and is the standard against which other fishers' organizations are to be measured. The Pacific Trollers' Association's members are the entrepreneurs and individualists whose views are rooted in their material basis of the long days of fishing alone and the nature of their markets. These conditions have been undergoing changes, and with them the Trollers have tended to reconcile themselves to the United Fishermen, negotiating accommodations during strikes and working together in the Survival Coalition. It is the United Fishermen, however, that represent the vast majority of industrial workers within the West Coast fishery, especially those aboard the seiners but also the gillnetters, whose markets are also industrial. They are the aggressive, hard-nosed fishing boat and plant workers who have often been in conflict with companies over conditions of work and incomes and have frequently struggled for their survival. The Prince Rupert Fishermen's Co-op members "look after themselves" by making their own collective way; they are co-operators, but only for their exclusive membership. They drive tough bargains with shore workers and crews without a financial stake in the enterprise. They reject both the big companies and the unions. These organizations are the Big Three on the West Coast in addition to the Native Brotherhood, whose activities are the most varied and complex because of the variety of practices they have adopted to attempt to represent the interests of the Native people.

The Pacific Trollers' Association has been the driving force behind other "associations" that have been formed. It has been the most aggressive (and successful) in opposition to the Union and toward government. The Prince Rupert Co-op has been a model of co-operative development, fighting against the unions and maintaining membership discipline while being successful on the market. It has been only moderately successful in maintaining co-operative principles for its membership, and there are internal divisions concerning control by management versus control by membership. In some ways the adversity the United Fishermen has faced (expulsion from labour congresses, anti-combines investigations, legal suits over the right to organize) has made the Union stronger. It has been able to join small-scale fishers (mainly gillnetters), intermediate- and large-scale crews (on seiners and trawlers) with plant workers into a unified force that clearly is an example of a proletarian ideology and practice. Small-scale fishers in the union are regarded and act as dependent commodity producers and intermediate- and large-scale crew as proletarian, all aligned with most of the West Coast's proletarian tender workers and shore workers.

Since British Columbia fishers are outside the legal framework of collective bargaining, they must build an infrastructure of practices and rules called boat clearances besides constantly having to be capable of enforcing these practices through extraordinary power. They must always guard against encroachments by others (this was especially true when they were outside the Canadian Labour Congress). These things have caused the United Fishermen to "be tough or die," and as a result they have been willing to exercise their power and to be seen to do so. The Union's legitimacy is not conferred by the state; it comes from the respect of others based on the solidarity of its membership.

On the East Coast the major actors have been narrowed down to the Maritime Fishermen's Union and its more hegemonic colleague, the United Food and Commercial Workers, 1252, or Fishermen's Union for short. The Maritime Fishermen's Union earned its spurs during a difficult ride, but its journey is far from over. It has been an aggressive, progressive labour force struggling against exploitation, but it has also made some astute alliances in recent years with the hegemonic Fishermen's Union, and its future seems to lie in that direction. The Fishermen's Union is a social movement that has settled into a solid, powerful industrial union held together in part by the charismatic leadership of Richard Cashin.

The United Maritime Fishermen is an example of a spent social movement. These charred remains, if not actual ashes, of the Antigonish movement reached their present state through stagnation in the 1970s and general decline in the early 1980s, succumbing to the prevailing economic weaknesses and a lack of membership loyalty. By the mid-1980s it was seeking to re-establish itself but within a new environment consisting of the Maritime Fishermen's Union and restructured private companies. In the chaos of the East Coast fisheries it is the Fishermen's Union that increasingly sets the tone, not only for Newfoundland but for the whole region, drawing together small-scale fishers, crew and skippers on intermediate-scale boats, trawler crews, and processing workers – the key elements.

An important "lesson" to be gained from this study is an assessment of the position of labour within the co-operative movement. It confirms the observations of A.F. Laidlaw, who has written about the co-op as employer as follows:

The relationship between employer and employee is no different from that in private business generally. Co-operatives claim to be different, and actually are different, in purpose and method, but in matters of employment and treatment of employees, they are usually no different, no more imaginative or innovative than the ordinary company or big corporation. They have simply failed to take advantage of their special nature and unique position as co-operatives. In short, most co-operatives try to be no more than conventional employers.[1]

Stating the point even more bluntly, labour is the Achilles heel of the co-operatives in both philosophy and practice. If co-ops combine capital and labour, it is only capital that is collectivized, not labour, and even then there is still a large gap between the personal capital of individual members and the corporate capital of the co-op. Every co-op in the fishing industry has to focus on the most serious of its problems, the relations between capital and labour.

Ironically, the most truly co-operative organization within the fishing industry is the Fishermen's Union, which includes among its members, as mentioned, skippers on intermediate-scale boats. Aside from the fact that this arrangement has removed a potential source of opposition, it has meant that the union has become very active in marketing through over-the-side sales and creation of co-operative-like agencies such as the shrimp company in Labrador. At the same time the Fishermen's Union has maintained a most militant stance against large-scale capital, has exhibited extraordinary solidarity internally, and each sector has led a major strike at some point.

At the time of writing, the fishing industry is still in a state of disarray. To understand its difficulties this study has argued that it is necessary to look at the material basis underlying the politics of the fishery. It is not enough to look at surface appearances. It is not sufficient to argue, for example, that "some [fishers] see themselves as independent entrepreneurs to be organized into a businessmen's association, others as members of the cooperative movement, and yet others as a proletariat to be unionized. No doubt there are yet others who change identity from season to season according to their fishing activity. This identity conflict . . ."[2] Fishermen do not have a perceptual problem or an identity conflict. There is a material basis for their perceptions and understandings. Their ideologies then lead them to various political practices. It is not enough simply to observe attitudinal differences; they need to be explained.

That explanation requires an understanding of property relations focused upon the relations between capital and labour. This has been most difficult for government officials to grasp. The naïve character of their observations is illustrated by the draft paper called, boldly, "Property Rights in Fishing" and circulated on March 3, 1980, as an internal Fisheries and Oceans document to area managers from the Director of the Field Services Branch. Aside from advocating quotas and an end to "all subsidy programs" with a return to the illusory (nineteenth-century) free market, the paper reads: "Since we assume that the end result is profitability, it is obvious that if fishing is profitable, the benefits of this wealth from the sea can then be shared with all Canadians through an equitable taxation system." The author obviously not only fails to understand the tax system and assumes that only profits matter but is also under a fundamental misunderstanding about the differences between capital and labour participants in the industry. What is profitable for one may not even be beneficial for the other.

The confusion (at least among many people) is understandable because the relationship between capital and labour is complex in the fishery. Most fishers have experienced the *real* subordination of labour but not the *formal* subordination. Those who continue to own (nominally) or rent boats have possession but not real economic ownership, and crews have neither possession nor real economic ownership, yet neither group has been formally subordinated to capital in the sense of becoming wage labour employees. Even those trawler crew in the Fishermen's Union with a guaranteed per diem continue to bargain the price of fish and the lay arrangement as their mode of payment (albeit as a thinly veiled proxy for a wage level).

To delve into the world of the fisheries is to enter a morass of illusions and contradictions, even, at times, anarchy. The state is omnipresent, but it is guided by class forces and operates in the context of class struggle. For the most part the state in Canada has been reactive, seeking to implement its policies primarily through private capital or, when that fails, at the behest of dominant financial capital through such enterprises as Fisheries Products International, which the Fishermen's Union found as reactionary as the old fishocracy. In many ways and places the state continues to impede progressive forces through regressive labour legislation (British Columbia, Nova Scotia, and Prince Edward Island) and policies designed to salvage large corporate participants, leaving the fishers and plant workers to fend for themselves.

In the fisheries people have organized in complex ways, reflecting the complexity of the industry. There have been patterns traceable to the material basis of the industry that have become expressed through organizational forms as political and ideological practices. In the fisheries, as in most areas of existence, people make their own history but not under conditions of their own choosing. Class struggle does matter.

Homer Stevens, by the way, retired from the United Fishermen's executive in 1981 and returned with his wife, Grace, to gillnetting for salmon, using a rented combination boat. He was forced by the sale of the rental fleet to buy the boat in 1982. His advice is still sought by his colleagues and he continues to make his own history.

SOURCE NOTES

CHAPTER ONE
1. All quotations not attributed to published sources are based on interviews conducted for this study. Tapes are deposited with the Labour Studies Resource Centre, Carleton University, Ottawa.

CHAPTER TWO
1. Kenneth Johnstone, *The Aquatic Explorers: A History of the Fisheries Research Board of Canada* (Toronto: University of Toronto Press, 1977), p. 5.
2. See ibid., pp. 12-15.
3. W.A. Black, "The Labrador Floater Codfishery," Association of American Geographers, *Annals* 50, 1960: 269-70.
4. See ibid., pp. 282-84. Thanks to Peter Sinclair for additional information.
5. For information about the Fishermen's Protective Union, see G.E. Panting, "The Fishermen's Protective Union of Newfoundland and the Farmers' Organizations in Western Canada," Canadian Historical Association *Report*, 1963; Ian McDonald, "W.F. Coaker and the Balance of Power Strategy: The Fishermen's Protective Union in Newfoundland Politics," Atlantic Canada Studies Conference, Fredericton, 1974; Robert Brym and Barbara Neis, "Regional Factors in the Formation of the Fishermen's Protective Union of Newfoundland," *Canadian Journal of Sociology* 3:4, 1978.
6. For information on the Bank fishery, see Frederick W. Wallace, *Roving Fishermen: An Autobiography Recounting Personal Experiences in the Commercial Fishing Fleet and Fishing Industry of Canada and the United States 1911-1924* (Gardenvale, Quebec: 1955); Raoul Anderson, "The 'Count' and the 'Share': Offshore Fishermen and Changing Incentives," Proceedings of the 4th Annual Congress of the Canadian Ethnology Society, Ottawa: National Museum of Man Service Paper #40, 1977; Raoul Anderson, "Social Organization of the Newfoundland Banking Schooner Cod Fishery, circa 1900-1948," International Commission for Maritime History Meetings, Bucharest, 1980.

7. *Canadian Fisherman* 32:4, 1945, 24.

8. B.A. Balcom, *History of the Lunenburg Fishing Industry* (Lunenburg: 1977), p. 28.

9. Ruth Fulton Grant, *The Canadian Atlantic Fishery* (Toronto: Ryerson Press, 1934), p. 70.

10. Gene Barrett, "Underdevelopment and Social Movements in the Nova Scotia Fishing Industry to 1938," in R.J. Brym and R.J. Sacouman, eds., *Underdevelopment and Social Movements in Atlantic Canada* (Toronto: New Hogtown Press, 1979), pp. 130-31, 142; see also Gene Barrett, "Development and Underdevelopment, and the Rise of Trade Unionism in the Fishing Industry of Nova Scotia, 1900-1950," Master's thesis, Dalhousie University, 1976, p. 32.

11. Barrett, "Rise of Trade Unionism," pp. 65-67.

12. Ibid., pp. 72, 75, 80.

13. See F. Homer, "Atlantic Salt Fish Industry Reviewed," *Canadian Fisherman* 32:7, 1945, 30.

14. Barrett, "Rise of Trade Unionism," p. 192.

15. Ibid., pp. 206-7.

16. See William Warner, *Distant Water: The Fate of the North Atlantic Fisherman* (Toronto: Little, Brown, 1983), pp. 32-44.

17. Ibid., p. 310.

18. See Kent O. Martin, "Play by the Rules or Don't Play at All: Space Division and Resource Allocation in a Rural Newfoundland Fishing Community," and Raoul Anderson, "Public and Private Access Management in Newfoundland Fishing," both in R. Anderson, ed., *North Atlantic Maritime Cultures* (The Hague: Mouton Publishers, 1979). Concerning rights to berths by draw, see James Faris, *Cat Harbour: A Newfoundland Fishing Settlement*, Institute of Social and Economic Research, Social and Economic Studies No. 3 (St. John's: Memorial University, 1972), p. 36, and on rights by inheritance, M.M. Firestone, *Brothers and Rivals: Patrilocality in Savage Cove*, Institute of Social and Economic Research, Social and Economic Studies No. 5 (St. John's: Memorial University, 1967), p. 93.

19. See Ellen Antler, "Women's Work in Newfoundland Fishing Families," *Atlantis* 22 (Spring) 1977.

20. Concerning longliners, see Bonnie Jean McCay, " 'Appropriate Technology' and Coastal Fishermen of Newfoundland," Ph.D. thesis, Columbia University, 1976.

21. John F. Kearney, "A History of the Port Market in the Bay of Fundy Herring Gillnet Fishery," *Sou'Wester* 1 May 1984: 4.

22. Ibid.

23. See *Sou'Wester* 15 Feb. 1983: 28.

24. See Task Force on Atlantic Fisheries, *Navigating Troubled Waters: A New Policy for the Atlantic Fisheries* [Kirby Report] (Ottawa: Minister of Supply and Services, 1983), p. 10.

25. See F.H. Leacy, ed., *Historical Statistics of Canada*, 2nd ed. (Ottawa: Statistics Canada, 1983), N1-11.

26. Economic Council of Canada, *Reforming Regulation*, Final Report (Ottawa: Economic Council of Canada, 1981), p. 69.

27. Kirby Report, p. 12.
28. See ibid., pp. 31-32.
29. Ibid., p. 48.
30. Ibid., p. 318.

CHAPTER THREE
1. See W.A. Carrothers, *The British Columbia Fisheries* (Toronto: University of Toronto Press, 1941), pp. 11-12; Lorraine Carter, "The First Cannery ... A Vision of the Future," *Western Fisheries* 98:6, 1979, pp. 142-43.
2. Duncan Stacey, "The China Contract," *Fisherman* 11 Dec. 1981: 19.
3. Duncan Stacey, *Sockeye and Tinplate: Technological Change in the Fraser River Canning Industry, 1871-1912*, British Columbia Provincial Museum Heritage Record No. 15 (Victoria: 1982), p. 7.
4. Commission on Pacific Fisheries Policy Final Report, *Turning the Tide: A New Policy for Canada's Pacific Fisheries* [Pearse Report], Vancouver, September 1982 (Ottawa: Department of Fisheries and Oceans, [1982]), p. 151.
5. See Joseph Forester and Anne Forester, *Fishing: British Columbia's Commercial Fishing History* (Saanichton: Hancock House, 1975), p. 22.
6. See Percy Gladstone and Stuart Jamieson, "Unionism in the Fishing Industry of British Columbia," *Canadian Journal of Economics and Political Science* 16:1, 1950, 154n.
7. See Mick James, "These Were the Pioneers," *Fisherman* 20 Dec. 1968: 17.
8. Harry K. Ralston, "The 1910 Strike of Fraser River Sockeye Salmon Fishermen," Master's thesis, University of British Columbia, 1965, p. ii.
9. See Jim Sinclair, "1913 Strike: A Unity Forged Among All Races," *Fisherman* 10 Dec. 1982: 10.
10. See Percy Gladstone, "Native Indians and the Fishing Industry of British Columbia," *Canadian Journal of Economics and Political Science* 19:1, 1953, 32.
11. See ibid., pp. 26-27.
12. See Mickey Beagle, "Segregation and Discrimination in the West Coast Fishing Industry," *Canadian Issues* 3:1, 1980, 143, quoting *Fisherman* 10 July 1945.
13. *Canadian Fisherman* 32:4, 1945, 26-27.
14. See A.V. Hill, *Tides of Change: A Story of Fishermen's Co-operatives in British Columbia* (Prince Rupert: Prince Rupert Fishermen's Co-operative Association, 1967), p. 78.
15. Ibid., p. 49.
16. Pearse Report, p. 10, Table 2-2.

CHAPTER FOUR
1. *Toronto Star* 15 July 1978: C6.
2. *Canadian Fishing Report* 5:4, 1983, 17.
3. See David Alexander, *The Decay of Trade: An Economic History of the Newfoundland Saltfish Trade, 1935-1965*, Institute of Social and Economic Research, Social and Economic Studies No. 19 (St. John's: Memorial University, 1977), pp. 141-42.

4.   *Globe and Mail* 26 May 1984: B3.
5.   *Financial Post* 9 Apr. 1983: 9.
6.   *Globe and Mail* 30 June 1984: B3.
7.   Task Force on Atlantic Fisheries, *Navigating Troubled Waters: A New Policy for the Atlantic Fisheries* [Kirby Report] (Ottawa: Minister of Supply and Services, 1983), p. 155.
8.   British Columbia Packers, *Seventh Annual Report 1934* (December).
9.   For 1933, see ibid.; for 1983, see *Globe and Mail* 13 Apr. 1983: B8.
10. See *Financial Post* 31 Mar. 1984: S7.
11. Calculated from F.H. Leacy, ed., *Historical Statistics of Canada*, 2nd ed. (Ottawa: Statistics Canada, 1983), N49-58.
12. Kirby Report, p. 204.
13. See *Report* of the Committee on Federal Licensing Policy and Its Implications for the Newfoundland Fisheries, David Alexander and G. M. Story, co-chairmen (St. John's: Memorial University, 1974), p. 11.
14. Commission on Pacific Fisheries Policy Final Report, *Turning the Tide: A New Policy for Canada's Pacific Fisheries* [Pearse Report], Vancouver, September 1982 (Ottawa: Department of Fisheries and Oceans, [1982]), pp. 164-65.
15. *Fisherman* 20 Jan. 1984: 11.
16. Kirby Report, pp. 40-41.
17. See *Canadian Business* July, 1982: 137.
18. Pearse Report, pp. 163-64.
19. See *Financial Post* 29 Sept. 1984: 13.
20. See *Fisherman* 7 Jan. 1972: 1, 8.
21. Kirby Report, p. 67.
22. Ibid., p. 97.
23. *Sou'Wester* 1 Apr. 1983: 16.
24. *Toronto Star* 20 Feb. 1983: F1.
25. C.L. Mitchell, *Canada's Fishing Industry: A Sectoral Analysis* (Ottawa: Fisheries and Oceans, 1980), p. 6.
26. See *Globe and Mail* 15 Sept. 1984: B4.
27. *Globe and Mail* 12 July 1980: 4.
28. Kirby Report, p. 61.
29. *Globe and Mail* 13 Jan. 1983: 3.
30. Peter R. Sinclair, "Fishermen Divided: The Impact of Limited Entry Licensing in Northwest Newfoundland," *Human Organization* (forthcoming), p. 20.
31. Pearse Report, p. 119.
32. Kirby Report, p. 216.
33. Reprinted in *Sou'Wester* 15 Mar. 1983: 11.
34. Gene Barrett, "The State and Capital in the Fishing Industry: The Case of Nova Scotia," Canadian Political Science Association Meetings, Dalhousie University, 1981, p. 19.
35. Bonnie McCay, " 'Fish Is Scarce': Fisheries Modernization on Fogo Island, Newfoundland," in R. Anderson, ed., *North Atlantic Maritime Cultures* (The Hague: Mouton Publishers, 1979), p. 167.
36. *Union Forum* 1:7, 1977, 3.
37. Donald Patton, *Industrial Development and the Atlantic Fishery:*

Opportunities for Manufacturing and Skilled Workers in the 1980s
(Ottawa: Canadian Institute for Economic Policy, 1981), p. xvi.
38. Ibid., p. 18.
39. *Canadian Fisherman* 66:1, 1979, 13.

CHAPTER FIVE
1. For a fuller account of the meaning of "class" and "property" as concepts, see "Class and Property Relations: An Exploration of the Rights of Property and Obligations of Labour" and "Property and Proletarianization: Transformation of Simple Commodity Producers in Canadian Farming and Fishing," Chapters 9 and 10 in Wallace Clement, *Class, Power and Property: Essays on Canadian Society* (Toronto: Methuen Publications, 1983).
2. See Karl Marx, *Capital*, vol. I (New York: International Publishers, 1967), p. 714.
3. See Nicos Poulantzas, *Classes in Contemporary Capitalism* (London: New Left Books, 1975), pp. 18-19. Poulantzas derives the distinctions possession, economic ownership, and legal ownership from C. Bettelheim, *Calcul économique et formes de propriété* (Paris: Maspero, 1970).
4. H. Scott Gordon, "The Economic Theory of a Common-Property Resource: The Fishery," *Journal of Political Economy* 62, 1954: 135.
5. John Peter Frecker, "Militant and Radical Unionism in the British Columbia Fishing Industry," Master's thesis, University of British Columbia, 1972, p. 29.
6. The Commission on Pacific Fisheries Policy Final Report, *Turning the Tide: A New Policy for Canada's Pacific Fisheries* [Pearse Report], Vancouver, September 1982 (Ottawa: Department of Fisheries and Oceans, [1982]), p. 76.
7. Michael J. Kirby, "Statement on the Release of the Report of the Task Force on Atlantic Fisheries," 17 Feb. 1983, p. 6.
8. Task Force on Atlantic Fisheries, *Navigating Troubled Waters: A New Policy for the Atlantic Fisheries* [Kirby Report] (Ottawa: Minister of Supply and Services, 1983), pp. 211-12.
9. See Charles Steinberg, "The Legal Problems in Collective Bargaining by Canadian Fishermen," *Labour Law Journal* October, 1974: 642-54.
10. Charles Steinberg, "Collective Bargaining Rights in the Canadian Sea Fisheries: A Case Study of Nova Scotia," Ph.D. thesis, Columbia University, 1973, p. 51.
11. See H.W. Arthur, D.D. Carter, and H.J. Glasbeek, *Labour Law and Industrial Relations in Canada* (Toronto: Butterworths, 1981), pp. 159, 179.
12. Rick Williams, "Inshore Fishermen, Unionization and the Struggle Against Underdevelopment Today," in R.J. Brym and R.J. Sacouman, eds., *Underdevelopment and Social Movements in Atlantic Canada* (Toronto: New Hogtown Press, 1979), p. 179.
13. As quoted in Craig R. Littler, *The Development of the Labour Process in Capitalist Societies* (London: Heinemann, 1982), p. 59.
14. See *Fisherman* 12 Dec. 1980: 17.
15. *Fisherman* 29 May 1970: 11.
16. *Fisherman* 19 Oct. 1979: 8.

17. See Anthony Davis, Arthur Hanson, Leonard Kasdan and Richard Apostle, *Utilization of Offshore Banks by the Small Boat Fisheries in Southwest Nova Scotia* (Halifax: Institute for Resource and Environment Studies, Dalhousie University, 1982).

CHAPTER SIX

1. John Boyd, *The Industrial Relations System of the Fishing Industry*, Task Force on Labour Relations Project No. 55a (Ottawa: Privy Council Office, 1968), p. 1.
2. James Sacouman, "Underdevelopment and the Structural Origins of Antigonish Movement Co-operatives in Eastern Nova Scotia" in R.J. Brym and R.J. Sacouman, eds., *Underdevelopment and Social Movements in Atlantic Canada* (Toronto: New Hogtown Press, 1979), p. 122.
3. Ronald J. Macneil, "The Origins and Development of the United Maritime Fishermen," Extension Department, St. Francis Xavier University, Antigonish, N.S., 1945, p. 23.
4. Gene Barrett, "Development and Underdevelopment, and the Rise of Trade Unionism in the Fishing Industry of Nova Scotia, 1900-1950," Master's thesis, Dalhousie University, 1976, p. 85.
5. United Maritime Fishermen, *UMF: The Cornerstone of the Co-op Fisheries Movement* (Moncton: United Maritime Fishermen, 1975), p. 14.
6. J.H. Mackichan, United Maritime Fishermen's *Brief* to the Royal Commission on Co-operatives, Halifax, 7 March 1945, p. 31.
7. Ibid., p. 39.
8. See *Canadian Fisherman* 31:7, 1945, 13.
9. See Rudolf Cujes, *Fishermen's Co-operatives in Nova Scotia*, Co-operative Economy Series No. 1 (Montreal: CIRIEC, 1969), p. 33.
10. United Maritime Fishermen, *UMF*, p. 17.
11. R.J. Chiasson, Chairman, UMF Committee on Structure, Extension Department, St. Francis Xavier University, Antigonish, 1965, pp. 6-7.
12. Charles Steinberg, "Collective Bargaining Rights in the Canadian Sea Fisheries: A Case Study of Nova Scotia," Ph.D. thesis, Columbia University, 1973, p. 186n.
13. Donald Snowden, *The Co-operative Movement in Newfoundland: An ARDA Study of Co-operative Organization from the Viewpoint of Industrial and Social Development* (Ottawa: Co-operative Union of Canada, 1965), pp. 69, 88.
14. See Ottar Brox, *Newfoundland Fishermen in the Age of Industry: A Sociology of Economic Dualism*, Institute of Social and Economic Research, Social and Economic Studies No. 9 (St. John's: Memorial University, 1972), p. 79.
15. David Macdonald, 'Power Begins at the Cod End': The Newfoundland Trawlermen's Strike, 1974-75, Institute of Social and Economic Research, Social and Economic Studies No. 26 (St. John's: Memorial University, 1980), p. 47.
16. Elias Stavrides, "8-hour day, Increased Pay 29 Day Strike in 1946 by Networkers," *Fisherman* 12 Dec. 1980: 23, 27.
17. Alicja Muszynski, "The Organization of Women and Ethnic Minorities in

a Resource Industry: A Case Study of the Unionization of Shoreworkers in the B.C. Fishing Industry, 1937-1949," *Journal of Canadian Studies* 19:1, 1984, 91.

18. See John Gibson's review of *Tides of Change* in *Western Fisheries* 75:6, 1968, 41.

19. A.V. Hill, *Tides of Change: A Story of Fishermen's Co-operatives in British Columbia* (Prince Rupert: Prince Rupert Fishermen's Co-operative Association, 1967), pp. 207-8.

20. See M.J. Friedlaender, *Economic Status of Native Indians in British Columbia Fisheries 1964-1973*, Technical Report Series PAC/T-75-25, Pacific Region, Fisheries and Oceans Branch (Ottawa: Environment Canada, 1975), p. 6.

21. Stuart Jamieson, "Native Indians and the Trade Union Movement in British Columbia," *Human Organization* 20:4, 1961/62, 222-23.

22. H.B. Hawthorn, C.S. Belshaw, and S.M. Jamieson, *The Indians of British Columbia: A Study of Contemporary Social Adjustment* (Vancouver: University of British Columbia Press, 1958), p. 474.

23. Ibid., p. 121.

24. See Boyd, *Industrial Relations*, p. 13.

25. Hill, *Tides*, p. 213.

26. See *Fisherman* 14 Oct. 1960: 1.

27. *Western Fisheries* 64:1, 1962, 12.

28. See Stuart Jamieson, *Times of Trouble: Labour Unrest and Industrial Conflict in Canada, 1900-66*, Task Force on Labour Relations, Study No. 22 (Ottawa: Privy Council Office, 1968), p. 373.

29. *Western Fisheries* 60:1, 1960, 15.

30. See Stan Stanton, "We Decided to Slug It Out," *Western Fisheries* 66:4, 1963, 4.

31. Prince Rupert Fishermen's Co-operative Association [PRFCA], *Tenth Annual Report 1949*, p. 2.

32. PRFCA, *Twelfth Annual Report 1951*, p. 3.

33. Boyd, *Industrial Relations*, p. 16.

34. See PRFCA, *Thirteenth Annual Report 1952*, p. 1.

35. See PRFCA, *Eighteenth Annual Report 1957*, p. 1.

36. PRFCA, *Twentieth Annual General Report 1959*, p. 2.

37. Hill, *Tides*, p. 130.

38. *Fisherman* 26 July 1963: 1.

39. *Western Fisheries* 74:1, 1967, 9.

40. PRFCA, *Twenty-eighth Annual Report 1967*, p. 2.

41. *Fisherman* 14 Apr. 1967: 5.

42. *Fisherman* 16 July 1967: 6.

43. See PRFCA, *Twenty-ninth Annual Report 1968*, p. 2.

CHAPTER SEVEN

1. See Silver Donald Cameron, *The Education of Everett Richardson: The Nova Scotia Fishermen's Strike, 1970-71* (Toronto: McClelland and Stewart, 1977).

2. See Robert Chodos, "The First Strike," *Last Post* 1:5, 1970, 45.

3. *Western Fisheries* 80:2, 1970, 50.
4. *Fisherman* 8 Jan. 1971: 1.
5. Ibid.
6. See Robert Chodos, "Fishermen Fight the Companies' Union," *Last Post* 1:8, 1971, 13.
7. *Union Forum* 1:2, 1977, 10.
8. *Union Forum* 1:3, 1977, 13.
9. Gordon Inglis, "Lawyers, Priests and Gangsters from Chicago: Factors in the Development of the Newfoundland Fishermen, Food and Allied Workers' Union," Canadian Sociology and Anthropology Meetings, University of British Columbia, 1983, p. 3.
10. Ibid., p. 4.
11. See *Union Forum* 1:6, 1977, 15.
12. David Alexander, *The Decay of Trade: An Economic History of the Newfoundland Saltfish Trade, 1935-1965*, Institute of Social and Economic Research, Social and Economic Studies No. 19 (St. John's: Memorial University, 1977), p. 141.
13. *Union Forum* 1:4, 1977, 11.
14. *Union Forum* 1:3, 1977, 6.
15. Ibid.
16. See *Union Forum* 2:2, 1978, 16.
17. David Macdonald, *'Power Begins at the Cod End': The Newfoundland Trawlermen's Strike, 1974-75*, Institute of Social and Economic Research, Social and Economic Studies No. 26 (St. John's: Memorial University, 1980), pp. 71-72.
18. See *Union Forum* 2:3, 1978, 6.
19. See *Fisherman* 24 Mar. 1972: 1.
20. *Fisherman* 17 July 1973: 1.
21. See *Fisherman* 29 June 1979: 1.
22. See *Fisherman* 16 Mar. 1979: 3.
23. *Fisherman* 7 Jan. 1972: 1.
24. *Fisherman* 22 Mar. 1968: 1.
25. *Native Voice* Mar./Apr. 1984: 2. Reprint of letter to United Fishermen and Allied Workers' Union from Native Brotherhood of British Columbia in 1959.
26. *Native Voice* Mar. 1971: 1.
27. *Native Voice* Sept. 1974: 4, editorial.
28. *Western Fisheries* 83:5, 1972, 37.
29. *Western Fisheries* 84:1, 1972, 9.
30. *Western Fisheries* 85:4, 1973, 44.
31. *Western Fisheries* 87:5, 1974, 14.

CHAPTER EIGHT

1. M.M. Coady, "The Social Significance of the Co-operative Movement," reproduced in United Maritime Fishermen, *UMF: The Cornerstone of the Co-op Fisheries Movement* (Moncton: United Maritime Fishermen, 1975), p. 38.
2. United Maritime Fishermen, *UMF*, p. 18.

3. Ibid., p. 24.
4. See *Union Forum* 1:1, 1977, 10, 2:4, 1978, 9, 3:9, 1979, 7.
5. *MFU* 2:1, 1981, 13 [the official publication of the Maritime Fishermen's Union].
6. *MFU* 2:1, 1981, 3.
7. See *Globe and Mail* 18 Feb. 1978: 8.
8. Article VI, Maritime Fishermen's Union Constitution, January 1980.
9. Ibid., Article II.1g.
10. Fundy Weir Fishermen's Association, *Fact Sheet*, n.d., p. 1.
11. See *Sou'Wester* 15 Oct. 1983.
12. See John F. Kearney, "The Transformation of the Bay of Fundy Herring Fisheries 1976-1978: An Experiment in Fishermen-Government Co-management," in C. Lamson and A. Hanson, eds., *Atlantic Fisheries and Coastal Communities: Fisheries Decision-making Case Studies* (Halifax: Dalhousie Ocean Studies Programme, 1984).
13. Ibid., p. 174.
14. See *Canadian Fishing Report* 1:3, 1979, 7.
15. *Canadian Fishing Report* 1:1, 1979, 1.
16. See Kearney, "Fundy Herring," p. 195.
17. *Canadian Fishing Report* 1:2, 1979, 1, 3.
18. *Union Forum* 2:7, 1978, 3-4.
19. See *Union Forum* 2:8, 1978, 3.
20. See *Union Forum* 2:9, 1978, 4.
21. See *Financial Post* 3 Nov. 1979: 7, Special Report: Atlantic Canada.
22. See Dennis Bartels, "Markets Without Merchants: The Political Economy of the Newfoundland Fishermen, Food and Allied Workers Union's Direct Sales to Bulgaria and Sweden," *Canadian Journal of Anthropology* 2:1, 1981, 102-3.
23. *Union Forum* 3:1, 1979, 19.
24. See *Union Forum* 3:4, 1979, 13.
25. *Union Forum* 4:3, 1980, 8.
26. *Union Forum* 4:1, 1980, 13.
27. David Close, "Unconventional Militance: Union Organized Fish Sales in Newfoundland," *Journal of Canadian Studies* 17:2, 1982, 10.
28. Roger Carter, "The Fogo Island Co-operative: An Alternative Development Strategy?" Master's thesis, Memorial University, 1984, pp. 111, 120, 126-27.
29. *Union Forum* 1:1, 1977, 14, 1:3, 1977, 9.
30. *Union Forum* 2:4, 1978, 16-17.
31. *Fisherman* 1 Aug. 1975: 4.
32. *Native Voice* Nov./Dec. 1975: 7.
33. See Will McKay and Julie Healey, "Analysis of Attrition from the Indian Owned Salmon Fleet, 1977 to 1979," Appendix to Native Brotherhood submission to Pearse Commission, 1981, pp. 13, 28.
34. See *Native Voice* June 1975: 3.
35. See *Native Voice* July 1975: 4; Mar. 1976: 11.
36. *Native Voice* July 1975: 2.
37. See *Fisherman* 18 July 1975: 1.

38. See *Fisherman* 25 July 1975: 1.
39. See *Native Voice* Sept/Dec. 1976: 19, Jan. 1977: 7, Mar. 1977: 10.
40. *Native Voice* Feb. 1977: 1-2.
41. See *Canadian Fishing Report* 2:5, 1980, 10.
42. See *Fisherman* 26 Apr. 1976, 1.
43. *Fisherman* 3 Nov. 1978, 1.
44. Prince Rupert Fishermen's Co-operative Association, *Thirty-ninth Annual Report 1978*, p. 3.
45. See PRFCA, *Thirty-seventh Annual Report 1976*, p. 3; *Thirty-eighth Annual Report 1977*, p. 3.
46. *Fisherman* 6 Oct. 1978: 1; also, see 22 Sept. 1978: 6, 4 Aug. 1978:1, 26 Nov. 1976: 11.

CHAPTER NINE

1. *MFU* 3:1, 1982, 5-6.
2. *Voice of the MFU* 5:2, 1984, 5-7 [name changed from above].
3. See *Financial Post* 2 June 1984: 42.
4. See *Canadian Fishing Report* 4:11, 1982, 1.
5. See *Sou'Wester* 1 June 1984: 9.
6. *Sou'Wester* 1 Aug. 1984: 7.
7. See *Atlantic Fishermen* 4 Jan. 1985: 6.
8. *MFU* 2:1, 1981, 8.
9. See *Sou'Wester* 1 June 1983: 7.
10. *Sou'Wester* 15 Dec. 1984: 11.
11. See *Atlantic Fishermen* 4 Jan. 1985: 6.
12. *MFU* 2:2, 1981, 2.
13. *MFU* 2:3, 1982, 4.
14. See *MFU* 3:2, 1982, 6.
15. See *Chronicle-Herald* [Halifax], 25 May 1982: 26.
16. *MFU* 3:5 1983, 5.
17. See *MFU* 4:2, 1983, 8.
18. See *Sou'Wester* 15 Jan. 1984: 2, 15 July 1984: 7, 1 June 1985: 5.
19. See *Canadian Fishing Report* 4:11, 1982, 1, 19.
20. *Sou'Wester* 1 Feb. 1985: 10.
21. See *Canadian Fishing Report* 1:11, 1979, 2.
22. See *Chronicle-Herald* 10 Apr. 1982: 18.
23. See *Chronicle-Herald* 2 Apr. 1982: 3.
24. See *Canadian Fishing Report* 5:4, 1983, 18.
25. See ibid.
26. See *Sou'Wester* 1 Jan. 1985: 7; *Atlantic Fisherman* 30 Nov. 1984: 9, 17.
27. See *Canadian Fishing Report* 6:4, 1984, 14.
28. *Chronicle-Herald* 17 June 1982: 25.
29. See *Canadian Fishing Report* 4:8, 1982, 13.
30. See *Canadian Fishing Report* 5:9, 1983, 10.
31. *Sou'Wester* 1 Jan. 1985: 3.
32. Task Force on Atlantic Fisheries, *Navigating Troubled Waters: A New Policy for the Atlantic Fisheries* [Kirby Report] (Ottawa: Minister of Supply and Services, 1983), p. 331.

33. See *Atlantic Co-operators*, April 1982: 3.
34. See *Sou'Wester* 15 July 1984: 5, 1 Feb. 1985: 7.
35. See *Union Forum* 5:3, 1981, 11.
36. See *Nova Scotia Worker* 2:3, 1982, 1.
37. *Chronicle-Herald* 9 Mar. 1982: 17.
38. See *Union Forum* 6:1, 1982, 8, 6:2, 1982: 17, 6:4, 1982, 7-8.
39. See *Sou'Wester* 15 May 1983: 10.
40. *Union Forum* 8:2, 1984, 12.
41. *Globe and Mail* 19 Jan. 1980: 8.
42. Kirby Report, pp. 35-36.
43. *Canadian Fishing Report* 5:7, 1983, 15.
44. *Union Forum* 2:2, 1978, 2.
45. See *Union Forum* 2:3, 1978, 19.
46. See *Union Forum* 5:1, 1981, 7-8.
47. *Canadian Fishing Report* 2:8, 1980, 2.
48. *Canadian Fishing Report* 2:6, 1980, 14.
49. See *Union Forum* 4:5, 1980, 9-10.
50. *Union Forum* 6:4, 1982, 21.
51. See *Union Forum* 1:1, 1977, 10, 2:4, 1978, 9, 3:9, 1979, 7.
52. *Union Forum* 7:3, 1983, 13, 8:6, 1984, 22.
53. *Canadian Fishing Report* 2:6, 1980: 18.
54. See *Union Forum* 7:1, 1983, 23.
55. See *Union Forum* 7:4, 1983, 8.
56. *Canadian Fishing Report* 6:3, 1984, 31.
57. See *Globe and Mail* 29 Aug. 1981: B20.
58. See *Financial Post* 19 Mar. 1983: 5.
59. See *Globe and Mail* 8 Dec. 1981: 9.
60. See *Canadian Fishing Report* 5:1, 1983, 14-15.
61. Kirby Report, p. 33.
62. Ibid., p. 23.
63. See ibid., pp. 22, 48, 52.
64. *Canadian Fishing Report* 5:2, 1983, 2.
65. *Globe and Mail* 6 July 1983: 6.
66. See *Financial Post* 28 Jan. 1984: 20, 12 May 1984: 6; *Globe and Mail* 7 Nov. 1983: 7, 17 Mar. 1984: B4, 22 May 1984: B13.
67. *Globe and Mail* 5 Nov. 1983: 10.
68. See *Globe and Mail* 21 Nov. 1984: B2.
69. *Union Forum* 7:6, 1983, 10.
70. *Financial Post* 27 Oct. 1984: 6.
71. *Financial Post* 21 July 1984: 44.
72. See *Union Forum* 8:1, 1984, 10.
73. *Union Forum* 8:3, 1984, 5.
74. See *Globe and Mail* 2 Feb. 1985: B4.
75. See *Sou'Wester* 1 Feb. 1985: 4.
76. See *Chronicle-Herald* 18 Aug. 1982: 21.
77. *Globe and Mail* 7 June 1984: 13.
78. See *Voice of the MFU* 5:2, 1984, 4.
79. *Sou'Wester* 15 Nov. 1984: 3.

80. See *Sou'Wester* 15 Dec. 1984: 5.

81. See *Sou'Wester* 1 Feb. 1985: 7.

82. *Globe and Mail* 10 Feb. 1984: 4.

83. See *Financial Post* 11 Feb. 1984: 3.

84. See *Union Forum* 8:1, 1984, 37.

85. See *Canadian Fishing Report* 5:8, 1983, 1.

86. See *Le Devoir* 7 mars 1981: A21, 8 sept. 1981: 12; *La Presse* 16 sept. 1981: D1.

87. See *Canadian Fishing Report* 4:10, 1982, 1.

88. See *Sou'Wester* 1 June 1983: 13-14.

89. See ibid.

90. See *MFU* 4:1, 1983, 11.

91. See *Canadian Fishing Report* 6:2, 1984, 1.

92. See ibid.

93. See *Atlantic Fisherman* 4 Jan. 1985: 2.

94. See *Canadian Fishing Report* 2:11, 1980, 16.

95. See *Pacific Trollers' Association Newsletter* 7:2, 1982, 1.

96. *Canadian Fishing Report* 4:8, 1982, 5.

97. See *Pacific Trollers' Association Newsletter* 7:4, 1982, 4.

98. PTA *Newsletter* [new name for Pacific Trollers' paper] 8:2, 1983, 6.

99. *Fisherman* 1 Mar. 1984: 15.

100. See *Beachline* 1:2, 1981, 5.

101. See *Fisherman* 10 Sept. 1982, 9.

102. See PTA *Newsletter* 8:3, 183, 1.

103. See *Current: Pacific Trollers' Association Newsletter* 1:2, 1984, 14.

104. *Current: Pacific Trollers' Association Newsletter* 1:1, 1984, 10.

105. *Native Voice* Jan. 1983: 1.

106. See *Native Voice* Feb./Mar. 1983: 1, June/July 1983: 1.

107. See *Native Voice* July/Aug. 1982: 2.

108. *Fisherman* 11 June 1982: 1.

109. The Commission on Pacific Fisheries Policy Final Report, *Turning the Tide: A New Policy for Canada's Pacific Fisheries* [Pearse Report], Vancouver, September 1982 (Ottawa: Department of Fisheries and Oceans, [1982]), p. 155.

110. *Globe and Mail* 2 Apr. 1984: B3.

111. See *Globe and Mail* 19 June 1984: B3.

112. *Globe and Mail* 18 Oct. 1982: B1.

113. See Geoff Meggs, *In Unity Lies Strength: The Structure, Benefits and Policies of the United Fishermen and Allied Workers Union* (Vancouver: 1981), pp. 13, 17, 22.

114. United Fishermen and Allied Workers' Union Special Bulletin, Nov. 1980.

115. *Fisherman* 13 May 1983: 1.

116. *Fisherman* 12 Feb. 1982: 1.

117. *Fisherman* 13 Aug. 1982: 5.

118. See *Fisherman* 17 Feb. 1984: 3.

119. See *Fisherman* 20 July 1984: 1.

120. *Fisherman* 17 Feb. 1984: 1.

121. See *Western Fisheries* 57:5, 1957, 77.

122. See John Gibson, "Licence Limitation: Economic Necessity Will Force a Sacrifice of Principle," *Western Fisheries* 69:5, 1965, 16-17.
123. See *Western Fisheries* 63:1, 1961, 24.
124. See *Western Fisheries* 77:6, 1969, 18.
125. Pearse Report, p. 81.
126. See *Fisherman* 7 Nov. 1973, 5.
127. See *Canadian Fishing Report* 2:5, 1980, 10.
128. *Canadian Fishing Report* 2:8, 1980, 13.
129. *Canadian Fishing Report* 5:7, 1983, 2.
130. See *Fisherman* 20 July 1984: 2.
131. See *Fisherman* 12 Dec. 1983: 18.
132. See *Canadian Fishing Report* 5:9, 1983, 2.
133. *Fisherman* 23 Oct. 1981: 1, 6.
134. *Current [PTA]* 1:1, 1984, 10, 23.
135. *Current* 1:2, 1984, 4.
136. See *Fisherman* 12 Dec. 1984: 6, 18 Jan. 1985: 1.
137. See *Financial Post* 12 May 1984: 1.
138. See *Financial Post* 23 June 1984: 9.
139. Jack Nichol quoted in *Fisherman* 19 July 1985: 3.

CHAPTER TEN

1. A.F. Laidlaw, "Co-operatives in the Year 2000," a paper prepared for the 27th Congress of the International Co-operative Alliance, Moscow, 1980, p. 53.
2. R.D.S. Macdonald, "Fishermen's Incomes and Inputs and Outputs in the Fisheries Sector: The P.E.I. Case," *Canadian Issues* 3:1, 1980, 30.

INDEX